Crime and the Criminal Classes in Ireland, 1870–1920

Studies in Irish Crime History

Crime and the Criminal Classes in Ireland, 1870–1920

Brian Griffin

CORK cup UNIVERSITY PRESS

First published in 2024 by
Cork University Press
Boole Library
University College Cork
Cork T12 ND89
Ireland

Library of Congress Control Number: 2024934638

Distribution in the USA Longleaf Services, Chapel Hill, NC, USA.

British Library Cataloguing in Publication Data
A CIP catalogue record for this book is available in the British Library.

ISBN: 9781782055990

Printed by Hussar Books in Poland

Design and typesetting by Alison Burns at Studio 10 Design, Cork

Cover image: C.W. Cole, 'Murder Scene on a Village Road', 1880.
Courtesy of the National Library of Ireland

www.corkuniversitypress.com

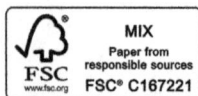

MIX
Paper from
responsible sources
FSC
www.fsc.org   FSC® C167221

Contents

Contents

Studies in Irish Crime History

SERIES EDITORS: Richard Mc Mahon and Ciara Molloy

This book series explores how crime history can offer new ways of understanding Irish society. It maps and critically engages with the actions and beliefs of those who often held a marginal position in Irish society, their relationship to the broader population and, crucially, their interactions with those in positions of authority. The history of the murderer, the prostitute, the thief, the bank robber, the vagrant, the white-collar criminal, among others, and their relationship to the police officer, the lawyer, the jury, the judge and the hangman will be explored to arrive at a deeper sense of the conflicts and contradictions that underpinned Irish life and continue to shape it into the present. The series also aims to explore the construction and meaning of key concepts such as 'crime' and 'evil' and the impact of such concepts on the individual, society and the state. In doing so, the series will embrace but also cut across key aspects of political, legal, economic, social and cultural history and raise questions about the nature of Irish society over time in fruitful and novel ways.

1. Brian Hanley, *Republicanism, Crime and Paramilitary Policing in Ireland, 1916–2020.*

2. Aogán Mulcahy, *Crime and Conflict in Northern Ireland, 1920–2022.*

3. Brian Griffin, *Crime and the Criminal Classes in Ireland, 1870–1920.*

Acknowledgements

It gives me great pleasure to thank the staff of the following institutions for the invaluable help that they gave me in the researching of this book: Bath Spa University Library (especially the hard-working interlibrary loan team), the British Library, the National Archives of Ireland, the National Library of Ireland, the Public Records Office of Northern Ireland, Trinity College Dublin Library and the United Kingdom National Archives. A special thanks goes to Barbara McCormack, Russell Library Special Collections and Archives, Maynooth University, for permission to reproduce two cartoons from *Zozimus* magazine. I am particularly indebted to my two editors, Dr Richard Mc Mahon and Dr Ciara Molloy, for their painstaking editorial work and numerous helpful suggestions regarding the various drafts of the book manuscript: the finished product is immeasurably stronger as a result of their input. Our beautiful dogs, Oisín and Enda, helped in ways that only owners of greyhounds can understand. As always, my greatest debt is to my wife, Sally, without whose understanding and encouragement this book could not have been written. The book is dedicated to her, as a small token of love and affection.

List of Figures and Tables

Introduction

At first glance, it might appear understandable to view Irish society between 1870 and 1920 as exceptionally violent and crime-ridden. Not only was the start of the period notable for an outbreak of agrarian violence and crime in parts of the midlands, but at the end of the period the country was scarred by the simultaneous political violence of the Irish Republican Army (IRA) and the counterinsurgency campaign of the security forces during the War of Independence.[1] Other notable instances of crime and disorder between these starting and terminal years would appear to lend weight to this view, which featured prominently in the pages of *Punch* and other contemporary British newspapers and magazines.[2] These included the murders of William Clements, third earl of Leitrim, in County Donegal in April 1878,[3] of Lord Frederick Cavendish, chief secretary for Ireland, and his undersecretary, Thomas Henry Burke, in Dublin's Phoenix Park in May 1882,[4] and the widespread violence and disorder associated with the Land War of the 1880s and the Ranch War in the early twentieth century. Periodic outbreaks of large-scale sectarian rioting in Belfast in the last three decades of the nineteenth century also undoubtedly added to the perception of Ireland as an exceptionally violent society.[5] The bloodiest of these outbreaks was the series of three separate phases of rioting that occurred between June and September 1886, which resulted in the killing of some thirty-two people, including one Royal Irish Constabulary (RIC) head constable, and the wounding of hundreds of policemen and civilians.[6] The authorities' fears of the possibility of outbreaks of communal disorder – whether this took the form of crimes in rural areas linked with agrarian agitation, sectarian rioting in Ulster, or republican attempts at armed rebellion – help to explain why Ireland had a heavier police presence than other parts of the United Kingdom throughout this period.[7]

This book has a number of main goals. Firstly, it looks closely at agrarian crime, probably the most commented-upon aspect of lawbreaking in Ireland in this period: the aim is both to illustrate the chief features of agrarian crime and also to show how it was often misunderstood by contemporaries, a misunderstanding that has persisted into the recent past. Particular attention will be paid to agrarian crime as *organised* crime: it will be shown that, while most violent agrarian crime certainly needed some form of organisation, insofar as the perpetrators needed to combine together in order to plan and carry out their violent acts, this should not necessarily be taken as evidence of secret-society involvement, notwithstanding frequent police claims to the contrary. Another main aim is to put agrarian crime in this period into perspective: while it was undoubtedly a very significant aspect of Irish lawbreaking, agrarian crime was merely one of many different types of crime that were committed between 1870 and 1920. Most crimes, whether they were violent or non-violent, minor or serious, that Irish people committed in this period had nothing to do with agrarian issues: in fact, Ireland's cities and towns tended to have

2

significantly higher recorded rates of indictable crimes than rural areas. When historians initially explored the topic of crime in late nineteenth- and early twentieth-century Ireland, they concentrated mainly on lawbreaking that was associated with the Land League agitation from 1879 to 1882, the Plan of Campaign from 1886 to 1891 and the Ranch War from 1906 to 1909.[8] More recently, there has been a welcome broadening of historians' interests in Irish crime in this period, to include examinations of 'ordinary' or non-agrarian crime.[9] Important explorations of such topics as homicide and assaults,[10] rape,[11] infanticide,[12] domestic violence[13] and illegal blood sports[14] have substantially widened and deepened our understanding of crime in Ireland in the years between 1870 and 1920. This book will extend this knowledge and understanding, by offering the first in-depth general overview and discussion of crime – both agrarian and non-agrarian – in Ireland in the last three decades of the nineteenth century and the first two decades of the twentieth. This will include an examination of the role of the police in the prevention and detection of crime. What emerges in the book is a picture of the ordinariness or unexceptional nature, by international standards, of most Irish crime in this period.

Chapter 1

Agrarian Crime

IN THE PERIOD from 1870 to 1920, there were several widespread outbreaks of agrarian crime in Ireland, many of which were supported by considerable sections of the community. These episodes affected most areas of the country at one time or another. From 1868 to 1871 Westmeath experienced a relatively high rate of agrarian crime, as did, to a lesser extent, parts of King's County (Offaly), Meath and Mayo. The Land War from 1879 to 1882 was a much more widespread affair, involving much of the country outside of Ulster, but with particularly high levels of violence, intimidation and other agrarian crimes in Kerry, Galway, King's County, Leitrim, Limerick and Tipperary;[1] during the Plan of Campaign from 1886 to 1891, Galway, Clare, Cork, Kerry, Limerick and Tipperary were the most affected counties.[2] Crimes connected with the Ranch War in the first decade of the twentieth century were committed in various parts of the country, but were most numerous in Galway, Clare, Meath, Westmeath, Sligo and Roscommon.[3] The last major outbreak of agrarian crime, from 1917 to 1920, affected up to sixteen counties at one stage, with Galway, Mayo, Sligo, Leitrim, Roscommon and Clare experiencing the highest number of crimes.[4] Several scholars, including Samuel Clark, James Donnelly Jr, David Fitzpatrick, Joseph Lee and W.E. Vaughan, have examined the topic of agrarian unrest in post-Famine Ireland,[5] and while they have documented the often extensive geographic spread of agrarian crime and disorder, it is important to note that, for most of the period, most of the country was unaffected by serious crime and disorder of an agrarian nature. This chapter will discuss the extent and nature of agrarian crime in the last decades of the nineteenth century and the first decades of the twentieth, highlighting key aspects of the main outbreaks of rural disorder in this period. Agrarian crime as a collective enterprise, including the putative role of secret societies, will be a major focus of the discussion.

Before the Land War

Agrarian offences were the most common form of collective crime in Ireland. The portrayal of Irish agrarian crimes of an often brutal nature formed a key element in contemporary British depictions of the rural Irishman in particular as a cruel and violent barbarian,[6] although such views were not confined to British observers. For example, in 1870 a barrister in Dublin lamented 'the deep reproach upon the country' that 'in no spot in Europe were so many crimes committed and so few of the perpetrators brought to justice as in Ireland', and he drew particular attention to 'the position of the country districts, where the roads were patrolled by Fenians in day light, and by night assassins lurked under hedges with revolvers to tumble any stray landlord or agent'.[7] Such alarmist views may not have seemed unfounded at the time, given the relative prevalence of agrarian crime in parts of the midlands and in Mayo. Westmeath was in a particularly disturbed state: from July 1869 to February 1871, a total of 327 agrarian offences were recorded in the county, which made a striking contrast with the total of 235 such crimes that were reported in the seven years from 1862 to 1868.[8] The fact that some six murders were committed in Westmeath from 1868 to 1871 caused special concern to the authorities. The victims were a landlord, Howard Fetherstonhaugh, who was shot in April 1868: the presumed motive was revenge for his having raised rents on two townlands on his estate; the railway station-master at Mullingar, Thomas Anketell, was shot in March 1869, possibly because he had dismissed a railway servant; Captain Rowland Tarleton, a landlord, was shot in April 1869 for having dismissed a herdsman; Michael Kerrigan, a small tenant farmer, was shot in February 1870, allegedly as a result of a dispute with a neighbour over five acres of land; a steward, Francis Dowling, was shot in November 1870, possibly because he had replaced the cousin of an alleged 'Ribbon' captain, James Duffy; and Duffy's landlord, Reverend James Crofton, was shot in December 1870 after he had served notice of ejectment on 'Captain' Duffy.[9]

Such was the widespread alarm at the state of Westmeath that a parliamentary select committee was established to explore the causes of the outrages in that county and in neighbouring parts of Meath and King's County. Statistics supplied to the select committee by the Royal Irish Constabulary (RIC) showed that from 1 January 1870 to 28 February 1871 there were three agrarian murders and five cases of attempted murder in Westmeath, as well as sixty-two cases of sending threatening letters or posting threatening notices, thirty-five cases of intimidation (including five of firing shots at victims), two cases of arson, two cases of administering illegal oaths, and one case each of malicious injury and killing cattle. The agrarian outrages in Meath in the same period consisted of one case of attempted murder, fifty-six cases of sending threatening letters or posting threatening notices, fifteen cases of intimidation (one of which involved firing shots at the victim), five cases of administering an illegal oath, two cases of firing into dwellings and three cases of illegally levying money, while those in King's County consisted of three cases of attempted murder, thirty-two cases of sending threatening letters or posting threatening notices, six cases of intimidation and one of arson.[10] Many of the crimes discussed by the select committee had nothing to do with disputes between landlords and tenants or with disagreements between tenants, but instead concerned disputes between employees and employers and intra-employee disputes;[11] the murder of Thomas Anketell, the Mullingar railway stationmaster, for instance, probably arose from his having sacked an employee some months previously, an action that many believed was motivated by sectarian prejudice.[12]

One contemporary observer, A.M. Sullivan, drew from his reading of some of the latest medical theories when he attributed agrarian crime to 'a moral epidemic … as contagious as typhus fever'. According to Sullivan, it had been 'well ascertained by medical investigation' that certain crimes 'burst occasionally on a community, and that they were promoted, intensified, and inflamed by the public excitement, panic, and alarm caused by their appearance'.[13] The RIC and others charged with maintaining law and order advanced a more prosaic, but still alarming, alternative explanation for the crime engulfing much of Westmeath and other counties: a secret, oath-bound Ribbon organisation, which drew its members from a wide range of rural and urban society, and enforced its will through organised intimidation and violence, was at the root of the disorder which so alarmed contemporaries. The select committee's report reflected this view when it asserted:

> That there is at present existing within the county of Westmeath and certain adjoining portions of the county of Meath and of the King's County, an unlawful combination and confederacy of a secret nature, generally known by the name of the Ribbon Society. That this Ribbon Society has existed for a considerable length of time, and has within the last three years, as compared with those immediately preceding, increased in power and influence.
>
> That owing to the prevalence of this Society, murder and other crimes of the most serious nature have been perpetrated within the district above referred to, and that by reason partly of sympathy with the perpetrators of such crimes, and still more by the terror created by the existence and action of the Society, it has been found to be almost impossible to obtain evidence on which to bring offenders to justice.[14]

The existence of an oath-bound secret society that used violence to enforce its will seemed patently obvious to the select committee, not only because this was attested to by numerous seemingly knowledgeable police, magistrates and other witnesses,[15] but also because it offered a plausible explanation for the widespread outrages that had taken place, as well as for the reluctance of witnesses to testify in court or to give evidence to the magistrates or RIC in the affected districts. Numerous agrarian secret societies had existed in various parts of Ireland and at various times before this period, so it did not take a huge leap of the imagination to believe that such a society was responsible for the outrages that had prompted the establishment of the select committee. However, notwithstanding claims by police and other contemporary observers about the widespread ramifications of Ribbonism in Westmeath at the beginning of our period, A.C. Murray presents a compelling argument that there is scant evidence to support the notion that a secret society was behind the outrages that were committed in Westmeath in the late 1860s and early 1870s, or even that such a society existed there at all.[16] Instead of a highly organised combination that carried out agrarian and other crimes throughout the county, it is very likely that the offences were committed either by individuals (such was probably the case with the sending of threatening letters, which constituted the largest single category of outrages)[17] or by different groups of men with no direct links with one another, with no central direction of any kind or without any of the features traditionally associated with Ribbonism, and acting from a variety of motives.

Most of the recorded outrages did not involve disputes between landlords and tenants, but arose out of disputes between tenants. These included somebody posting a notice on 19 February 1870 at Ballinamuddagh, which threatened one Nathaniel Lowe: a disputed car-way to a bog was the issue at stake in this instance. The houses of John Farrell, Honora Naughton and John Moran at Ardnagranagh were fired into on 8 November 1869, because they had 'told their landlord that they had no complaints'; James Hiney died as the result of an assault by two men at Toorphelum on 3 October 1870, the assault being the result of 'a drunken row, and dispute about land'. On 13 August 1870 a sheep belonging to Dominick Nugent was killed at Russagh, because he had 'prevented a man from crossing his field some short time' previously; Michael Looram of Cuminstown received a threatening letter on 26 November 1870, the purpose of which was to force him to give up seven acres of land that he had purchased some twenty-eight years previously; and Patrick Daly was threatened at Clare townland on 20 February 1871 by a man with a revolver, who fired a shot into his hedge after warning him to give up twenty acres of land that had been in his possession for the previous twenty years.[18] Nobody was found guilty of these offences, and the perpetrators of most of the other outrages also got away with their crimes; in most cases, the RIC failed to identify suspects or to bring charges against suspects. Given the scattered locations of the crimes, and the unwillingness of most victims and witnesses to aid the police in their investigations, either out of sympathy with the perpetrators or fear of retribution, it is easy to see why the RIC and other officials ascribed the outrages to a secret conspiracy with ramifications throughout the county. As Murray points out, this was an illusion 'created by their failure to maintain law and order in the countryside', and 'the terms Ribbonism, Ribbonman, and Ribbon society were labels affixed by the police and magistrates to crimes they could not solve, criminals they could not catch, and gangs they could not break up'.[19] According to Murray, one of these 'gangs' was closely associated with a small farmer named James Duffy, who farmed around fifteen acres in Cloneyhague townland in the south of the county. Land pressure was particularly acute in Cloneyhague, and Murray suggests that this could help to explain the prevalence of agrarian crime in Cloneyhague and the general Kilbeggan district. Such pressure was also evident in other parts of Westmeath: a variety of factors, including a poor potato harvest in 1868, increased competition for grassland 'which invited the more adventurous landlords to raise their rents', and possibly 'exaggerated rumours of what the approaching land legislation would bring', all 'combined to make existing disputes concerning land and employment more flammable'.[20] Duffy committed outrages himself or persuaded others to do so, and his 'gang' could also be hired by those 'anxious to have a man threatened or given a beating'. A high proportion of the serious agrarian crimes committed in Westmeath were committed by Duffy's men or those associated with him.[21] Other groups unconnected with Duffy's 'gang' ('small knots of miscreants', according to the Catholic bishop of Meath, Dr Thomas Nulty) carried out many of the agrarian crimes that were committed in other parts of the county.[22]

According to W.E. Vaughan, Ribbonmen's supposed activity continued to shape RIC perceptions of agrarian crime's origins, not only in Westmeath but also in the rest of the country during the Land War.[23] Some historians have also perpetuated the idea of 'Ribbon' or other secret society responsibility for agrarian crime – which is probably understandable, given historians' heavy reliance on RIC records when researching this topic. For example, Donald Jordan believes that a 'significant degree of responsibility' for the increase in agrarian crime in Mayo in the late 1860s and early 1870s rests with members of the Irish Republican Brotherhood (IRB). The Fenians' membership certainly grew in the county in these years, but the only tangible evidence of direct IRB involvement in agrarian crime in this period that Jordan provides is not compelling, consisting as it does of a claim made to the Irish Folklore Commission in 1938 that IRB members threatened landlords and 'land grabbers' who took land from which tenants had been evicted.[24] While there is stronger evidence that some Fenians carried out agrarian crimes in Mayo and elsewhere in Ireland during the Land War of 1879–82, there is nothing to indicate that they did so as members of agrarian secret societies along the lines identified for the pre-Famine period.[25] Pádraig Lane argues that herdsmen and rural labourers also committed agrarian crimes, often, but not always, as members of secret societies: what he describes as the herdsmen's and rural labourers' '*jacquerism*' 'could be either organised or spontaneous'. He does not offer any tangible evidence that such organised violence emanated from anything as structured as a secret society in the late nineteenth or early twentieth centuries, however.[26]

Many lawbreakers took advantage of the constabulary and magistrates' predisposition towards ascribing agrarian crime to secret societies, by sending threatening letters that were designed to create the impression that they were sent by members of a secret confederacy – in reality, such letters were, in many cases, the work of individuals with personal, rather than communal, agendas.[27] For example, on 31 August 1870 the tail of a cow belonging to Colonel Ansley of Malcomfield, County Carlow, was cut off and found hanging from the mouth of a plaster of Paris figure of a lion; at the end of the cow's tail was a letter stating that 'the writer would not have Catholics put out for Protestants, and that no Protestants were wanted in Carlow'. On the following day, a boy in the colonel's employment found another letter which stated that Ansley's head 'would be put where the tail of the cow was put', and that 'We are the boys who fear nothing', after 'some few sentences of uncomplimentary remarks about Colonel Ansley'. Instead of being the work of a confederacy dedicated to preventing the dismissal of Catholics from Colonel Ansley's employment in favour of Protestants, the two letters were written by a workman who had been several times dismissed for drunkenness by the colonel.[28] In March 1870 several people who were believed to be interested in attending the sale in Louth of a farm belonging to Matthew O'Reilly Dease, MP, received notices signed by 'Rory of the Hills', warning them not to offer bids for the farm in excess of a certain amount per acre. One of those threatened, a 'mercantile gentleman', received a minatory letter signed 'on behalf of the entire county'. This letter appeared, at first inspection, to have been the work of two or three individuals, as parts of it were written in 'a bold free hand', while others 'appeared as the almost indecipherable scrawl of a party devoid of education'. However, a handwriting expert believed that the letter was the work of just one writer; similar notices were posted on the chapel gates of Rathkenny, County Meath.[29]

Other attempts to give the impression that threatening missives were sent on behalf of a collective include a letter sent in November 1870 by 'Rory of the Hills' to William Campbell of Clogher, in County Tyrone, in which Campbell was threatened with death in a dispute over £10 given as security in a legal transaction, and a letter sent by James Dornan (alias 'Rory of the Hills') to Elizabeth Ann McClelland of Banbridge in March 1874, in which McClelland was warned that Rory, who was 'sworn in by the Brotherhood to put down all tyranny of landlords', was about to pay her a visit from the south of Ireland and shoot her if she did not pay one Wallace his 'tenant right'.[30] In an arson compensation case at Armagh assizes in February 1874, a farmer whose four stacks of turf were allegedly maliciously burned testified that he had been warned in a threatening letter in May 1873 that 'We have Orange and Home Rule together blended most beautifulle' and that he should give a person named Roleston some turf.[31] In March 1875 William James Watson, a rent agent from Aghavilla, Warrenpoint, received a letter decorated with 'rude drawings of a coffin and a gun'; the letter warned Watson that emissaries from the south were going to 'pop you soonner [sic] or later'. According to the letter's author (who, police suspected, was an old carpenter whom Watson had discharged earlier in the year), 'Tipperary boys will meet you should it be in railway or rent office, or at your own dore [sic]'.[32]

It is impossible to know how many such letters were sent with genuine threatening intent and how many were hoaxes. Some were sent as ill-conceived jokes, arguably similar to the phenomenon of hoax telephone calls to ambulance services, police and fire services today.[33] An example of one such hoax threatening letter was sent by Helen Waters, the wife of the RIC sub-inspector of the Castletown district, and her friend Mrs Ogilvy, the wife of the local coastguard commander, to the Church of Ireland curate of Adrigole at some time between 1874 and 1877. The curate, newly arrived from England, was regarded by his flock as 'an objectionable prig, who looked on us all as a sort of savages'. His sermons, in which he reminded his audience of their 'misfortune in having to live in such a God forsaken country, thus being unable to realise the delights of London life to which he had been accustomed', did nothing to endear him to his listeners. The two officials' irate wives tried to drive the curate away by sending him a letter, decorated with a huge sketch of a skull and crossbones, and threatening him with the fate of one O'Rourke, a proselytising mission-ary preacher whom local Protestants believed had been murdered some years previously (his death had prob-ably been caused by an accidental fall from a horse). Sub-inspector Waters had some difficulty in covering up the case, but was unable to prevent his wife and her friend from subsequently committing an assault on the curate by their poisoning him with a powerful laxa-tive. This made him ill for several days and achieved the desired effect of driving him away from the parish.[34]

Opinions regarding threatening letters varied. Some viewed them as representing genuine threats and as symp-toms of general lawlessness; one such individual was the lord chief baron, David Richard Pigot, who told the grand jury at the Queen's County (Laois) assizes in March 1870 that no crime required greater attention from them than that of sending threatening notices, as this crime was the prelude to worse outrages.[35] Lord Justice Fitzgibbon told the grand jury at the Monaghan assizes in July 1879 that the case of a process-server who was threatened by 'a large number of people' while he tried to perform his duties was less serious than another case where 'notices were ex-tensively posted through the country threatening persons who would come to an amicable arrangement with their landlord'.[36] Not everyone viewed threatening notices as evidence of a deeper malaise in society: in March 1872 the *Evening Telegraph* played down their significance, de-scribing them as 'compositions which are generally the offspring of mischief and folly rather than deliberate crime',[37] while in February 1881 the *Freeman's Journal* argued that 'Every one concedes that those threatening letters are the works of fools or madmen, and that such "outrages" are not to be taken into any serious account'.[38] The *Freeman's Journal*'s view received support from some surprising sources. For example, Justice Charles Robert Barry, who told the Antrim assizes in August 1872 that 'There was no greater or more serious offence than that of writing a threatening letter. It is a thing that menaces the happiness and security of the community at large', had completely changed his tune regarding this category of crime during the Land War of 1879 to 1882. In July 1881 he told the Cork assizes that he 'did not regard them as being in one case in a thousand indicative of an intention on the part of the writer to carry out his threat or get it carried out', and that 'they are obviously written with a view on the part of the writer sometimes, and indeed very often, as I think, for a private purpose of his own, to take advantage of what he knows or believes to be a system of terrorism and intimidation prevailing in the district'.[39] Alfred Turner, who was appointed assistant to Sir Redvers Buller, special commissioner for Kerry and Clare in 1886, was also sceptical about the idea that threatening letters were sent by members of collectives engaged in agrarian crime; he believed that 'The Irish are very much given to writing threatening letters, which, in the vast majority of cases, mean nothing at all, and are often written by way of a joke or to work off exuberance of spirits in a fit of bile.'[40]

Although some contemporary commentators dismissed the idea that threatening letters and notices were manifestations of a deeper malaise in Irish rural society, one should not be too quick to accept such views. W.E. Vaughan, in particular, has argued that for most of the period between the end of the Famine and the outbreak of the Land War, much of rural Ireland was relatively peaceful and prosperous, as rents generally failed to keep pace with prices for agricultural produce, evictions were relatively rare and agrarian crime much less widespread than previously.[41] However, this image of a generally peaceful and prosperous rural Ireland does not present the full picture. Even in the relatively prosperous decades that Vaughan discusses there was still considerable poverty and land hunger in much of rural Ireland. Many rural malcontents, even if they did not always carry out the blood-curdling threats that they made, found at least a temporary outlet for their grievances and resentments in sending threatening letters to and posting threatening notices directed against such targets as landlords and their agents, 'landgrabbers', or 'stranger' labourers or herdsmen who were deemed to have unfairly taken employment that rightly belonged to locals.[42]

The Land War

Sending threatening letters formed a considerable portion of the agrarian offences recorded during the Land War of 1879 to 1882 and during the Plan of Campaign from 1886 to 1891. Almost two-thirds of the agrarian crimes committed in Ireland between 1879 and 1882 – some 7,035 offences out of 11,320 – consisted of sending threatening letters.[43] During the Plan of Campaign period, such offences did not feature quite as prominently in constabulary outrage returns as they did during the earlier Land War years, but nevertheless they still represented a very high proportion of the overall total of Irish agrarian crimes, constituting some 40.2 per cent in 1886, 33.1 per cent in 1887, 37.7 per cent in 1888, 36.3 per cent in 1889, 38.3 per cent in 1890 and 45.6 per cent in 1891.[44]

The numerous threatening missives during the two phases of the Land War were part of a larger catalogue of agrarian crime.[45] The period from 1879 to 1882 witnessed the largest spate of agrarian crimes since 1849:[46] recorded agrarian outrages rose from 863 in 1879 to 2,585 in 1880 and peaked at 4,439 in 1881, before declining to the still very high number of 3,433 in 1882. These constituted some 24.7 per cent of the total crimes committed in Ireland in 1879, 45.6 per cent of those committed in 1880, 57 per cent of those committed in 1881 and 54.8 per cent of those committed in 1882.[47] In addition to the numerous threatening letters and notices, there were some sixty-seven agrarian homicides, 156 cases of firing at people, 907 cases of arson and 3,155 other agrarian offences committed in these years.[48] A large proportion of these agrarian crimes were carried out in support of the Land League's agitation. The agitation began in Mayo in 1879 as an anti-landlord campaign that aimed at peasant ownership of the land, but, as the Land League spread from Mayo to more prosperous parts of the country, it gradually developed into a campaign that aimed instead at securing sizeable rent reductions, and other reforms that reflected the aspirations and leadership roles of middling or well-to-do farmers in the expanded organisation.[49] The image of an oppressed peasantry bravely combating tyrannical landlords was a potent element in the propaganda that was produced by agrarian agitators in the 1880s.[50] This traditional interpretation of the origins and nature of the Land War, as involving a heroic defence by rack-rented peasants against predatory landlords, has, however, been challenged by a number of revisionist interpretations.[51]

Kerry, with some fifty-two reported agrarian outrages per 1,000 of its population, had the highest recorded rate of agrarian outrages from 1880 to 1882, followed closely by Galway, with a reported rate of fifty-one outrages per 1,000 of its population; the next highest reported rates were those for King's County (forty-three), Leitrim (forty-two), and Limerick and Tipperary (both forty-one).[52] Some districts had unusually high numbers of violent agrarian crimes: in the 'murder triangle' around Craughwell, in County Galway, for instance, there were some eight agrarian murders between May 1881 and June 1882. The victims were a landlord and his guard, Lord Clanricarde's agent and the agent's driver, a constable in the RIC and three tenants who had taken land from which other tenants had been evicted.[53] The Plan of Campaign, which attempted to force landlords on some 203 estates to accept reduced rents, was, like the Land League movement before it, ostensibly a peaceful agitation, but much of the agrarian violence between 1886 and 1891 was undoubtedly committed in support of its aims.[54]

Although agrarian outrages in the later period never reached the same high numbers as in the years of the Land League agitation, they were still, relatively speaking, at an extremely high level when looked at in the context of crimes committed in the post-Famine decades. The agrarian outrages that were reported by the RIC during the Plan of Campaign years consisted of some thirty-four homicides (twenty-four of which were murders), eighty-one incidents of firing at the person, 457 cases of arson and 3,550 other crimes.[55] These statistics do not provide a full picture of the crimes that were committed during this period, as many offences were never reported to the RIC: for example, according to one observer in 1886, 'not a tithe of the predatory visits made to farmhouses is made public, owing to the unwillingness of the victims to make representations to the authorities, thus provoking prosecutions and bringing down on their own heads future punishment either by boycotting or by attempts on life and property'.[56]

The scale of agrarian crime in much of the country from 1879 to 1882 posed a severe challenge to the authorities' ability to maintain law and order,[57] a challenge that was heightened by the widespread tactic of the boycott against those who had defied the wishes of the Land League, particularly those who took farms from which tenants had been evicted. Although boycotting had been occasionally used as a tactic in agrarian protest before the Land War, in the early 1880s it was used on a more widespread scale and more systematically than ever before.[58] The numerous examples of obstruction of, or violent resistance to, evictions by large crowds of people, as well as of crowds interfering with sheriffs' sales of cattle that had been distrained for non-payment of rent,[59] convinced many police and other observers that law and order had collapsed under the pressure of what seemed like a tenants' revolt in much of rural Ireland. The widespread boycotting of landlords and of 'obnoxious' tenants – boycotts that were often enforced by violence – added to this conviction.[60] The widespread tenants' campaign of obstruction against fox-hunting in late 1881 and early 1882, which led to the suspension of fox-hunting activity by most of Ireland's hunts (and often to the establishment of 'people's hunts' in their stead, which amounted to a form of mass poaching), added further weight to these fears.[61]

The widespread extent of the agrarian disorder led one Irish alarmist to inform British politician (and future chief secretary for Ireland) John Morley in 1882 that Ireland was 'literally a society on the eve of dissolution'.[62] This opinion was shared by many figures in authority, such as William O'Connor Morris, who served as a county court judge in Kerry from 1878 to 1886. In his memoirs, O'Connor Morris presented a particularly bleak overview of the deteriorating law and order situation in the early 1880s:

A reign of terror was witnessed in some counties as the [Land] League struck back at the Government and the law. A series of frightful murders took place; the victims were sometimes of the upper classes, but often from the ranks of the peasantry, for disobedience of the League meant peril to life, and more than one farmer who paid his rent was shot. A system of persecution, ingenious and cruel, was devised to insult and worry the gentry; domains were ravaged by 'Land League hunts', wild assemblages of excitable mobs; the sports of the field were strictly forbidden to landlords who 'made themselves obnoxious'; the horses, hounds, and flocks of many a squire were destroyed.

But the power of the League was most severely exercised against those – often in the humbler walks of life – who dared to transgress its barbarous edicts. The vengeance inflicted on 'grabbers of derelict farms', and threatened under tremendous penalties, was extended to all who crossed the will of the League; and petty juntas of tyrants in their local conclaves pronounced and carried out the detestable sentence of 'boycotting' against those who did not yield to their bidding.[63]

While many members of the Land League committed crimes in pursuit of one or other of that organisation's aims,[64] there is no evidence to support claims that the league's leadership, at either national or local level, condoned such illegal activity.

In an attempt to explain why such crimes were committed, the police pointed to familiar culprits: secret societies. Colonel Henry Brackenbury, appointed assistant undersecretary for police and crime in May 1882, was convinced that political and agrarian crimes were 'solely and entirely promoted by secret societies'.[65] His view echoed that of numerous police officers, who were convinced that agrarian outrages were the work either of 'Ribbon' societies or of Fenians and Ribbonmen working in tandem in furtherance of the aims of, and as members of, the Land League.[66] Fenians certainly played key national leadership roles in the Land League, and they were also leaders – often militant ones – at the local level in many parts of the country.[67] However, whether they played an active role in committing agrarian outrages either on an organised basis, as claimed by the constabulary, or as individuals who were members or supporters of the Land League, is far from clear. Secret societies were deemed to be behind such notorious episodes as the murder of Maria Smythe of Barbavilla, in County Westmeath, in April 1882,[68] the murder of five members of the family of John Joyce at Maamtrasna on 18 August of the same year,[69] and the so-called Crossmaglen Conspiracy, an alleged plot by a society called the 'Patriotic Brotherhood' to commit murder and carry out other outrages in Armagh and Monaghan in the early 1880s.[70] The evidence for secret-society involvement in these cases is speculative. Much of Donnacha Seán Lucey's account of agrarian violence in Kerry during the Land War rests on evidence that was given at the Parnell Special Commission in 1888; while Lucey accepts that this evidence was 'contested' at the special commission, and that some of it 'appeared to be fabricated', it nevertheless constitutes an important part of his evidence for the alleged involvement of secret societies (with Fenian leadership) in agrarian outrages in Kerry. However, Lucey also offers a useful corrective to James Donnelly's assertion that a secret society committed agrarian outrages in north-west Cork in the early 1880s. According to Donnelly, this outfit called itself the 'Royal Irish Republic', and was commanded by a discharged soldier named Connell (or O'Connell). Donnelly argues that this group of over fifty men acted as 'jury, judge, and executioner whenever their unwritten agrarian code was violated'.[71] Lucey shows how unreliable O'Connell's evidence was regarding this alleged secret society. According to O'Connell, the society consisted of some 1,500 to 1,600 members, armed with over 1,000 rifles and dynamite, and it was responsible for the agrarian outrages in the Millstreet region. He claimed that the Millstreet group was part of a 'district, county and national network'. It is indeed likely that O'Connell was involved in committing agrarian outrages, but the fact that the constabulary were able to convict a mere four individuals on O'Connell's evidence, and failed to find any of the large stores of arms that O'Connell claims were hidden in the area, casts strong doubt on his claims regarding the existence of the 'Royal Irish Republic' network.[72]

Although the special commission went to considerable lengths to portray the Land League and its successor, the National League, as criminal and traitorous conspiracies that were behind the agrarian and political violence of the 1880s,[73] it failed in its efforts to prove that secret societies were behind the agrarian violence of the period. Indeed, it is significant that it accepted the statement that Charles Stewart Parnell made in the House of Commons on 7 January 1881, to the effect that agrarian secret societies no longer existed in Ireland, as well as Matthew Harris' claim that no secret societies existed in Ireland, apart from the IRB.[74] In March 1887, Judge Peter O'Brien gave a perceptive assessment to the grand jury at the Kerry spring assizes of the supposed secret-society involvement in agrarian outrages, when he stated that:

> it is unhappily in the power of a few persons to engage in this system of nightly invasion of houses, and by means of terror and intimidation to appear as a conspiracy embracing a large number. At the same time there can be no doubt that there must be many such combinations in the county acting entirely independent of each other.[75]

Agrarian murders, arson, house attacks and mutilation of animals often required men from the same townland or perhaps the same parish to combine together to plan and carry out their crimes and, possibly, to prepare alibis for themselves, but this could be done without necessarily forming anything as formal or permanent as an oath-bound secret society: while O'Brien's assessment relates to how agrarian crimes were carried out in the late 1880s, it may also apply to how most of such offences were perpetrated in the earlier phase of the Land War.

Regardless of whether agrarian outrages were committed by secret societies, by combinations of men gathered together on an ad hoc basis to commit a specific crime or by lone individuals, the ferocity of many of these crimes led to a reluctance on the part of witnesses, even if they were victims, to supply evidence to the constabulary or to offer evidence in court. An appalled Baron Richard Dowse gave evidence of witnesses' fear of retaliation if they should help the police, when he informed the grand jury at the Connacht winter assizes in 1880 that, although in the previous four months there had been 236 indictable offences committed in Mayo, there were only twelve cases for trial at the assizes – in some 215 cases, nobody had given information to the RIC. There were some 291 indictable offences committed in Galway, and the victims in 278 cases refused to give evidence that would aid in bringing a prosecution.[76] A similar state of affairs existed in many parts of the country. The apparent paralysis of the judicial system when dealing with agrarian cases was one of the main reasons why four Coercion Acts were passed in the 1880s. These helped the authorities to at least disrupt the organisation of the Land League and of the Plan of Campaign through various wide-ranging measures, including authorising the arrest and detention of suspects without trial, as well as establishing special courts to try suspects in agrarian and political cases.[77]

While it is perhaps understandable that the police and judicial authorities should have highlighted those aspects of the agrarian agitation that suggested the existence of criminal conspiracies that appeared to have either willing or unwilling support from large sections of the community, one should not lose sight of the fact that, to a considerable extent, agrarian crimes were also committed that had nothing to do with either the Land League agitation or the Plan of Campaign. Approximately 39 per cent of agrarian offences between 1848 and 1880 arose out of such factors as competition for farms, trespassing, disputes between tenants and sub-tenants and disagreements about succession to farms, and another 23 per cent had a miscellany of origins, none of which were directly a product of communal agitation.[78] This suggests that real and compelling conflicts over the control of land were present in Irish rural society but that the formation of secret societies with elaborate structures to carry out violent acts to deal with these conflicts was rare by the closing decades of the nineteenth century (an unusual and later exception to this general rule was a secret society that was active in Craughwell, County Galway, during the Ranch War of the early twentieth century).[79] Instead, co-operation and campaigning to deal with conflicts over land were more likely to be directed into more formal political organisations such as the Land League or, on a more conspiratorial level, the Fenians. Both organisations appear to have had little or no desire to be actively involved in carrying out violent acts in pursuit of advantage in disputes over land, preferring to generate political and moral pressure rather than sponsoring agrarian outrages. This meant that outrages, while not unconnected to broader political movements, were distinct from them and were often the product of more immediate personal and familial concerns that arose from the unstable and unequal system of landholding and landownership.

Some interesting cases from the 1870s show how outrages frequently arose from a complex mix of local and family grievances, often of an apparently trivial character. For example, in May 1870, two siblings, Lawrence and Margaret Shiels, were hanged in Tullamore jail for having murdered a man named Patrick Dunne three months previously, in revenge for Dunne's having testified against their brother in an assault case, as a result of which their brother was sentenced to six months in prison. The original source of the discord between the two families was a dispute over rights of way to a turf plot.[80] In August 1873 Laurence Smith, of Lackenmore, County Cavan, a blind man, was hanged for having stabbed to death a fellow tenant farmer from the same townland on 3 July 1872. A 'miserable scrap of useless bog had caused warm words, many years ago', to pass between Smith and his victim, Patrick Lynch, which led to 'Vexatious litigation' between the two. Smith, who lost the court case over the bog, which was valued at ten shillings, had nursed a grievance ever since, and eventually killed his neighbour in revenge.[81] Also in August 1873, a 55-year-old woman, Mary McCallion, was brutally murdered in Muff, County Donegal – she was savagely beaten in the head, her brains and teeth scattered over the floor of her small cottage. McCallion had been the housekeeper of Patrick Feeney, who owned a small farm of some six or seven acres and who bequeathed it to her in his will, to the chagrin of other members of the Feeney family. The small farm was a particularly desirable property as it contained a pit of freesand, which was used extensively to scour houses in Derry city. The RIC believed that the murder was committed by William Doherty, who occasionally worked in the sandpit, but that the crime was committed at the behest of one of Patrick Feeney's nephews, James Feeney.[82]

David Fitzpatrick argues that many examples of rural unrest in nineteenth-century Ireland may be interpreted as arising from family disputes: conflicts that apparently involved different classes within rural society may often have involved struggles within families, and conflicts within classes may be viewed as struggles within family factions.[83] Fitzpatrick's argument certainly holds true for some of the agrarian violence committed during the 1880s, although it pays insufficient attention to the underlying social and political circumstances that gave rise to these disputes. According to Samuel Clark, the personal and the collective often dovetailed in the outrages that were committed during the Land War, as those behind the outrages 'usually had some personal stake in the case, or were friends of individuals who were personally involved'. Furthermore, many assaults on 'landgrabbers' were designed not to restore a former occupant, but to promote the interest of one or more parties who wished to obtain possession of the disputed farm instead, and many outrages involved disputes among relatives over inheriting land, or attacks on parents (usually widows) for not turning land over to their children.[84] Timothy Harrington, one of the Land League leaders and one of the main organisers of the Plan of Campaign, claimed before the Parnell Special Commission in 1888 that 'the most difficult cases out of those we had to deal with, and the cases out of which most of the agrarian crimes arose were the cases where one member of a family had taken land from another member'.[85] While this probably exaggerates the significance of internecine family disputes as a cause of agrarian crime, it nevertheless suggests that the idea that agrarian offences involved only the enforcement of an unwritten agrarian code does not fully represent the complexity of the issues that were involved.[86] The system of landholding itself gave rise to conflicts, which could divide families and communities and lead to bitter disputes between individuals and relatives.

The RIC in Queen's County recorded three agrarian homicides during the period from 1879 to 1893, one of which was probably a case of fratricide. A 68-year-old farmer from Boley Upper, Patrick Dunne, was found dead on his bed on 18 December 1881 – he was killed by blows to his head, which were probably inflicted by a hammer and chisel. The chief suspect was Patrick's brother, Timothy, who had been living on bad terms with him since his return from the United States of America in 1878 or 1879. Timothy had helped Patrick pay off part of the debt on his ten-acre farm, expecting to get at least a share of the holding; when this was not forthcoming, Timothy carried out some revenge attacks against his brother, such as burning a stack of his oats and tying his donkey to a beehive, which resulted in its being stung to death.[87] A case of murder in Clonboo, County Galway, in December 1883 at first appeared to bear the hallmarks of a typical agrarian homicide, when a tenant farmer named John Moylan was allegedly fired on and killed by a large group of men when he was walking home accompanied by his wife. A note was left on his body threatening one Thomas Brown, 'who was unpopular in the neighbourhood'. At first it appeared that Moylan had been murdered in a case of mistaken identity, but when the RIC investigated the crime suspicion quickly fell on the dead man's wife, Mary. According to local rumour, she had been having an affair with Michael Downey, a labourer on the Moylans' farm, while her husband was working in the United States of America to earn money to pay off rent arrears (which had only been partly paid, despite the large sums of money that he sent home). Eventually, Mary confessed that Downey had murdered her husband and that the threatening letter had been placed on his body as a ruse to trick the police into thinking that a gang of gunmen had shot him in mistake for Brown. Downey, who claimed that the dead man's wife had paid him to kill her husband, was hanged in Galway jail in January 1885.[88]

Another complicating factor to bear in mind when examining agrarian crime is that of bogus outrages – crimes that were committed either to fraudulently claim compensation or for other reasons. George Garrow Green, who served in the RIC from 1868 to 1889, believed that 'at least 50 per cent' of supposed outrages, such as threatening letters, cattle-maiming and arson attacks, were 'uncoupled with malice'.[89] He instanced several examples in his memoirs, such as the case of a landlord who got his steward to write him a threatening letter because a police barrack, for which he received government rent, was about to be discontinued, and another landlord who wrote himself a similar letter and fired a gun-shot at his own window so that he could have some policemen stationed in his house, 'whom he used to employ in various ways, and have driving him about as a sort of guard of honour'. Two head stewards wrote threatening missives to themselves, to increase their worth in their employers' eyes and have their wages increased. Most bogus outrages were committed by farmers so that they could claim compensation under the Malicious Injury to Property Act. As Green explained, 'It is no doubt a great temptation to avaricious and unscrupulous persons to do themselves, say, a £10 injury and mulct their neighbours of five times as much by exaggeration'.[90] Michael J.F. McCarthy, writing in 1911, stated that the system that prevailed in Ireland, whereby county court judges awarded compensation to victims of outrages, which was levied on the districts in which the outrages occurred, 'only punishes the innocent and lets the delinquent go scot-free'. As the RIC struggled to detect the perpetrators of outrages, and the judges usually awarded high levels of compensation in such cases, there was 'undoubtedly a temptation to struggling farmers to destroy their own property in the assurance that they will be handsomely remunerated for the loss'.[91]

The constabulary often found it difficult to prove that a compensation claim was really a case of fraud. For example, they believed that a servant of F.C. Garvey of Carrowkeel, County Sligo, had burned Garvey's house and offices in October 1898 on Garvey's orders, as the latter wished to fraudulently claim compensation for the destruction to his property. Although they built up a strong body of circumstantial evidence against Garvey, they were unable to convince the Sligo grand jury that Garvey's claim was a fraudulent one.[92] In another incendiary case at Tullerboy, near Bruff, in October 1914, the RIC were convinced that they knew who had set fire to a haggard containing about eighty tons of hay, but they were unable to secure evidence to convict her, 'largely due to the ease with which compensation can be had'. The *Royal Irish Constabulary Magazine* claimed that 'If compensation depended more on the assistance given to the police in such cases by the parties concerned, these fires would be fewer', and the guilty parties would be punished more frequently than was the case.[93]

An unusual bogus outrage was committed by a rabbit-trapper in Raheen, County Clare, in the years before the First World War. The trapper, John Foley, had paid the owner of the Raheen lands for permission to trap rabbits, but found that the preserve was also targeted by local poachers. To trick the constabulary into keeping a close watch on the rabbit preserve, and thereby protecting his own traps, Foley's son fired a shot one night and was sent by his father to the local constabulary to claim that the Foleys had been fired at, thereby ensuring future police protection for their traps.[94] District Inspector John Regan, who was transferred to Lisnaskea in 1914, records that one of his fellow district inspectors in Fermanagh retained his job as a result of committing a bogus outrage. The officer in question was an alcoholic, who, 'if he took a drink at all he had to keep at it for some weeks and nearly got the DTs'. He nevertheless managed to keep his job in the constabulary, mainly as a result of a battle of wits with his county inspector. On one occasion he concocted a case of agrarian outrage with the help of his landlady and her relative, in order to satisfactorily cover up his drunken absence when the county inspector came to visit him.[95]

As the preceding discussion illustrates, agrarian crimes were committed from a variety of motives. Many were carried out in pursuit of the aims of the Land League and Plan of Campaign, respectively, and probably had at least the tacit approval of a sizeable section of the communities in which the crimes were committed. It is probable that most of the perpetrators met on an ad hoc basis to carry out crimes in their local area: while this suggests that at least some level of rudimentary organisation and planning was involved in the short term, this is not the same as saying that secret societies carried out these crimes or that the perpetrators in different communities acted under central direction as part of a wider organised conspiracy. In addition to offences that were committed in pursuit of the Land League and Plan of Campaign's aims, some of the agrarian crimes during the Land War did not originate from any form of communal grievance: instead, they arose from a complex mix of family, intra-tenant and neighbours' disputes rooted in the land system itself. Rural Ireland during the Land War was a complex society and the historian should be wary of simplistic or one-dimensional readings of its agrarian crime.

The Ranch War

At the time that Michael J.F. McCarthy claimed that the compensation system in cases of outrages failed to deter lawbreakers from attacking property, some parts of the west of Ireland were still periodically in a state of disturbance as a result of outrages directed against graziers. These outrages were designed to compel the graziers to give up their holdings as a prelude to their redistribution among the landless and those with farms that were too small to be economically viable.[96] The anti-grazier campaign had its roots in the simmering discontent among many small farmers in the west at both the slow pace of land redistribution and the insufficient land available for this redistribution. The main organising body behind the agitation was the United Irish League (UIL), formed in Mayo in 1898 by a veteran of the Land War of 1879 to 1882 and the Plan of Campaign, William O'Brien.[97] In the first years of its existence, the UIL's main weapon was the boycott: graziers were the main targets for this form of intimidation, with the aim of forcing them to cease taking lands on the eleven-month system (which meant that the lands were outside the scope of the various remedial Land Acts that had been passed since the early 1880s), but landlords who persisted in letting grazing lands and shopkeepers who did not join the UIL were also subjected to boycotts. In 1901, William O'Connor Morris gave a typically alarmist assessment of what he regarded as the UIL's malign influence:

Steadily adhering to the precepts laid down by Parnell, the United Irish League has brought the detestable system of 'boycotting' to a hideous perfection in several counties; whole districts are subject to this secret but villainous tyranny; the results are seen in numbers of derelict farms, in hundreds of victims writhing under ever-present terror, in an infamous interference with trade and industry.[98]

The UIL's anti-grazier campaign spread considerably beyond its original Mayo base in the early years of the twentieth century; a notable turning point came in 1906, when Laurence Ginnell, MP for Westmeath North, advocated the new illegal tactic of driving graziers' cattle off their lands, in an effort to intimidate the graziers into giving up their lands for redistribution.[99] There were some 1,071 cattle drives in Ireland at the height of the campaign from 1907 to 1909, with the RIC in Galway, Meath, Clare, Westmeath and Roscommon recording particularly high occurrences of this offence.[100] These often involved crowds of hundreds of people.[101] In addition to cattle drives and boycotts of individual graziers, other intimidatory tactics included bands playing at or near the homes of 'objectionable' graziers – while these bands did not break the law, their ostensibly festive actions were clearly meant to intimidate. Newspapers that published in detail speeches at UIL meetings, in which graziers and other 'obnoxious' individuals were named or had hostile resolutions passed against them, also heightened the impact of the UIL's campaign of intimidation.[102] The anti-grazier agitation in the district of Riverstown, in County Sligo, included an unusual sectarian element. The Protestant community, which refused to join or subscribe to the UIL, was boycotted in a blatantly sectarian campaign of intimidation that began in the summer of 1908.[103]

Not all supporters of the anti-ranching campaign were content to intimidate by merely boycotting persons considered obnoxious by the UIL, or by driving their cattle or playing music at or near their homes – as in the agrarian agitation in the 1880s, the Ranch War of the early twentieth century also involved a degree of violence, which included maiming cattle, arson, assault, and firing shots at graziers or into their homes.[104] There was a marked rise in the number of violent agrarian crimes in the three years after Ginnell advocated cattle-driving as a tactic to be used against graziers. In the three years from 1904 to 1906, there were a mere six recorded cases of firing at the person that the RIC considered to be agrarian crimes, and thirty cases of firing into dwellings; in the three years from 1907 to 1909, the totals were 39 and 144, respectively.[105] One similarity between the agrarian outrages committed in the early twentieth century and those committed in earlier decades was the relatively high proportion of threatening letters or notices recorded by the RIC. In 1908, for example, some 233 of the 576 recorded agrarian offences (40.5 per cent of the total) consisted of threatening letters or notices, 'many of them of very trivial importance'.[106] The most serious spate of violence occurred in the Craughwell district in County Galway, where a secret society of more than 200 members, under the leadership of Tom Kenny, a blacksmith, carried out numerous agrarian outrages, including cattle drives, arson and firing into the houses of people deemed 'obnoxious' by the conspirators.[107] The most noted victim of Kenny's secret society, which appears to have mainly consisted of members of the IRB, was Constable Martin Goldrick, who was shot and killed on 21 January 1909 while protecting two labourers who were working for an 'obnoxious' farmer at Templemartin, who had been on the receiving end of a sustained campaign of intimidation by Kenny's organisation.[108] Goldrick was one of only two fatalities during the Ranch War; the other person killed during the agitation, John Stenson, was shot by the Riverstown RIC during an attack on the police by a stone-throwing mob of thwarted cattle-drivers on 29 October 1908.[109]

Although the Ranch War did not involve violence or disorder on anywhere near the scale of that witnessed during the 1880s, it nevertheless demonstrated how sections of rural society were prepared to countenance collective illegal activity if they believed that this would further their interests. Robert Lynd commented in 1909 that it was probable that 'the cattle-drivers would be quite as uneconomic farmers as the red-faced grazier who rolls about the country on his car with his armed policemen following him on their bicycles',[110] but this rather misses the point: the landless, and those with uneconomic holdings, believed otherwise, and there was enough dissatisfaction with the slow pace of purchase of landlords' estates and with land redistribution after the 1909 Land Act to ensure that attacks on graziers continued in various parts of the country in the period leading up to the First World War, even if these did not reach the high levels recorded between 1906 and 1909.[111]

Agrarian crime during and after the First World War

While agrarian crime persisted as a problem after the outbreak of the war, it remained at a relatively low level until a new campaign against graziers (and others) was begun in parts of the country, particularly in the west, in the winter of 1917 and spring of 1918. Republican activists, or on some occasions people for whom the republican tricolour simply represented a temporary flag of convenience, were often to the fore in this new bout of agrarian agitation.[112] In south Sligo, Sinn Féin activists took advantage of the prevailing nationwide concern about wartime food supplies, as well as the knowledge that farmers had not complied with compulsory tillage orders, to seize grass farms and divide them up ('in the name of the Irish Republic') among small farmers for conacre. These land seizures were often made by large crowds, accompanied by bands with republican flags and banners. Many Sinn Féin-orchestrated cattle drives also took place in different parts of the west.[113] The year 1918 saw a marked increase in the number of recorded agrarian outrages across the country, with some 355 in total, compared with just 168 in 1917; some 245 cattle drives took place in 1918, compared with just 64 in the previous year.[114] While the number of cattle drives fell to 92 in 1919, agrarian offences as a whole rose to some 488 in that year.[115] While it is important not to dismiss the strength of nationalist and republican feeling in the country at the time, some of those involved in committing agrarian crimes showed surprising flexibility in their professed political allegiance. For example, Robert Brown of Kilmanihan, County Kerry, assisted by others in the neighbourhood, seized the lands and house of Edward O'Connor after subjecting him to a campaign of intimidation, including shooting his horse, throwing a bomb at his house and shooting and wounding O'Connor. After seizing control of O'Connor's house and land 'in the name of the Irish Republic', Brown then sought the legal protection 'of an Act of an alien Parliament, which he did not recognize – the Increase of Rent and Mortgage Act – to retain possession of these premises'. Brown was, rather surprisingly, originally awarded possession by the county court of the lands and house that he had forcibly seized, but this judgement was overturned at the Kerry assizes in July 1919.[116] In some places, the agrarian agitation in 1919 involved murder: in March, a resident magistrate was killed in Mayo because he had convicted several Sinn Féiners allegedly involved in the agrarian campaign, and in Galway a herdsman was beaten to death because he did not give up his employment.[117] On 31 October the IRA killed Constable William Agar in an attempted arms raid on Ballivor barracks, County Meath. Although this was not an agrarian murder, a notable feature of the raid is that the IRA attackers gained access to the barracks by one of the party pretending to be a local farmer who was reporting a cattle raid, a crime 'which was quite common in the area at the time'.[118]

There was a marked increase in the number of land seizures and other agrarian crimes in 1920, especially in Connacht and Munster, which were facilitated by the RIC's abandoning, in late 1919, of hundreds of rural barracks that were considered too difficult to defend from IRA attacks. Sinn Féin and the IRA were behind many of these crimes in Tipperary, Clare, Galway and Sligo,[119] and almost certainly in other parts of the country. In County Longford, the IRA burned Currabola House in June 1920, in the belief that the house was about to be converted for use as an RIC barracks; the local IRA commander, Seán Mac Eoin, later admitted that he had been tricked into burning the house by local people who wanted the lands of the Currabola estate.[120] This was merely one of hundreds of examples of IRA arson attacks on 'big houses' during the War of Independence. Terence Dooley argues that many of these burnings were carried out for a complex mixture of military and agrarian reasons.[121] Furthermore, some IRA attacks on crown forces in Galway may have primarily had an agrarian motivation, suggesting the often intimate link between the political and the agrarian in Irish society.[122]

In addition to the intimidation, arson attacks, threatening letters and cattle drives that had become a staple of agrarian agitation by this time, some seven people were murdered as a result of disputes about land.[123] One of the murder victims, Frank Shawe-Taylor, was probably killed by the Galway IRA in March 1920; Shawe-Taylor, a landlord and grazier, had stubbornly resisted repeated demands that he give up his lands for redistribution to locals.[124] In an unusual twist, one IRA member was murdered in an agrarian dispute in Meath in 1920. The victim, Mark Clinton, was shot dead on 10 May while he was ploughing on his uncle's land at Cormeen; his two plough horses were also shot. It was believed that the attack was originally meant just to intimidate the Clintons, who had secured the farm in question in controversial circumstances and 'in the face of strong local opposition', but when carrying out the attack one of the gunmen decided to 'finish' the dispute, by killing Clinton.[125]

The attempt by elements of the IRA and Sinn Féin in the west and elsewhere to align their political goals with people's land hunger[126] had some unforeseen consequences: for example, in Clare, according to Seán McNamara, commander of the IRA's 6th Battalion, 'all sorts of fantastic claims began to be made and people who had been put out of farms several generations earlier endeavoured to regain possession'. In some instances, 'persons began to agitate for their neighbours' lands on no better grounds than that they had it from local gossip that they were the rightful owners'.[127] In May 1920 an alarmed Roscommon auctioneer and Sinn Féin member, Graham Sennett, summed up the state of apparent anarchy in his county as a result of the widespread land seizures that were taking place, and called on the Dáil to restore order and thereby win the confidence of those who felt threatened by the flagrant disrespect for the rights of property shown by the 'Cattle Drivers, Marauders, Terrorists and Hooligans'. He asserted that:

> Every man in the county who has anything will stand by Sinn Féin and the Republic, if we can prove that we restore order and do justice, where England could do neither ... the ranks of the land agitators are bristling with bad eggs, who have come into Sinn Féin to look for land and who, if they had it tomorrow, would set it on the eleven months and drink the proceeds.[128]

The opportunism of at least some of those involved in what *The Irish Times* on 20 April 1920 called 'Agrarian Bolshevism' is shown by an incident in Kilbride, County Roscommon, where a cattle drive was about to take place, 'with a tricolour in readiness to lead the advance'; when the owner of the cattle declared that he would take his case to the Dáil, the white and orange were torn from the flag and the drive was carried out in the name of the Ancient Order of Hibernians instead.[129] Arthur Griffith responded to the alarming reports from the west by authorising the establishment of arbitration courts, which, he hoped, would bring some semblance of order to the rural agitation in much of the country. Griffith was motivated by a number of factors: the land seizures could threaten the cross-class alliance on which Sinn Féin was based, and internal social conflicts could distract from the war against the British. Furthermore, those who openly flouted the law in the agrarian campaign were regarded as a potential threat to Sinn Féin and Dáil Éireann's authority. In order to establish their credentials as state-builders, the republican leadership had to assert their authority over the rural agitators.[130] A semblance of order was eventually brought to the disturbed areas by the network of Dáil courts, with IRA action (or threats of IRA action) often being used against the recalcitrant to enforce the courts' decisions.[131] The IRA became the *de facto* police in many parts of the country in the enforced absence of the RIC, and attempted to suppress various offences including burglary, theft, assault (including domestic violence), pocket-picking, sheep-stealing, trespass, drunkenness and contravening the licensing laws, in addition to clamping down on the illicit distillation of poteen.[132]

Although Ireland was not the only part of the United Kingdom in which periodic outbreaks of agrarian disturbances occurred,[133] the frequency and wide geographic range of such outbreaks, as well as the violence that accompanied them (although intimidation through threatening letters, boycotting and, in the twentieth century, cattle-driving were more common instances of agrarian crime than physical violence), were exceptional in Ireland's case. This would suggest deeper and more enduring conflicts and insecurities at the heart of the country's system of land ownership compared to other parts of the UK and, more broadly, western Europe.[134] As the preceding discussion notes, many valuable local and regional studies of agrarian crime in the period under review have been written, and several historians have also provided useful brief works that provide general discussions of agrarian crime throughout Ireland.[135] While it is difficult to advance a comprehensive explanation for agrarian crime from 1870 to 1920, as the contexts that gave rise to each major outbreak differed, nevertheless the Land League's beguiling slogan of 'The land for the people' may serve as a useful explanation of what drove many offenders to commit agrarian offences in this period. Who 'the people' were, of course, varied from time to time and from place to place, as did the desired object of 'the land'. For some, 'the people' were small tenant farmers in general, or those in a specific parish or landed estate; for others, 'the people' were one's own immediate or extended family or, indeed, oneself alone; for some, crime could be a means to securing 'the land' at current or reduced rents, while for others it was a means to try to secure land ownership or to compel graziers to give up their lands for redistribution among the landless or those with small, uneconomic farms. One can say that 'land hunger' in one form or another was sufficiently strong to drive large numbers of people, acting either as individuals or in tandem with others, to commit much of the agrarian crime in the period under study. Often this had a regional dimension, as evidenced by how often agrarian crimes were committed in different areas of Connacht, but the lure of 'the land' was never confined to just one particular region of the country; instead, it emerged from and reflected deep-rooted conflicts and divisions in Irish society in general. The hunger for land was a potent factor in the period, which was often manifested in agrarian crime: it was a factor that numerous political and military organisations, such as the Fenians, the Land League, the United Irish League, Sinn Féin and the IRA, tried to harness with varying degrees of success.

Chapter 2

'Ordinary' Crime and Its Policing

Introduction

WHILE THE PRECEDING DISCUSSION focuses on the numerous outbreaks of crime and disorder of an agrarian nature that punctuated the period, these episodes need to be placed in their proper context. Although many parts of Ireland *were* periodically disturbed by widespread agrarian offences, this should not obscure the important fact that even at the height of the most serious outbreak of agrarian disorder during the period, namely the Land War from 1879 to 1882, some areas of the country remained virtually unaffected by the violence that accompanied the agrarian agitation.[1] Even during the Land War, as Bernard Becker pointed out, the extent of crime in the supposed lawless areas where the agrarian agitation was at its highest was exaggerated, especially by outsiders. He documents the alarmed reactions of Dubliners when they learned that he proposed going on a tour of the disturbed districts, and records that 'It was in vain that I pointed out that every stone wall did not hide an assassin, and that strangers and others not connected either directly or indirectly with the land were probably as safe, if not safer, on a high road in Mayo than in Sackville-street, Dublin.'[2] This chapter will focus on 'ordinary' or non-agrarian crime in Ireland, indicating some of the main patterns and exploring some of the possible factors that helped to shape these trends.[3] Key differences between occurrences of crime in Ireland's urban and rural areas will be highlighted, particularly the higher rates of certain crimes in urban areas, and put in the context of wider debates about the incidence of crime in cities in Europe and elsewhere. The chapter will include a consideration of the Irish police's crime deterrent and detection roles and methods,[4] including their use of technology and forensic science. In particular, the constabulary's role in the prevention and detection of the illicit distillation of poteen will be discussed in detail, as a case study to illustrate how effective the RIC could be in certain circumstances when it came to preventing and detecting crime.

Recorded levels of non-agrarian crime

Notwithstanding the periodic prevalence of agrarian crime and disorder in some areas, the underlying, overall trend in the late nineteenth and early twentieth centuries was one of a general stability and, at times, decline in violent crime in the country.[5] Similar patterns have been noted in Britain during the same period.[6] Many historians' concentration on agrarian crime has meant that urban patterns of crime, and how they relate to the national picture, are often ignored. This has also resulted in a loss of perspective on the ordinariness of much Irish offending and a failure to recognise the degree to which Irish society 'at least in certain regions for prolonged periods, was not endemically or abnormally violent'.[7] The idea that Ireland was relatively free from serious crime was alluded to by *Zozimus* magazine as early as 29 July 1871, in a cartoon titled 'The Idle Assizes', which depicts a succession of 'Irish judges, crown prosecutors, jailers, hangmen' boarding an emigrant ship and disconsolately wailing, 'We have no work to do-o-o-o-o' (see Figure 1).[8]

THE IDLE ASSIZES.

CHORUS OF IRISH JUDGES, CROWN-PROSECUTORS, JAILERS, HANGMEN, &c.—" We've got no work to do-o-o-o-o. We're got no work to do-o-o-o."
They are compelled to emigrate to England, where " trade is flourishing."

Figure 1: 'The Idle Assizes', *Zozimus*, 29 July 1871. Reproduced by permission of the Librarian, Maynooth University, from the collections of St Patrick's College, Maynooth

In most of rural Ireland, for most of the period, the nature of crime was remarkably similar, consisting mainly of non-indictable offences of a trifling nature.[9] Evidence from contemporaries presents a broadly similar picture, supporting the *Evening Telegraph*'s generalisation in March 1872 that 'the pettiest of petty larceny rogues, a couple of sheep stealers comprised most of the defendants at Irish assizes'.[10] Later in the decade, the *Freeman's Journal* described Ireland's 'almost Arcadian state of repose', when commenting on the low levels of serious crime in the country.[11] Christopher Lynch-Robinson, who was appointed as resident magistrate in County Donegal in May 1912, recorded that the majority of crimes committed there consisted of minor cases of drunkenness, 'with and without disorderly conduct', as well as 'failure to have a light on the donkey cart at night, using obscene and threatening language to a neighbour whereby the said neighbour had just cause to apprehend a breach of the peace, and allowing cattle to wander upon the public road'.[12] The RIC at Leenane told a tourist in 1914 that there 'was really very little crime' in that district, 'but a sheep would be missing now and then, or a bit of poaching would be done, or perhaps a quarrel would arise between some farmer and his labourers and a horse would be lamed'.[13] James J. Comerford recorded of life in his native area, Muckalee parish in County Kilkenny, in the years before the War of Independence, that 'there were no criminals living in Muckalee parish and no criminal acts happening in the area'. The RIC's duty in County Kilkenny was similar to that performed in other rural areas of Ireland. Ensuring that the local public houses opened and shut within the times prescribed by law was a major part of their job, and on Sundays the constabulary watched these establishments 'like hawks'. During the rest of the week, 'the RIC chased grazing cows off the roads and issued summonses to their owners. At night time they gave summonses to owners of horses and carts if the cart[s] did not have a lighted lamp. Riders of bicycles without lights also got summonses.'[14]

Recorded instances of serious crimes such as aggravated assault in Ireland show rises in the 1880s and 1890s, and then a fall in the years before the First World War.[15] The post-Famine trends in the homicide rate is illustrated by Ian O'Donnell's figures, which show that the annual average homicide rate per million population from 1841 to 1850 was 38.7 and from 1851 to 1860 was 37.7; from 1861 to 1870 the rate was 23.7, and remained fairly steady thereafter at 24.5 between 1871 and 1880, 25.6 between 1881 and 1890 and 23.0 between 1891 and 1900. This was followed by a noticeable drop in the early twentieth century, to 15.9 between 1901 and 1910 and 14.4 between 1911 and 1919. It should be noted, however, that these figures include infanticides as well as other homicides, and that most of the recorded decline in homicides in the late nineteenth century was due to a marked fall in recorded infanticides. When one excludes cases of infanticide from the statistics, there were minor fluctuations in the recorded homicide rate from decade to decade: the recorded rates from 1870 to 1900 were not much different from the rate in the 1850s, while

O'Donnell suggests that there was a decrease in the recorded homicide rate in the first two decades of the twentieth century.[16]

There is anecdotal evidence to reflect the relative stability of the country and possibly a decline in at least some violent crime in Ireland in the late nineteenth and early twentieth centuries. Patrick Lyons, who served in the RIC from 1886 to 1920, recorded that he had so little police work with which to occupy himself that he was able to devote much of his time to becoming a keen amateur antiquarian. He took numerous photographs of, and made copious notes on, sites of archaeological and antiquarian interest in the various counties in which he served.[17] Stephen Crane, who visited Ireland in September 1897, was struck by both how peaceful the countryside of County Cork was and how numerous, and apparently idle, were the RIC. The latter appeared to the novelist to devote most of their time to fishing. He wrote of one sergeant that 'He probably caught more trout than any three men in county Cork. Some people had never seen him in any other posture but that of crowding forward on his stomach to peer into a pool. They did not believe the rumour that he sometimes stood or walked like a human.'[18] In 1912, the former Nationalist MP Tom Kettle also commented on the apparent lack of useful activity on the part of the RIC due to the relative absence of crime, when he remarked that 'The Royal Irish Constabulary was formerly an Army of occupation. Now, owing to the all but complete disappearance of crime, it is an Army of no occupation.'[19] Although both Crane and Kettle were writing for comic effect, their general point concerning the comparatively peaceful state of much of the country in the twenty years or so before the First World War appears a valid one.[20] In much of the period under discussion, the quotidian duties of most rural Irish policemen, which rarely involved the prosecution of major offences, largely mirrored those of their rural British counterparts.[21]

The fact that in the 1890s magistrates often gave offenders the benefit of the Probation of First Offenders Act of 1887[22] – in effect, letting them off with a warning as to their future behaviour – perhaps also suggests a contemporary perception that Irish crime levels were not at an alarmingly high level, otherwise magistrates would undoubtedly have imposed harsher sentences more regularly as a deterrent. Indeed, such was the 'wholesale application of the First Offenders Act' by magistrates, according to Fr P.B. Donnelly, of the Philipstown reformatory, in 1899, that young offenders were losing their fear of punishment in the courts, which was leading to a 'multiplication of criminals over 16 years of age'.[23] This was merely an assertion, which was not supported by any tangible evidence from the frustrated clergyman. He was correct, however, in his view that lawbreakers were frequently accorded lenient treatment under the act's provisions in the 1890s. Some representative examples from Belfast court cases illustrate the point. Magistrates were often inclined to apply the act in cases where parents intervened on behalf of their offspring, as, for example, when the mother of James Gamble, an 'artful youth' who obtained a parcel of clothing under false pretences from a shopboy in July 1891, 'promised to look after him' in future, and in the following month when Robert Spence's father gave bail for his son's future good behaviour, after the latter stole a shovel belonging to Belfast Corporation.[24] Three boys who stole two boxes of sweets from a cart on a Belfast street on 30 March 1892 also received the benefit of the act after their parents went bail for their future good conduct, as did a 'lad' named Butler in October 1893, whose father assured the court that up to the point that his son stole a pair of opera glasses from a man living in Smithfield he 'had always been a very dutiful boy'.[25]

There are a number of possible explanations for the apparent stability in crime levels in the late Victorian and Edwardian periods. The high levels of emigration may help to account for stable or declining levels of certain crimes. As Ian O'Donnell states in his study of violent crime in the post-Famine period, the massive exodus from the country meant that Ireland became 'an exporter of potential criminals': put simply, far fewer people residing in Ireland meant fewer crimes were being committed there.[26] Some astute killers were even able to take advantage of the fact that large numbers of people were emigrating from Ireland to hide evidence of their crimes, at least temporarily, by fooling relations of their victims that the homicide victims had emigrated. For example, Hugh Monahan killed his wife Isabella on Meenakeerin mountain, in County Tyrone, on 24 July 1872 while they were en route to Lough Derg. To account for his wife's disappearance, Monahan spun a yarn, which was believed, to the effect that she had returned to Glasgow, where the couple had wed in October 1871. Unfortunately for the killer, his wife's badly decomposed body was found a month after the killing, less than 130 yards away from where Monahan and his wife were last seen together, but luckily for him the body was in such an advanced state of decomposition that it was impossible to prove that she had been murdered, and he was found guilty of manslaughter instead.[27]

In a similar case, William Sheehan got away with homicide for somewhat longer than Monahan did, again hiding his crime by pretending that his victims had emigrated. Sheehan murdered his mother Catherine, his sister Hannah and his brother Thomas on their farm near Castletownroche in October 1877, because his mother objected to his marrying a neighbour's daughter on the grounds that her proposed 'fortune' was not big enough; his mother's objection meant that the marriage could not proceed and that Sheehan could not inherit the farm. Sheehan explained the sudden disappearance of his mother and siblings by claiming that they had emigrated to America, the fares being paid for out of the dowry that his prospective bride's family had allegedly paid him; in reality, he had thrown their bodies down a 72-foot-deep well on the farm. The crime was not discovered until 30 August 1884, when a labourer found the remains of the bodies when he was working on clearing the well, and Sheehan, who had emigrated to Australia in July 1883 after being evicted for non-payment of rent, was arrested.[28] Likewise when Joseph Fee, a Clones butcher, robbed and murdered John Flanagan, an egg-dealer, on 16 April 1903, Flanagan's sudden disappearance was explained away as a case of his having emigrated to America. The truth did not emerge until later that year, when Flanagan's butchered body was discovered under a manure heap behind Fee's premises on 15 December.[29] On 12 July 1909, William Scanlan of Feenagh, County Limerick, murdered (and probably raped) his sister-in-law Bridget Gayer near Charleville and managed to successfully allay suspicion by claiming that she had emigrated to America. Gayer's partly concealed body was discovered in a dyke some eight days later, which prompted a remarkably intricate and ultimately successful RIC investigation into the murder.[30] Although it is impossible to know precisely how often Irish murderers were able to get away with their crimes as a result of their claiming that their victims had emigrated, it is unlikely that the examples outlined here are the only instances when killers adopted this ruse.

The Ballot Act of 1872, which introduced the secret ballot in general elections, also probably had at least some impact in reducing numbers of recorded cases of violent assault, as the riots and assaults that frequently characterised elections in Ireland before the 1870s[31] became much less frequent thereafter. It is also possible that the gradual reduction in arrests for drunkenness and attendant disorderly conduct reflected a real decline in such unruly behaviour in this period.[32] The Sunday Closing Act of 1878, whose provisions extended to most of the country, almost certainly led to a reduction in drunkenness, at least on Sundays, in many of the areas covered by the act.[33] Under the 1878 legislation, alcohol could still be sold on Sundays, but during restricted hours, in the cities of Dublin, Belfast, Waterford, Cork and Limerick, and these restrictions probably also had the effect of decreasing the total number of arrests for drunkenness. Other factors that probably also led to a fall in public drunkenness include the fact that the consumption of spirits had been declining since the 1850s and that of beer was rising (but, on the whole, the overall consumption of alcohol dropped since the late 1870s).[34] Illicit distillation of spirits was also at a much lower level in the period under study than in the decades before the 1870s.[35] In the last three decades of the nineteenth century in parts of Ulster, the popularity of ether drinking, which did not tend to lead drinkers into inebriated acts of violence, also probably played some part in keeping the statistics of drunkenness down.[36]

That Ireland was the most heavily policed part of the United Kingdom[37] also possibly had a deterrent effect on potential lawbreakers, even if this effect is impossible to quantify. Because there were more police per head of population in Ireland than in Britain, this meant that the Irish police had a much greater knowledge of the individuals and communities that they policed. This is shown, for example, in the statistics that were kept regarding the characters of the people who were charged with various offences in Ireland and in England and Wales. These demonstrate that from 1870 to 1881 the proportion of people prosecuted in Ireland whose characters were previously unknown to the police ranged from a high of

21 per cent in 1878 to a low of 14.7 per cent in 1881; these contrast with a high of 36.3 per cent in each of 1879, 1880 and 1881 and a low of 31.4 per cent in 1875 in England and Wales. Over the next twelve years, the

Year	Ireland (%)	England & Wales (%)
1870	19.5	32.3
1871	18.2	32.9
1872	16.4	33.6
1873	18.3	33.3
1874	20.4	32.9
1875	19.2	31.4
1876	17.9	33.7
1877	18.8	32.5
1878	21.0	32.6
1879	19.3	36.3
1880	17.2	36.3
1881	14.7	36.3
1882	14.1	
1883	13.8	
1884	15.4	
1885	16.2	
1886	16.9	
1887	16.0	
1888	16.4	
1889	13.8	
1890	14.2	
1891	15.5	
1892	12.9	
1893	12.8	

Table 1: Proportion of prosecuted people whose characters were previously unknown to the police, 1870–93.

Source: *Irish Judicial Statistics*, 1870–93

Irish statistics ranged from a high of 16.9 per cent in 1886 to a low of just 12.8 per cent in 1893, the final year in which these particular statistics were recorded by the registrar-general. The relatively large police presence in Ireland probably also resulted in an increase in the annual rate of prosecution of a wide range of minor, non-indictable offences in the last decades of the nineteenth century.[38]

Historians disagree about what official statistics reveal about crimes that were committed in nineteenth- and twentieth-century Britain,[39] and it is also far from clear what the statistics tell the historian about crime in Ireland in this period.[40] This point was noted by Robert Lynd in 1909, when he stated that such statistics could be read as indicating that the Irishman was either 'The least criminally-inclined of all the inhabitants of Europe' or 'A murderer, a maimer of cattle, a carder of women's hides'.[41] It is impossible to quantify how variables such as, for instance, the varying police strengths in different parts of the country or the foibles of individual officers (which determined whether certain offences were either overlooked or suppressed vigorously at different times)[42] affected the police recording of crimes. Nor is it possible to know the 'dark figure' of crimes that went unrecorded by the police.[43] There are also serious methodological objections to using statistics of crime collected by the Irish and British police, respectively, as a basis for comparing and contrasting crime rates in the two countries. These objections relate not just to the significant differences in the levels of policing on both sides of the Irish Sea, but also to the fact that the police in Ireland and Britain sometimes used different yardsticks when recording crime. To take the example of the recording of murder: William Neilson Hancock, who compiled the Irish judicial statistics in the 1870s and early 1880s, explained in 1872 that in Ireland the statistics reflected the crime that was charged at the commencement of the prosecution, which corresponded closely with the verdicts of coroners' juries, whereas in England and Wales the police returns reflected the decision of juries in murder cases.[44] This meant that Irish crime returns inevitably recorded a higher rate of murder than those of England and Wales. Another complicating factor is that not only did different English and Welsh police forces use different criteria when defining and recording violent crimes, but, according to one historian, they also often tended to record unexplained or suspicious deaths as suicides or accidental deaths rather than as murders, as investigating the latter cases ate into their limited budgets.[45] There is enough evidence, therefore, to suggest that one is not always comparing like with like when comparing Irish and English and Welsh statistics of crime, which calls into question S.J. Connolly's assertion, based on a study of the official crime statistics for these countries, that they 'leave little doubt that the common perception of Ireland as a more violent society than other parts of the United Kingdom was firmly based in fact'.[46]

Rural versus urban crime rates

While one needs to approach official crime statistics with caution, they are probably accurate in suggesting that Ireland's urban areas generally had higher crime rates than rural areas: for instance, the statistics would suggest that Belfast's crime rate was significantly higher than that of other areas of Ulster in the late nineteenth century[47] and Dublin always featured to a disproportionate extent in the annual police returns of serious crime.[48] From 1882 to 1914, the various registrars-general who compiled the annual Irish judicial statistics recorded the crime rates in each county and urban police district. These show that in every year, the Dublin Metropolitan Police (DMP) district had either the highest or, occasionally, the second-highest overall crime rate in the country, and that it always had the highest rate of serious or indictable crimes. Simple larceny constituted the majority of indictable crimes recorded in Ireland in any year, and the vast majority of these were recorded in the DMP district. For instance, a perusal of the returns of simple larceny committed in the ten years from 1885 to 1894 reveals the extent to which this crime was heavily concentrated in the capital. In 1885, 88.8 per cent of cases of simple larceny were committed in the DMP district; the statistics for the following years were 1886: 88.9 per cent, 1887: 89.7 per cent, 1888: 88.3 per cent, 1889: 90.8 per cent, 1890: 87.4 per cent, 1891: 89.9 per cent, 1892: 85.3 per cent, 1893: 86.7 per cent and 1894: 86.8 per cent.[49] The DMP district, along with Belfast, Limerick city, Waterford city, Cork city and Galway town, usually had the highest rates of crime. At the other end of the scale, Donegal, Antrim, Down, Fermanagh, Wexford and Mayo featured most frequently among the counties with the lowest rates of crime.

John McKenna, who joined the RIC in 1891, provides anecdotal evidence in his memoirs of the different crime rates in rural and urban areas. McKenna spent the first twelve years of his police service in rural County Galway, where 'there was really nothing to be done except to summons a man for being drunk at a fair, or a farmer for occasionally allowing his pig or dog to walk on the road. An ambitious policeman thought himself lucky when he found an ass or pig [wandering] on the road, as it meant a "case" opposite his name in the monthly summary prosecutions which had to be prepared for the inspecting officers.' McKenna found that the situation was very different in his next posting, Ballymena, in which town he soon found out that 'it was impossible to avoid making almost daily arrests for drunkenness and disorderly conduct, etc'.[50] Ian Bridgeman, in his discussion of the higher crime rate in Irish towns, suggests that 'The greater incidence of theft in towns reflected a greater opportunity to steal, a greater … chance of avoiding detection, and a greater willingness on the part of the aggrieved to involve the authorities in the recovery of his [sic] property'.[51]

The Leicester School's concept of the existence of a 'rough working class' – a section of the lower working class, economically insecure, alienated from the wider society and from the police, and prone to violence[52] – seems applicable to the conditions of life in the slum areas of Dublin in the late nineteenth and early twentieth centuries,[53] and also seems applicable in helping to explain why Dublin had a massively disproportionate level of indictable crime in this period. Such episodes as the street violence of the 'Boltoneer' and 'Georgeite' gangs between 1871 and 1874,[54] the widespread rioting and looting that ensued after a fire consumed a large Thomas Street timber-yard in June 1873,[55] and the bacchanalian disorder that followed a massive fire at Malone's bonded whiskey stores in Chamber Street, in the Coombe, in June 1875, which resulted in several people, including children, falling seriously ill or dying as a result of drinking the sewage-contaminated streams of burning whiskey which gushed along the streets,[56] showed the potential for riotous disorder which existed in many of the poorer parts of the city, as did the frequent crowd attacks on members of the DMP, especially when they arrested people for being drunk.[57] The DMP did not only have to contend with crowd attacks, but some individuals were also noted for their propensity for assaulting policemen. These included a 'rough', John Carty, who by June 1880 had been convicted of 143 offences, mainly of assaulting policemen; according to Constable Eastwood, 'he never works, and the first young constable he can meet in the street he strikes him to knock him down without saying a word to him'.[58] Another formidable police-hater was Francis Lacy, a 'stout, well-built fellow, of powerful physique', who served several terms in prison, including one of five years for assaulting DMP men. According to the *Freeman's Journal*, Lacy 'has always been regarded with dread by [even] the stoutest members of the metropolitan force', and on his arrest in July 1880 it took the entire Sackville Street station party to restrain him. Lacy was a member of the 'Band Boys', a gang that specialised in assaulting policemen.[59]

Many of the street battles between rioters and the DMP during the 1913 Lockout[60] may be at least partly interpreted as further expressions of the long-standing hostility that existed towards the police among Dublin's 'rough working class': as Constable Dockery explained, regarding the 'very low specimens' who rioted in the Thomas Street area: 'They were mostly of the working class. I know that locality; there is a very dangerous class of people there, and the crowd was mostly composed of them – a crowd that never work.'[61] The looting that occurred in the centre of Dublin during the Easter Rising in 1916 also involved many of the capital's 'rough working class' taking advantage of the temporary absence of their accustomed enemy, the DMP. An English eyewitness described the events that he saw at the corner of Sackville Street and North Earl Street on 26 April:

> The gamins take charge of a hat-shop, and come out dressed in 'toppers', hunting caps and bowlers, which give them the most grotesque appearance imaginable – seeing that the rest of their garments are nothing but rags of the filthiest description. They loot a sports' emporium, and rush out into the road to play mock cricket and golf. They seize a cheap book-shop, and immediately offer to sell armfuls of the paper volumes to the now rapidly-growing crowd. The more adult hooligans, intent on more profitable spoils, smash a huge plate-glass window of a boot-shop and emerge with

stacks of expensive footwear and hurry away to their hovels ... The younger members of this high-spirited rabble mount the abandoned tramcars, dressed in some of the astonishing garb they have stolen, and wave their sporting trophies proudly in the air, what time the more mercenary of the mob purloin the entire stock of a Sackville Street jewellers', returning at intervals to scrape over the very dust on the shelves in case they may have missed something.[62]

A DMP detective, Ned Broy, later recorded similar impressions of the looting that occurred during the rebellion:

One could see some bizarre sights from the windows during that week: corner-boys wearing silk hats, ladies from the slums sporting fur coats, a cycling corps of barefooted young urchins riding brand new bicycles stolen from some of the shops, and members of the underworld carrying umbrellas. One citizen was carrying a large flitch of bacon on his back, with another walking behind cutting off a piece of bacon with a large knife.

Although the detectives, in common with the whole DMP force, were by Commissioner's orders confined to barracks, members of the housebreaking squad were revolted at the sight of so much stolen property being flaunted before their eyes. They sailed out and soon filled the cells of College St[reet] police station with prisoners who could not be dealt with until the following week when the courts were opened.[63]

In many ways, the exhausting and frequently dangerous daily round of DMP men in Dublin or RIC men in Belfast was more akin to that of policemen serving in British cities such as Liverpool, Middlesbrough, Manchester or Glasgow than that of members of the constabulary who served in rural Ireland during periods of agrarian tranquillity.[64] An examination of the crime that was committed in Irish cities between 1870 and 1920 offers little support to those scholars who argue that European and North American cities tended to be less affected by crime, especially violent crime, than rural areas.[65]

Policing and the prevention of crime: the case of illicit distillation

Foreign observers were often struck by what they regarded as the relative ubiquity of policemen in Ireland.[66] Not only did the police seem to be everywhere, but they also seemed to have an intimate knowledge of the character and habits of the people in their districts.[67] This was particularly the case in rural areas. The apparent omniscience of the Irish police was aided by their keeping a number of detailed registers of the population in the various constabulary sub-districts, which were regularly updated: these allowed newly appointed policemen to quickly familiarise themselves with the people who lived in their area, and they also made it easier to spot strangers. Under the terms of the Habitual Offenders Act of 1869, an alphabetical list was compiled of the names, physical descriptions and criminal histories of persistent re-offenders, and each year 1,700 copies were circulated to prisons, post offices and police stations.[68] By the 1890s, the particulars of habitual criminals and released convicts were published twice a week for the information of the police.[69] The constabulary also used registers of the inhabitants of their local area to aid their surveillance efforts. The RIC register for Knocknacarry barracks, in County Antrim, for 1881 shows that these registers contained the names and addresses of registered keepers of public houses, as well as of blacksmiths and vendors of gunpowder. They also listed the names and occupations of every householder in each district, along with details of the relation of every house's inhabitants to the householder.[70] The RIC were also often able to arrest suspected persons as a result of reading their descriptions in another surveillance aid, the police gazette the *Hue and Cry*.[71] The constabulary's routine presence at railway stations, where they watched the arrival and departure of train passengers, led to the arrest of numerous suspects.[72] A correspondent for the British socialist *Clarion* newspaper who went on a tour of Ireland in 1896 commented unfavourably that 'to the free-born Englishman the appearance of the spiky-helmeted perishers on every railway station platform has a very irritating effect. They examine every carriage and "peruse the features" of every arriving and every departing passenger. And one especially perfervid polisman evinced a desire to put his nose down the throats of the passengers, and see what they had had for dinner.'[73] Police surveillance at Queenstown railway station was particularly important, as suspects were often arrested there as they passed through the station en route to trying to board passenger ships for America.[74] The case of two juveniles from Loughrea, named Catherine Keghane and James Farrall, aged sixteen and seventeen respectively, on 27 May 1875 on a charge of having stolen £20 from Keghane's father, was typical of many. The pair were eloping and, after failing in their attempt to get married in Limerick due to the refusal of a clergyman to marry them on account of their youth, they made their way to Queenstown in an effort to journey to New York. A telegram with details of their descriptions put Constable Mack on the alert and he arrested them when they arrived at Queenstown railway station.[75] George Bidwell, an American, who, along with his brother and other accomplices, swindled the Bank of London out of some £104,000 in January and February 1872, provides a graphic account in his memoirs of how difficult it was for him to evade the attention of Irish detectives and plainclothes policemen in various parts of Munster when he fled from England and tried to take a White Star steamer to the United States at Queenstown. He was rather fortunate, after several days of leading his police chasers a merry dance and several lucky escapes, to eventually make his way to Belfast, whence he caught a steamer to Glasgow. Along the way, he found it necessary to pass himself off variously as a priest who wished to travel incognito, a friend travelling to visit some officers stationed at Cahir, a Fenian leader on the run, a Russian prince and a French gentleman. Some of these guises led to his receiving help in his flight from the police.[76]

How effective was police surveillance? One result of the intense police surveillance of Irish society in this period was that the illegal manufacture of poteen could be carried out only in secret, and in relatively remote or inaccessible parts of the country. Lord Rossmore, in describing poteen-making in County Galway in 1912, explained that:

> Police surveillance is so close that the men fear to make the potheen with malt in the old-fashioned way, because the scent of the mash would be carried a mile over the mountain, and in that would lie their greatest risk of detection. To avoid this they now distil potheen from a mixture of sugar and water which produces the vilest of poisons, indeed, if it is dropped on a woollen fabric it immediately acts as a corrosive.[77]

A few examples should suffice to illustrate the general point about poteen-makers being forced to carry out their activity in secluded areas, as a result of police surveillance. In June 1877, the RIC seized a still in what was described as the 'almost inaccessible' mountainous district between Ballygawley and Pomeroy.[78] A visitor to the Inishowen peninsula in 1884 remarked that 'not a few of the peasants have made a hereditary profession' of making poteen in that region, and that 'What with the wild coast-lines, and the innumerable creeks, they can easily land the raw material and ship the manufactured article'. Stills tended to be set up 'in some secluded ravine where the smoke is most likely to escape detection', with children apparently lounging on the hillsides acting as lookouts.[79] Inspector General Andrew Reed told the royal commission on liquor licensing laws in March 1898 that the illegal manufacture of poteen was a problem in the RIC districts of Oughterard, Roundstone and Spiddal, and particularly around Carraroe, 'where the inhabitants are most persistent in the making of illicit whisky'. Reed explained that 'The locality ... favours the making of it, as there are a great many small islands, which are difficult of access, and, in consequence, the exertions of the police in their attempts to suppress the practice is [*sic*] considerably baffled'.[80] According to the November 1911 issue of the *Royal Irish Constabulary* Magazine, the Glencahy and Rossport RIC sub-districts, 'dreary mountainous wastes in North-West Mayo', were 'still noted for the distillation of illicit spirits', while the January 1912 issue of the same magazine stated that Glenlark mountain, in County Tyrone, 'forms a natural hiding place for distillers'.

The decline in the illegal poteen-making industry had set in before 1870, partly due to the exertions of the Revenue Police, and then those of the Irish Constabulary, which took over the Revenue Police's duties in 1857.[81] Although the RIC failed to suppress poteen-making in its entirety, they certainly made it more difficult for the 'smugglers', as the poteen-makers were often described, to carry out their activities. In the 1870s the islanders of Owey and of Inistrahull, off the coast of Donegal, frequently engaged in a battle of wits with the RIC and the coastguard in order to manufacture poteen. When the sea conditions were stormy Owey could be inaccessible from the mainland for weeks

at a time, which meant that the islanders could distil poteen in full view of the RIC, who were unable to prevent
them from flagrantly breaking the law. When the stormy
conditions abated, the islanders were usually able to hide
the poteen on the island or to transport it to public houses
on the mainland. The RIC also kept up an energetic campaign against the Inistrahull poteen industry, which was
a communal activity in this decade.[82] Innishmurray, off
the coast of Sligo, 'was the great headquarters of poteen
makers' in the 1870s, according to Sub-inspector Samuel
Waters, and during the winter months 'the islanders were
mainly employed in distilling poteen from grain supplied
by the farmers on the mainland'. A similar battle of wits
ensued between the Innishmurray poteen-makers and the
Sligo police as took place between their Donegal counterparts. Illicit distillation was suppressed on Innishmurray
when a permanent RIC presence was established there,
but this was removed in the early twentieth century, with
the result that the industry revived and the RIC on the
mainland once again had to attempt to catch the illegal
manufacturers unawares.[83]

Although there were swingeing fines for the manu-
facturing of poteen – £6 was the minimum amount that
magistrates could impose – a combination of extreme
poverty in the areas where poteen-making persisted, and
the profits that were to be made from the trade, ensured
that illicit distillation continued, especially in parts of the
west and in Ulster, despite the efforts of the RIC to suppress it.[84] A journalist commented on the link between
poverty and the attractions of poteen-making in the Erris
district of Mayo in 1883:

The principal industry in Erris seems to be the making of poteen. This, wherever carried on, has a demoralising effect on the people. It encourages idleness, drunkenness, evasion of the law, and irregular habits. But the people are so poor that without some accessory employment such as this it is hard to tell how they could live at all, especially when a storm has destroyed their oat or potato crop, as not unfrequently happens. This temptation to make money by illicit distillation is strong, and its strength, and the circumstances of the people, while they do not justify, certainly palliate the offence.[85]

Poor prices for cereals, or the failure of cereal crops due to wet weather, were also commonly cited as reasons why poteen-makers resorted to their illegal trade.[86]

Sympathy towards those who engaged in the illegal manufacture of poteen often came from surprising sources. When Jack McGee was sentenced at Falcarragh petty sessions in February 1872 to a fine of £12 or six months in jail in place of paying the fine (this was his second poteen-making offence), a memorial on his behalf was drawn up '[i]n consideration of the poor man's poverty' and among the reputed signatories was Sub-inspector George Maxwell.[87] A.B.R. Young, the Church of Ireland minister of Ballybay in the 1870s, records that 'a small and very poor farmer' in his neighbourhood frequently had no option but to make poteen from his oats when his crop failed, as often happened, in order to be able to pay his rent. Reverend Young states that 'my sympathies were entirely with him', and that he often helped him to fool RIC search parties by hiding the farmer's illicit produce in his own house. The clergyman was able to do this because his friend, the local sub-inspector, William Bingham Kelly, would invite himself to lunch with him on these occasions, always giving a few days' notice, thereby enabling the farmer and Young to hide the poteen from the RIC.[88] According to the Nationalist MP William O'Malley, members of the RIC at Carraroe in the 1880s 'very often' turned a blind eye to the local manufacture of poteen, with the exception of some individual policemen, 'anxious for promotion', who 'pried into the private affairs of the people and heavy fines were imposed on the distillers'.[89] District Inspector Vere Gregory, who joined the RIC in 1895, records that on one occasion he received information that 'a small and very poor farmer was to "make a run" one night on a desolate bog, bordering on his holding' in County Sligo. This was 'in the centre of a locality where poteen making was rampant'. Gregory's sympathies were with the lawbreaker when he and his men raided the poteen-maker's wretched cabin:

I knew the run had been made to the order of a well-to-do neighbouring farmer, and as I gazed on this scene of poverty and squalor, I fervently hoped that his unfortunate tool had not kept any of the poteen for his own consumption, but, alas, a small bottle of it, fresh run and still warm, stood on the chimney shelf, and the wretched man had to go to prison for three months, in default of paying the heavy fine which the law imposed on conviction under the Illicit Distillation Act.[90]

In 1919, Katharine Tynan recorded an Irish peer's 'disgust at the conduct of a magistrate who inflicted heavy fines for poteen-making, as though he interfered with an ancient and honourable industry. The peer seemed to look upon the magistrate as a horrid sort of new broom.'[91] The sympathy that was accorded to poteen-makers even by some leaders of Irish society illustrates the inherent challenges in trying to police and prosecute an activity that was legally, but not culturally or socially, considered a crime.

Many contemporaries suspected that the RIC connived to an extent in allowing the illegal manufacture of poteen to continue, as they received rewards for detections of the equipment that was used in the illicit trade. The suspicion arose from the discrepancy between the number of detections of illicit distillation each year, and the relatively small number of prosecutions. For example, in 1900, while the RIC discovered some 1,828 instances of illegal distillation, there were only twenty prosecutions for the offence: the tiny number of prosecutions makes the claim of one revenue commissioner, that the RIC did not press illicit distillers too closely for fear that they would cease production, seem less fantastic than it might otherwise appear.[92] Vere Gregory documents that a blacksmith in one part of County Sligo made the stills that were used by the local poteen-makers, and that he would periodically coerce them into ordering replacement stills; the blacksmith would then secrete the stills on 'unallocated' bog and inform the police, thereby earning a reward for himself, and the RIC party that found the stills would also share in 'the substantial reward prescribed by law for successful detections and seizures' in cases of illicit distillation. According to Gregory:

All this is somewhat reminiscent of the old story of the attempt by the British authorities to get rid of snakes in India, by offering a reward to the natives for every snake brought to the local police station. Far from having the desired effect, it only aggravated the evil, for the wily native at once perceived what a nice little source of income the scheme could be made to afford him. He at once started to rear snakes, and then claimed the reward for each carcass of the young broods he handed in, until the number of snakes and the amount paid in rewards reached such an alarming figure that the scheme had to be abandoned.[93]

Robert Lloyd Praeger claimed in 1895 that illicit distillers in the Antrim mountains had a similar cunning arrangement whereby they procured fresh funds to make new equipment. According to Praeger, once a still was past its working life, it was hidden in 'some out-of-the-way spot' and one of the distillers informed the constabulary of its location, thereby earning him £6 reward 'for his reverence of the law' but also allowing for the manufacture of a replacement still.[94]

Irrespective of how reliable or unreliable the claims of constabulary collusion in poteen-making may have been, the RIC were at least able to restrict the amount of poteen-making that was carried out, as Table 2 illustrates. As one historian points out, by the late nineteenth century

Year ending 31 March	Ireland	England	Scotland	Year ending 31 March	Ireland	England	Scotland
1870	2,215	40	5	1897	1,546	4	15
1871	1,813	34	15	1898	1,693	1	2
1872	1,115	21	8	1899	1,781	9	5
1873	1,033	14	10	1900	1,828	12	5
1874	796	12	6	1901	2,008	9	1
1875	731	5	2	1902	1,404	12	2
1876	796	8	1	1903	913	7	6
1877	979	3	2	1904	1,148	6	9
1878	745	10	2	1905	1,175	7	3
1879	683	8	2	1906	991	2	2
1880	685	5	5	1907	968	4	2
1881	700	9	3	1908	1,025	3	1
1882	881	5	8	1909	1,149	1	2
1883	883	11	16	1910	1,099	0	4
1884	782	6	13	1911	1,139	0	4
1885	829	5	22	1912	1,165	0	8
1886	864	7	16	1913	1,027	0	2
1887	1,186	9	17	1914	1,016	0	2
1888	1,808	3	40	1915	998	0	2
1889	1,739	11	31	1916	910	0	2
1890	1,819	14	28	1917	581	0	2
1891	1,518	1	15	1918	412	0	2
1892	1,205	12	19	1919	336	3	2
1893	1,208	6	21	1920	947	2	5
1894	1,392	6	16	1921	315	2	5
1895	1,107	4	10	1922	172	0	4
1896	1,338	5	6				

Table 2: Annual detections of illicit distillation in Ireland, England and Scotland, 1870–1922.

Sources: Fourteenth to fifty-second *Inland Revenue Commissioners' Reports*, 1870–1909; First to thirteenth *Reports of the Commissioners of Customs and Excise*, 1910–22 '[i]llicit distillation had been brought under control' by the constabulary;[95] indeed, the *Freeman's Journal* argued on 11 January 1900 that the spirit revenues that flowed into the exchequer as a result of the RIC's efforts against poteen-makers were the main reason why the force's strength was maintained at a very high level that bore no relation to the number of crimes committed in the country. It is perhaps a testament to the constabulary's success in disrupting and restricting the manufacture of poteen that, when the RIC were forced to abandon hundreds of rural barracks in late 1919 and early 1920, the illicit trade sprung up again in many parts of the country,[96] and the IRA often felt it necessary to carry out raids against the distillers or to confiscate poteen at fairs.[97] Such raids were particularly common in Mayo, Galway, Monaghan, Antrim, Tyrone, Sligo, Donegal and Longford,[98] counties that had been traditional strongholds of illicit distillation. In one of these raids in December 1920 in County Tyrone, where the manufacture of poteen was having a 'demoralising' effect on the population and where it was feared that members of the IRA 'might fall victims to the evil', a distiller named Mullen, an ex-member of the IRA, opened fire on the raiders and was shot in turn, and died of his wounds the next day.[99]

This case study of the RIC's generally successful efforts to suppress the illegal poteen industry is significant for what it suggests about police attempts to combat crime in the late nineteenth and early twentieth centuries. At first glance, it gives the impression that the constabulary were an effective crime-fighting body, as the RIC's pervasive presence in the countryside made it difficult for poteen-makers to conduct their activities. Although poteen-making was not entirely stamped out, illegal distillers had to resort to remote locations for fear of being caught in the act. The police also adopted a relatively subtle approach – targeting the confiscation of the still rather than the prosecution of the maker and thereby likely preventing undue or excessive resistance and resentment. However, one needs to be cautious about claiming that the RIC's undoubted success against the poteen trade was replicated in their fight against crime in general. Poteen-makers were vulnerable to being detected by the police because they had to light and maintain a fire as part of the poteen-manufacturing process: the smoke from their fire frequently alerted the local RIC to the fact that illicit distillation of spirits was taking place. Such an obvious tell-tale sign was not available to the RIC when it came to preventing or detecting other crimes. Their pervasive presence probably acted as a deterrent to lawbreaking to an extent, but they could not be everywhere at all times: most cases that came before the courts involved suspects who were charged after they had allegedly committed an offence, rather than their being caught red-handed in illegal activity. In these cases, the RIC's intimate knowledge of the people who lived in the communities where they were based was frequently invaluable in bringing successful prosecutions at petty sessions and other courts.[100]

Police methods

One of the main means by which the RIC built up their knowledge of what was happening in their communities, and thereby improving their surveillance over Irish society, was simply that of chatting with their neighbours. Ned Broy, who grew up in County Kildare in the late nineteenth century, recorded that the RIC would get work done at the local blacksmith's forge, 'the great social meeting place in rural areas', and thereby 'gradually collect all the local gossip'. The publican who had been prosecuted a number of times and whose licence 'was only hanging on by a cobweb' as a result would often 'be in a mood to supply all the local information which his occupation inevitably brought to him, and thus having helped the RIC he was secure from further prosecution for a long time to come'. According to Broy, 'Every area had its quota of loyal citizens', and as these were usually employers they had access to information that proved useful to the RIC. The constabulary acted as census enumerators and collected the annual agricultural statistics, and 'This entailed visits to practically every house in the country by members of the RIC and afforded an excellent opportunity, of which full advantage was taken, to gather all sorts of information during the course of conversation.' Moreover, 'Talking to children, who innocently supplied minute particulars which came to their keen perception of all local happenings' was another means of gathering useful information, and policemen's children were also a source of 'extremely valuable information that was available in abundance amongst other schoolchildren' and indicates the degree to which the force was integrated within the wider community. Broy added that barrack servants, who were mostly married women, 'happened to be just the type of gossip collectors, par excellence, that existed in all areas'.[101] In County Carlow, at the turn of the century, 'The usual procedure for acquiring information was to visit the local Post Mistress and shopkeepers and have a friendly chat'.[102] The constabulary's familiarity with local gossip and rumours provided them with useful leads when investigating cases of suspected infanticide and concealment of birth.[103]

The Sinn Féin activist P.S. O'Hegarty wrote perceptively of the RIC that 'Day and night they patrolled the roads and the lanes of Ireland, stopping and questioning whom they chose and as they chose, so that not a dog could bark without their knowledge'.[104] Cockfighting,[105] dog-fighting[106] and prize fighting[107] were among the casualties of policemen's intimate knowledge of their districts, as devotees of these pursuits found that their once popular recreational activities usually had to be conducted in secret in an effort to thwart crackdowns against them by both the RIC and DMP. Road bowls – 'throwing bullets', in Ulster – was another popular amusement that fell foul of the police and magistrates in this period, with the RIC, particularly in Belfast, making determined efforts to suppress it.[108] The reasons behind the authorities' suppression of road bowls were partly illustrated in a coroner's inquest in Belfast in 1894 in which it was alleged that one John Laverty, of 10 Second Street, died as a result of injuries to his head received when struck by a 'bullet' at an illegal road bowls match on 16 March.[109]

While a close knowledge of their local areas provided a crucial basis for the police's crime-fighting role, science and technology also played a part, if a less important one.[110] For example, the RIC first used photographic evidence in a criminal trial in 1889, in the prosecution of the men accused of murdering District Inspector William Martin at Derrybeg, in County Donegal. Several photographs of the murder scene were used as evidence in the trial.[111] The RIC used photographic evidence in other murder investigations thereafter,[112] as well as when investigating suspected cases of arson that were committed to defraud insurance companies.[113] The police found the telegraph system to be an important aid in their surveillance of strangers and capture of suspects,[114] as, to an extent, was the telephone. All of the DMP stations were linked to one another by telephone in January 1882,[115] but the RIC were slower than their metropolitan counterparts to make widespread use of the telephone, often due to the prohibitive costs involved. All of Belfast's RIC stations had telephones by October 1890,[116] but the force in most of the rest of the country lagged behind Belfast in this regard. For example, Derry Corporation discussed paying for telephones for Derry's RIC stations on a number of occasions in the 1890s, but it was not until 1900 that it eventually paid for the telephones to be installed.[117] Although this may appear to have been an extremely long wait, the RIC in Derry were luckier than most of their comrades stationed elsewhere. When Lisburn merchants petitioned Inspector General Neville Chamberlain in 1909 to have Lisburn RIC station provided with a telephone service, Chamberlain explained to them that there were no official funds provided to the RIC for such a purpose, and that any urban stations that had telephones had had them paid for by their local urban district council.[118] It is not surprising in these circumstances that many urban police barracks had no telephone service in the early twentieth century. Telephones were even rarer commodities in rural stations.[119]

The bicycle was another form of technology that the police began to use with increasing regularity in the 1890s, as it enabled the rapid pursuit and successful apprehension of suspects, often over long distances.[120] In cases where the RIC believed that members of a particular family had information that they needed, resourceful policemen would deliberately puncture their bicycle tyres with pins and use the puncture as an excuse to enter the house and engage the family in conversation. The conversation would eventually be steered around to the topic in which the police were interested, and members of the family would then 'quite innocently' supply the police 'with all the local gossip'.[121] Binoculars were another example of a technological aid that was sometimes used by the constabulary; they were occasionally employed to surreptitiously observe suspects, as in the case of a Bray sergeant who caught two poachers in the act in January 1905,[122] and the police from the Farmhill barracks in County Mayo who caught two men engaged in the illegal manufacture of poteen in November 1911 after observing them with binoculars.[123]

Forensic science played a relatively minor role in helping police to combat crime, although there were some useful developments in this area. From 1850 it was possible to identify a mark as a bloodstain, and in 1895 human blood could be distinguished from animal blood for the first time.[124] Cases in which the relevant scientific techniques proved essential included the investigation of the rape and murder of Anne McConn, a forty-year-old woman, in Trillick in 1902, and the attempted rape and the murder of Mary Walker, a nineteen-year-old woman, near Mullingar in 1909.[125] In the Trillick murder case, bloodstains (which were proven to be human) on the trousers and pocket knife of one of three suspects in the case, Joseph Moon, were crucial in proving his guilt. The other suspects were a tramp, John Burnett, 'who was unfortunate enough to have been in the area at the time of the murder', and a local man, Joseph Woods, who was initially suspected of the crime because he had scratch marks on his face. In the Mullingar murder case, the precipitin reaction test, by which human blood could be identified from other mammalian blood, also showed that the clothing and broken knife of the chief suspect, labourer Joseph Heffernan, contained human bloodstains.

Fingerprint evidence was also used increasingly in police investigations and prosecutions in the early twentieth century.[126] Two burglars, who 'both belonged to the criminal fraternity of Derry City', were among the first Irish lawbreakers to be convicted on fingerprint evidence. Towards the end of 1906 they broke into a grocer's shop in County Donegal, using a lighted candle to make their way through the premises in the dark. The fingerprint from the little finger on the left hand of one of the prisoners was found on an extinguished candle in the shop, and was used to prove him guilty of the crime.[127] A man was convicted of sacrilege in a church near Lisburn in November 1907, after he left a fingerprint on one of the church's windows when he broke into the building to commit a burglary. When he was arrested he claimed that he had been in Scotland at the time that the crime was committed, but the fingerprint evidence proved otherwise. Another man who committed sacrilege by breaking into a church at Dundrum, in County Dublin, in May 1910 was convicted as a result of his having left a fingerprint on one of the church's panes of stained glass. Like the culprit at Lisburn, the Dundrum burglary suspect (an ex-convict living in Kingstown) claimed to have been elsewhere – Belfast – at the time the offence was committed, but the evidence of his fingerprint at the crime scene convinced the jury of his guilt, and he was sentenced to five years' penal servitude.[128] There is evidence to suggest that from as early as 1911, Irish criminals were forensically aware and unsuccessfully tried to obliterate their fingerprints by tearing their skin with their teeth or with nails.[129] This was not the case with one Belfast crook, who stole a pair of boots in July 1908 and asked a boy to pawn them for him; his fingerprints on the stolen items were enough to demonstrate his guilt. On New Year's Eve in 1910, a public house in Belfast was burgled and liquor and other items, including a clock, were stolen. The hapless burglar once again left fingerprint evidence, this time on the glass of the window that he broke in order to gain entry to the public house. He, along with an accomplice, was found guilty of burglary. The fingerprint evidence was crucial in solving these cases.[130]

Not only did fingerprint evidence help to convict offenders, it was also useful in establishing the true identities of prisoners in police custody. This was particularly the case when English pickpockets travelled to Ireland to ply their trade among the crowds that gathered on such occasions as Horse Show week in Dublin, or King George V's visit to Ireland in July 1911.[131] On the latter occasion, some twenty English pickpockets were arrested in Dublin; their fingerprints were taken in Mountjoy prison and sent to New Scotland Yard, and by return of post the criminal records of most of these individuals were revealed. It was also discovered that in every case, the pickpockets had given a false name when they were arrested.[132] This was not the only instance in which fingerprint evidence helped to reveal the true identity of prisoners in Ireland. On 7 October 1911 the house of Miss Jones of Moyroe, in County Tipperary, was burgled and jewellery worth £50 was stolen. On learning that 'a suspicious looking tramp' had been seen in the neighbourhood, the Nenagh RIC scoured the countryside on their bicycles and eventually arrested a tramp some fifteen miles away: what drew their attention to the tramp was that he was sporting a white woollen sweater, 'a most unusual garment for a tramp to be wearing'. The tramp, who claimed that his name was John Mackesy, violently resisted arrest; all of the stolen jewellery, as well as other stolen items, were in his possession when he was searched. When his fingerprints were taken in Limerick prison, these showed that he was really Daniel Purcell, 'one of the most notorious criminals in the south of Ireland at the present day'. On 26 December 1910, Purcell had almost killed an old woman named Kate McCarthy, of Queenstown, in 'a most savage assault'. He was sentenced to ten years in prison for his crimes.[133]

Conclusion

The preceding discussion shows several patterns in non-agrarian crime in Ireland in this period. Rates of indictable crimes were higher in urban centres, with Dublin consistently recording the highest rate of these offences. Most crimes, however, were non-indictable offences, with such minor offences as drunkenness or allowing cattle to wander on the roads featuring prominently in rural Ireland's catalogue of lawbreaking. In general, crime rates remained stable and it is possible that there was a decline in at least some violent crime, which helps to explain why many contemporaries felt that Irish society was relatively peaceful – apart from periodic outbreaks of agrarian crime in some parts of the country – at the turn of the century. Ireland was the most heavily policed country in the United Kingdom. The RIC were relatively well integrated into Irish rural communities:[134] the case of illicit distillation illustrates how the constabulary's pervasive presence could help in curtailing or suppressing certain crimes, but their intimate knowledge of their local communities was probably of greater importance in tackling 'ordinary' or non-agrarian crime. Their adoption of new developments in technology and forensic science played a relatively minor role in this endeavour.

Chapter 3

Frequent Offenders, the 'Criminal Classes' and the Police

NUMEROUS COMMENTATORS in Victorian Britain wrote about the existence of what they termed 'the criminal classes' in British cities and large towns. These were perceived to be groups existing separate from the rest of society, pursuing lives of crime at the expense of the respectable and law-abiding majority. While the 'criminal classes' were members of the urban lower classes, they were perceived as different from them in that they did not earn honest livelihoods but instead lived off the proceeds of crime: they were, in effect, professional criminals.[1] Modern historians of crime argue that the idea of the existence of a professional criminal underworld which preyed on the rest of society was largely an exaggerated sensationalist construct of the press and ill-informed social commentators.[2] Although there were some individual professional criminals, the 'criminal classes' as a distinct social group or sub-group did not exist; nevertheless, belief in their existence was widespread and helped to shape much contemporary discourse about crime, criminality and criminal justice.[3] In Ireland's case, the influence of such discourse may be seen in how the country's annual returns of crime were tabulated in the late nineteenth century. It is noteworthy that the annual judicial statistics from 1870 to 1893 describe five separate categories of people whom the police recorded as constituting Ireland's 'criminal classes': these were habitual drunkards,[4] prostitutes, 'vagrants, tramps, and others without any visible means of subsistence', 'known thieves' and a nebulous group categorised simply as 'suspicious characters'.[5] With

Year	Prostitutes	Habitual drunkards	Suspicious characters	Vagrants, tramps, and others without any visible means of subsistence	Known thieves
1870	11,846	9,333	8,614	4,575	2,683
1871	10,456	8,500	7,837	4,032	2,454
1872	8,283	9,451	6,633	3,784	2,267
1873	7,999	7,472	6,217	3,794	1,927
1874	7,165	7,806	6,420	3,830	1,670
1875	7,064	7,184	6,600	4,048	1,561
1876	6,986	7,268	6,178	4,227	1,590
1877	6,899	6,667	6,157	3,864	1,600
1878	7,298	4,033	7,148	4,332	1,561
1879	6,550	3,316	6,926	4,371	1,595
1880	5,373	2,728	6,044	3,716	1,461
1881	5,139	2,781	6,740	3,440	1,671
1882	4,221	3,308	6,911	4,451	1,520
1883	4,694	2,831	7,206	4,595	1,496
1884	4,750	3,103	7,790	4,350	1,484
1885	4,587	2,950	7,092	4,510	1,698
1886	4,832	2,240	8,428	4,329	1,772
1887	5,352	2,308	9,012	4,349	2,003
1888	5,589	2,609	8,277	4,645	1,824
1889	5,471	2,773	4,678	4,017	1,655
1890	5,263	2,990	4,981	5,004	1,647
1891	5,063	3,430	7,121	5,142	1,423
1892	3,686	3,208	7,188	5,064	1,530
1893	3,374	3,223	6,453	4,002	1,308

Table 3: The 'criminal classes' in Ireland, 1870–93.
Sources: *Irish Judicial Statistics*, 1870–93

the possible exception of the 'known thieves', it is unlikely that these so-called 'criminal classes' could be regarded as professional criminals. However, the individuals noted by the police were undoubtedly on the receiving end of what they would have regarded as unwelcome attention from the authorities and were responsible for a large proportion of the crimes that were committed in Ireland. The fact that many of them committed crimes does not mean that they constituted a 'class' of professional criminals, however. Nevertheless, because they often came before the courts charged with various offences, in this chapter it is worth exploring the crimes committed by these putative 'criminal classes' (with the exception of the vaguely defined 'suspicious characters') and other frequent offenders.

Drunkards

Sophisticated techniques such as those that were discussed at the end of the previous chapter were unnecessary for investigating most of the offences that were committed in this period. For example, some individuals broke the law on such an open and regular basis that policemen's detective abilities were not particularly taxed when it came to bringing charges against them. This was particularly true of drunkards, many of whom combined inebriety with other offences, usually disorderly conduct or assault, and who were frequently hauled before the courts as a result. One of these notorious frequent offenders was an old woman, Jane Feeney, who by March 1870 had been charged with drunkenness 'upwards of 200 times' in Belfast. The RIC stated at one of Feeney's court appearances for drunkenness in April 1871 that it cost the town council some £30 annually to keep her in prison, which probably led to her being discharged with a caution on that particular occasion. In July 1871, when Head Constable Lamb agreed with Resident Magistrate J.C. O'Donnell that there was no 'earthly use' in punishing Feeney, that her latest drunkenness offence was committed purely for the purpose of getting overnight accommodation in a police cell and that sending her to prison for six months as a 'rogue and vagabond' would result in her death, she was again discharged from police custody.[6] Other disorderly Belfast drunkards with numerous convictions included a blind phrenologist, John McCallin, who had chalked up some 202 drunk and disorderly cases by February 1873;[7] Jane McCance, with 105 convictions for similar offences by March 1872;[8] Catherine O'Rorke, 'an inveterate drunkard', who allegedly appeared in Belfast's courts 'four or five times every week' on charges of drunkenness;[9] Mary Tierney, who was 'never out of jail', who had some 73 convictions for drunkenness by November 1876;[10] and an old woman named Annie Johnston, who failed in her attempt to avoid a six-month prison sentence in August 1882 by offering to take the total abstinence pledge when the presiding magistrate pointed out to her that she was appearing in court for the sixtieth time on a charge of drunkenness and disorderly conduct.[11]

There are fewer reports in Belfast newspapers of troublesome drunkards being repeatedly charged in the city's courts towards the end of the century, but some individuals still featured regularly in reports of court proceedings. These included Margaret Daly, whose 117th drunkenness prosecution occurred in July 1891, Lucy Mitchell, whose 103rd drunkenness offence was recorded in October 1893, and Margaret Ann Rocks, with some 236 convictions by August 1899, mostly for inebriety and disorderly behaviour.[12] These named individuals merely represented a small fraction of the number of habitual drunkards who appeared before Belfast's magistrates in the 1890s: according to District Inspector Henry Browne Morell in 1898, some 54 Belfast inhabitants (44 of whom were women) had been convicted of drunkenness more than 100 times, while one woman had over 260 convictions for drunkenness in the previous three years.[13]

Drunken recidivists also proved troublesome to the police in other parts of the country.[14] Mary Clarke, an elderly woman from Derry, served more than 500 prison sentences, with drunkenness featuring regularly on her charge sheet.[15] In Limerick in September 1873, one enthusiastic toper made his 500th appearance before the city's police court on a charge of drunkenness.[16] A Dublin woman, who was sentenced to seven years' penal servitude for stealing 15s. from a man's pocket in a house off Westland Row in September 1875, had already been in prison 118 times, mainly for drunkenness, disorderly conduct and robberies, since her first conviction in April 1859.[17] A young woman named Mary Reilly, who was arrested by Constable Thomas Rice on 15 October 1878 for disorderly behaviour in Pill Lane, had already been in prison some fifty-seven times. Reilly resisted arrest by stabbing Constable Rice twice in the face with a knife, declaring that 'She would earn twelve years before she went with him'; in the event, she only 'earned' five years' penal servitude on this occasion.[18] Frances Sinclair, alias Charlotte Molony, was another drunken character who made life difficult for the DMP: before her arrest in November 1883 for breaking a window in a confectionery shop on Stephen's Green, she had been convicted of sixteen assaults, eighty-two cases of drunkenness and 'a number of larcenies' since her first conviction in 1855.[19] John Curtis, a former soldier, was another disorderly drunk with an impressive police record: in October 1887, when he was charged with assault and being drunk and disorderly, it was the 141st time that he had been charged with drunkenness. He was treated rather leniently at Naas petty sessions, being given the option of a fine of 5s. and costs or four days in prison, in consideration of the fact that he never assaulted the police when he was arrested.[20] The number of women who were frequently charged with drunkenness or drunkenness and disorderly behaviour is a striking feature of press coverage of such cases in this period. This is arguably because the sight of women being drunk and disorderly in public was probably more shocking to police and other witnesses than the sight of men exhibiting the same behaviour. Women's public inebriety and violence went against conventional expectations of how women were supposed to behave. The drunk and violent woman was 'an affront' to society's norms,[21] which probably explains why drunken women featured so prominently in newspaper reports of Irish court proceedings.

Drink was a factor in many other offences, apart from that of being drunk and disorderly, a fact which Justice Harrison referred to at the opening of the County Waterford spring assizes in March 1893 when he stated that 'They who were connected with the administration of the criminal law knew that drink was at the bottom of all or nearly all cases that came into court'.[22] District Inspector Henry Browne Morell believed in 1898 'that 75 or 80 per cent of crime in Belfast was traceable either directly or indirectly to drink', with 75 per cent of child cruelty cases being drink-related. The National Society for the Prevention of Cruelty to Children noted that the main cause of the 68,007 cases of cruelty and neglect of children with which it dealt in Ireland between 1889 and 1911 arose from the abuse of alcohol.[23] It is not surprising that habitual drunkards were one of the five distinct groups of people categorised by the police as constituting Ireland's 'criminal classes' who committed a disproportionate amount of crime.

Prostitutes

It is impossible to state exactly how many prostitutes there were in Ireland in the late nineteenth and early twentieth centuries. The statistics that the RIC and DMP compiled each year of the number of women arrested for soliciting offer some indication of how widespread prostitution was, but such statistics provide, at best, an impressionistic snapshot. Many prostitutes were arrested on numerous occasions, which distorts the overall picture; another

problem with trying to gauge the number of Irish prostitutes is that the police often turned a blind eye to their
existence,[24] a fact that occasionally prompted groups of
people who were hostile towards prostitutes' presence to
take collective action against brothels. Householders in
the Upper Cross Roads and Portobello areas of Dublin in
1875 and 1876 formed one such group. They established
a prosecution fund, into which property holders paid 1s.
per £1 valuation on their property; this fund was used
to pay a private investigator £1 per week to bring prosecutions against brothels.[25] The White Cross Vigilance
Association, established in Dublin in 1885, was a longer-
lasting and more successful anti-prostitution collective.
In the late 1880s and early 1890s its members forced the
closure of dozens of Dublin brothels, through a combination of establishing patrols outside known 'evil houses',
accosting customers while they were leaving brothels and
bringing prosecutions against brothel keepers.[26] The first
two decades of the twentieth century saw remarkably
low recorded numbers of prostitutes arrested in Dublin,
which contrasts markedly with contemporaries' accounts
of the numerous prostitutes in the capital city,[27] raising
further doubts about using police statistics of prosecutions for soliciting as a means of measuring precisely the
extent of prostitution.

Most prostitutes in Dublin and elsewhere who ended
up in prison did so as a result of drunken or disorderly
behaviour or for robbing their clients, rather than for
plying their trade as prostitutes.[28] The DMP chief commissioner stated in 1881 that 'there is no class with whom

we are more frequently brought into contact in the discharge of our duties than female servants, brothel keepers and prostitutes',[29] which gives a good indication of how urban prostitution often involved criminal behaviour that went beyond mere soliciting, something that was also a feature of prostitution in British cities.[30] The *Freeman's Journal* of 6 May 1870, when reporting on the coroner's inquest into the death of an 'unfortunate', Annie Brown, despaired that 'there is no city in Europe where Vice parades itself more unblushingly than in some of the leading streets of our own metropolis'. It claimed that:

In former years its displays were reserved for the glare of the gas-lamps, and for the covering shelter of the night; but now it struts abroad in the open sunshine, and boldly confronts us as it flounces along the pathways, or is borne aloft enthroned in carriages and pairs. A mother can scarcely take her daughter with safety through the thoroughfares we allude to between the hours of three and six in the afternoon. If she do[es], she must forewarn her of the sights she may expect to see. She must tell her who these painted women are that will jostle against them as they pass – she must tell her not to be shocked at the odd scraps of conversation that will occasionally reach her ear ... Passing from our streets to our places of public recreation, and to our fashionable sea-side promenades, the evil is still the same, and the pleasantest of our suburbs is made almost unbearable by the presence of these pestilential creatures.

Few of the women seem to have been put off by the prospect of a spell in prison. On the contrary, in 1871 the inspectors-general of Irish prisons stated that 'our gaols, more especially those for females, are occupied chiefly by a class of prisoners (prostitutes and vagrants) who regard these more in the light of asylums and hospitals than as places of punishment or reformation'.[31]

In their report for 1875, the inspectors-general noted that Ireland's jails were:

chiefly occupied by prisoners of both sexes who are constantly re-committed for drunkenness, assaults, and petty thefts, and by females of the depraved class who have no honest means of livelihood. We may add that in no part of the world is the 'social evil' more troublesome, impudent, and degraded than in the cities and large towns of Ireland. The elevated and noble moral and religious tone which prevails even in the humblest classes of the Irish people has a reflex influence in driving unhappy women who live a life of sin into such a state of remorse and despair that they become more like wild beasts than women, and are a signal pest to the entire community.[32]

Not all contemporaries believed that prostitutes were completely desensitised to the influence of religion. Several institutions, most notably the Magdalene asylums, whose primary aim was to 'rescue' prostitutes from what was perceived to be their life of sin, as well as charitable organisations such as the Dublin and Belfast

Midnight Missions, believed that prayer and hard work were means by which prostitutes could redeem themselves.[33] The Quaker-run Prison Gate Mission, founded in Dublin in 1876, offered a combination of religious services and training in various occupations to women, including prostitutes, when they were released from prison.[34]

The inspectors-general of Irish prisons may have been correct when referring to Ireland's cities and large towns as the locations of the 'social evil': as Maria Luddy shows, the overwhelming majority of arrests of prostitutes in the period from 1870 to 1919 occurred in the largest urban areas, particularly in Dublin and Belfast.[35] Sailors in Cork[36] and soldiers at the Curragh[37] and in garrison towns and cities[38] were regular customers of prostitutes. In 1880, over one-third of the 4,357 soldiers stationed in Dublin were admitted to hospital suffering from venereal disease; 940 of these had syphilis. In 1881, over a ten-month period, some 43 per cent of the unmarried men in one regiment were incapacitated by venereal disease. Joseph V. O'Brien writes that 'one is tempted to suggest that the prostitutes of Dublin were doing far more than republican-minded nationalists to weaken the sinews of empire' at this time.[39] Prostitutes also profited from the custom of men who travelled to Irish cities and large towns on business. These were often the victims of robbery by prostitutes. Examples include the English boot-buyer who had £120 and a silver watch stolen from him by 'two unfortunate girls' in a house in Mountjoy Street in Dublin in March 1884; Andrew Brennan, a Mullingar farmer and cattle dealer, who was robbed of £55 by a prostitute in a house in Dublin's notorious Montgomery Street in April 1896; and another cattle dealer, Lawrence McCabe, whose purse containing £42 or £43 was robbed by two prostitutes in another Montgomery Street house in January 1898.[40]

Although Montgomery Street was the most notorious locale of prostitution in Dublin, it was by no means the only one. Bull Lane in the 1870s had a similarly formidable reputation for general lawlessness, until the brothels there were suppressed by the DMP, temporarily at least, in 1880. A newspaper report of the murder of a prostitute in Bull Lane in June 1870 – her throat was cut by Andrew Carr, a pensioner recently discharged from the 87th Regiment – casts some light on how the kind of people who lived there were perceived, when it describes how 'During Thursday night [the night of the murder] numbers of abandoned characters of both sexes remained in crowds in Bull-lane, the majority of them half-mad with the poison which they drank in the surrounding beer houses, and, indeed, the whole scene was horrible in the extreme'.[41] A reporter who visited the newly opened Chancery Street Police Office in September 1871 found it crowded with inhabitants of Greek Street and Bull Lane, 'the two great head-quarters of crime in the city'. The building was constructed to 'suit the convenience of some of their most constant customers' from the two aforementioned streets, as well as from nearby Pill Lane, Fisher's Lane, Mary's Lane, Church Street and Bow Street. Drunken prostitutes and other women, 'some of them looking like gorgons', were much in evidence. The local men were similarly unappealing to the journalist, who described how 'Heavy, muscular, drowsy-looking men now issued out of the lane and out of the low public houses which abound in the neighbourhood. Nearly all these men were dressed in greasy baragon [*sic*] clothes, some had black eyes and bruised faces, and there was not one of them that did not bear the marks of violence, inflicted in battles recent or remote.' These were 'professional "bullies" who lived on plunder when out of jail, and whose head-quarters when released from durance was Bull-lane, or other localities of the same character'.[42] Commenting on the murder of another prostitute in Bull Lane in October 1878, a barrister remarked that the witnesses were women 'who came from a nest of ruffians and villains of every kind, a nest where the worst of infamy was carried on, from a place which was a pest in the middle of the city', and that 'Even if they were to search hell itself, they could not find worst witnesses to come out of it than they could get in Bull-lane'. The revelations of lawlessness that arose during the criminal proceedings in this instance led the Dublin grand jury to petition the government to take steps to suppress Bull Lane's brothels.[43]

Although most prostitutes were women, an unknown proportion were children. On 31 October 1870 the *Freeman's Journal* drew attention to the plight of Dublin's homeless and vagrant children 'who infest the streets and obtain a precarious livelihood by begging, by petty thefts, and by other modes which we shall not further allude to than that they lay the foundation of all the misery and suffering of the female part of the population, whose lives average seven years from their entry on the career of vice'. Five years later a mother charged her own daughter with the theft of 'an old skirt', valued at about 2*s*., with the aim of keeping her daughter from living in a brothel at Upper Cross Roads.[44] In November 1876 Theobald Brophey, a painter residing at Johnson's Court, prosecuted his daughter, Maria Brophey, an 'interesting looking girl' aged around thirteen years, for stealing various 'articles of small value from him'; his purpose in doing so was to try to keep her from 'houses of bad character' in Bull Lane, Crampton Court and Crane Lane. According to the distraught father, 'nobody, neither the magistrate nor the priest, had the slightest idea of the amount of child degradation that was carried on in this city, but he had discovered it in his quest after his child'. He claimed that there were some ten child prostitutes in one brothel alone that was kept by 'apparently respectable women'.[45] Edward Dwyer Gray, MP, claimed in 1878 that he had ascertained that there were between 5,000 and 6,000 prostitutes in Dublin, 'exclusive of the upper class ... of women of this kind', and further referred to the 'melancholy and awful fact, that there were a great many of the unfortunate class who were children under 10 and 11 years of age'.[46]

In Belfast, the existence of a child prostitution ring came to light in April 1871 when Sub-constable Thomas Irwin charged Mary Coogan, a girl aged about fourteen years, for disorderly conduct in Albert Square. The policeman told the presiding resident magistrate,

J.C. O'Donnell, that Coogan was one of ten or eleven 'little girls' who lived in the Harper's Court house of Anthony McMahon, who lived on the money that they earned from prostitution. McMahon also prostituted his own daughters. The astonished resident magistrate ordered the RIC, who clearly knew about the nature of McMahon's house and livelihood, to suppress the brothel and to arrest this 'monster in human form'. McMahon and his wife Jane, who had been previously convicted of keeping a brothel in London in 1858, were successfully prosecuted by Sub-inspector James Ellis French and were sentenced to five years and six months in jail each.[47] French, who served as the RIC's detective director from June 1872 to September 1882, was arrested in July 1884 for his illegal sexual activity with homosexual Dublin Castle officials and others. In the course of his trial, the existence of at least three brothels that catered for homosexuals in Dublin came to light.[48]

In summary, one can say that prostitution in Ireland shared many features with prostitution in Britain in this period. There were some notable differences: for example, while there is some evidence that there were some child prostitutes in Belfast and Dublin, and adult male prostitutes in Dublin, there do not appear to have been as many of these as there were in some of Britain's largest cities, and particularly London.[49] The similarities between the two countries are more striking than the differences, however. Prostitution was a prominent feature of life in Irish and British cities: prostitution per se was not illegal, and the police tended to leave prostitutes in both countries alone, allowing brothels to operate without interference unless they were unruly and attracted complaints from prominent and influential citizens, in which cases the brothels would be suppressed, at least temporarily. Another common feature of policing prostitution in Ireland and Britain is that prostitutes were arrested mainly when they were drunk and disorderly in public. It was also common for prostitutes in both countries to be prosecuted for robbing their clients.[50]

Tramps

As well as prostitutes, tramps were another segment of the 'criminal classes' who came in for a lot of police attention.[51] Animosity towards, and fear of, the tramp were feelings that were widespread in the community.[52] The perception that tramps were an excessive burden on ratepayers partly explains the hostile feelings towards them. The press helped to strengthen the image of the parasitic tramp by publishing accounts of vagrants who travelled between Poor Law unions with the express purpose of securing accommodation in different workhouses, at the ratepayers' expense.[53] Sensationalist newspaper accounts of a general tramp 'plague' or nuisance also contributed to the 'moral panic' regarding vagrants.[54] The *Freeman's Journal*'s complaint in December 1878 concerning 'the screaming, scheming, professional beggar, who infests our streets, and extorts money by audacity and imposture', and the *Belfast News-Letter*'s reference in March 1893 to the problem of the 'lusty, happy-go-lucky tramps and vagrants' who received lodgings in the Belfast work-house, were typical of hostile contemporary newspaper commentary on tramps.[55] The perceived criminality of tramps[56] added to the fear in which they were held by much of Irish society.[57] Because 'the numerous outrag-es committed for some time past were supposed to have been perpetrated by tramps or others prowling about the country', in January 1875 the Dublin Castle author-ities sent Irish magistrates a summary of the Vagrancy Acts, in the hope that this would prompt firmer action from them against vagrants in their areas.[58] Lord Chief Justice James Whiteside told the Westmeath spring as-sizes in March 1875 that the 'tramp nuisance' was the greatest evil in the country. According to Whiteside, tramps 'were idlers, vagrants who did no good for them-selves or for any one else. They were the medium of crime throughout the country, and by tyranny and terrorism they levied "black mail" on the humbler classes.'[59] Some nine years later, John Jellie, a magistrate and one of the Carrickfergus Poor Law guardians, stated that it was no coincidence that local crime rates rose whenever tramps used the local workhouse 'as a place of refuge or conve-nience'. According to Jellie, 'That the men and women of this class are considered dangerous can be readily proved by many respectable farmers' wives and daughters, who, in the absence of the male members of the families, have often been terrified into giving alms, bread being occa-sionally refused and money demanded'. He added: 'That casuals or tramps are a suspected class may be inferred from the fact that they are regularly visited by policemen in workhouses to ascertain if any of them are "wanted" on account of the commission of some misdemeanour, or the perpetration of some felonious act'.[60] As late as July 1919 the grand jury at the Limerick summer assizes was told by Justice Arthur Samuels that four local burglaries and four cases of house-breaking were believed to have been committed by tramps, who were 'adepts at such offences'.[61]

The image of the tramp as a criminal did not just derive from generalisations such as those voiced by Samuels, but from numerous newspaper accounts of criminal acts by individual vagrants. These almost certainly deepened the feeling of insecurity of many people in rural Ireland regarding tramps. Examples include the case of William Tobin, a 'thickset and wretchedly attired man' described as 'a wandering tramp going about the country', who murdered Johanna Cotter, a farmer's wife, at Mondaniel, County Cork, on 1 August 1874, by battering her in the head,[62] and James McCormick, alias William Brennan, a 'low-sized and ill-looking' bricklayer 'of no fixed residence' (tramps were sometimes workmen who took to the road in search of employment, rather than being permanently unemployed and on the move) who was suspected by the DMP of murdering seventy-year-old Anne McQuirk, and of stealing her fowl, at Kimmage in October 1881.[63] The crime of another tramp, a former soldier named Patrick Hannon, who raped and killed eighty-four-year-old Alice Fleming at Garrintaggert, Spink, Queen's County on 21 December 1891, while he was drunk, would not have made rural dwellers feel more secure against the depredations of vagrants; nor would the killing of two girls, four-year-old Kate McGlynn and her sister, six-year-old Mary Anne McGlynn, near Monasterevin, by John Curran, 'a strong, hulking, young tramp', on 18 April 1905.[64] Hannon's defence was that he sometimes became 'temporarily insane' as a result of suffering sunstroke when he was serving in the British army in Egypt. The jury accepted his explanation, which was supported by a doctor, and Hannon was found guilty of manslaughter rather than murder. Pauline Prior shows that killers often escaped the hangman's noose as a result of being found guilty of killing while they were insane or temporarily insane.[65]

Of course, it was not just murders committed by tramps that led to suspicion and hostility towards vagrants in this period. Tramps were often viewed as a general threat to the rest of society, who, when they were not in the workhouse, lived by begging and thieving.[66] This helps to explain why even vagrants who were aged in their eighties and nineties were sometimes sent to prison.[67] An episode that occurred near the Mayo village of Cong in July 1914 is instructive for what it reveals about the rural community's attitude towards vagrants. A thirteen-year-old boy sparked a panic when he claimed that a tramp had shot him in the face, hands and chest with a revolver after he refused his demand for money. The boy, who was alone in his uncle's house at the time, ran for help and his bloodied state seemed to give weight to his story. The Irish Volunteers at Cong 'turned out in force' and assisted the RIC in scouring the neighbourhood for the fugitive tramp, while lurid rumours spread about there being a vagrant armed with three revolvers in the locality. Eventually the local RIC district inspector managed to get the boy alone and he confessed that he invented the entire story: he had received his injuries while playing with a gunpowder-filled cartridge which he lit with a match, and made up the tale about the tramp to escape being chastised by his uncle.[68]

On rare occasions, tramps elicited sympathy from those tasked with policing them. John Regan, who joined the RIC in 1908, recorded that 'I always pitied the unfortunate tramp. He never had any friends in the place, and the public often became most helpful in assisting the police in such a case, while local magistrates, who would never convict anyone they knew, would show their high regard for law and order in sending the unfortunate tramp to gaol for a couple of months for something quite petty.'[69] Regan's sympathetic sentiments were not typical of policemen's attitudes towards vagrants, however. According to Thomas Fennell, who joined the RIC in 1875, there were two types of tramp. The first type was the 'weary Willie', who 'would not work, even if offered it', but 'kept to the road all the time, begging on the way, where there seemed a chance of getting food or money'. Tramps of this kind were 'a worthless, unpopular lot; nobody wanted them'. The constabulary were ordered to visit the 'low lodging houses' and the workhouses to interview such vagrants, to see if any of them were suspected of committing crimes. The second type of tramp was the itinerant tradesman, addicted to drink, who never settled in one locality and usually ended his days in a pauper's grave.[70] It is not surprising that there was mutual animosity between tramps and policemen. For example, Robert Lynd met one tramp, a native of Thurles, in Kilkenny in 1912, whose view of the RIC was far from complimentary: '"They're tyrants, them fellows", he said, "and the lies they would tell on a poor man might be the means of getting him a week or maybe a month in gaol, and he after doing nothing at all but only going quietly from place to place. And thieves and robbers running loose that would murder you on the roadside and no one to say a word".'[71]

Because the IRA, during the War of Independence, consisted mainly of volunteers from farming backgrounds, it is not surprising that its view of tramps tended to reflect that of the society whence most of its volunteers originated. For generations, tramps had been objects of suspicion in rural areas, viewed as outsiders and as potential criminals, and the IRA did not take much convincing to turn its guns against them. Tramps were significantly overrepresented among the civilians who were killed by the IRA from 1919 to 1921, and, even when they were not shot, vagrants were often harassed by republican gunmen.[72] Tramps were shot, or were arrested by republican police, either because they were alleged spies or alleged criminals. James Comerford, of the Kilkenny IRA, explains that in the districts where the RIC had abandoned its barracks, 'In order to prevent scamps and tramps, drunks and bullies, adventurers and criminals from taking advantage of changes caused by the Guerilla

Warfare conditions, firm steps had to be taken by the IRA to prevent these fellows from doing unlawful things for their own selfish purposes and private profit'.[73] Timothy Dinneen recorded that the intelligence officer of the IRA's Kilnamartyra company, in County Cork, was so zealous in 'tracing suspicious characters such as tramps and individuals who were strangers in our area who were often taken to be spies' that the company referred to him as 'The Minister of Tramps'.[74] Seamus Babington, engineer of the 3rd Tipperary Brigade, describes where such zeal in tackling the perceived tramp problem could lead. He records how the Faugheen company had arrested an alleged spy, 'an old tramp' whom Babington recognised as a man to whom he had occasionally given alms over the previous five years when he visited Carrick-on-Suir. The evidence against the 'spy' consisted of the fact that he had been seen coming out of the local RIC barracks and was in possession of a soldier's pension book – not unreasonably, as he was an army pensioner, having served in the Boer War. The tramp, who was over seventy years old, was 'more or less defective in mental powers', and therefore could give no satisfactory explanation to the Faugheen IRA as to why he visited the RIC barracks, but Babington vouched for him and he was released on his orders, 'to the consternation and disappointment of a number of his captors' as they had already prepared a grave in which to bury the tramp after his execution.[75] It is possible that at least some of the vagrants who were shot as spies during the War of Independence were killed merely because they were strangers, victims of the IRA's paranoia that British agents were disguising themselves as tramps:[76] such men were simply unfortunate that they did not have a sympathetic IRA advocate like Babington to fight their corner.

Professional criminals

Professional criminals, as opposed to people who were perceived as having criminal tendencies, formed a relatively small proportion of the 'criminal classes' over whom the police kept watch. Many of these were ticket-of-leave convicts, prisoners who received conditional early releases from prison: unlike the case in Britain, where there was a relatively lax police surveillance of such individuals, in Ireland they were required to report their arrival at the RIC barracks in the area in which they lived, and on the first day of each month thereafter.[77] The *Freeman's Journal* claimed on 1 May 1878 that most crime in Dublin was committed by a hardened minority of recidivist criminals, a 'venomous residuum'; it stated that 'it is a standing sore which is in our midst – a population of jail birds – which does most of the harm'. Prisoners who completed their jail terms, and criminals released on tickets-of-leave, often fell back into a life of crime. The recorder for Dublin from 1878 to 1905, Frederick Richard Falkiner, frequently called for Dublin's recidivist or hardened criminals to be deported to a special penal colony, believing it was folly to release them back into the general population after they had served prison terms, as they would inevitably re-offend.[78]

In February 1884, William Patrick O'Brien of the Irish General Prisons Board stated that the difficulty that ex-prisoners encountered in securing employment accounted for their relapsing into crime, and argued that their only hope of avoiding this was to emigrate.[79] There was some hope for female prisoners in Dublin of finding an alternative to a return to crime, however, through the efforts of the Discharged Female Prisoners' Aid Society: from 1882 to 1900, some 850 women found employment through the auspices of the society, or were helped to emigrate, after they had served their sentences. As Fr John Hughes, a member of the society, explained in January 1900, 'Habitual criminals can only be practically put down in one way, and that is by cutting off the supply.'[80]

In Dublin, which each year had a disproportionately large share of Ireland's recorded larcenies from the person, pickpockets constituted probably the largest single professional criminal element. Pickpockets particularly liked to operate where crowds gathered, such as at railway stations and the port terminals,[81] at fashionable shopping streets such as Grafton Street,[82] outside churches at the end of religious services,[83] or at events that were guaranteed to attract crowds, such as the religious revival meetings of Dwight Lyman Moody and Ira David Sankey or entertainments at the Royal Dublin Society grounds at Ballsbridge.[84] Outside of Dublin, race meetings and fairs also proved attractive environments in which pickpockets could ply their trade.[85] When Winston Churchill travelled to Belfast on 8 February 1912 to give a speech at Celtic Park in support of home rule for Ireland, among the thousands who congregated in the stadium were skilled pickpockets, as evidenced by the fact that the RIC reported that more than £400 in cash was stolen from members of the audience, as well as 300 watches.[86]

Burglars, counterfeiters and confidence tricksters of various kinds also ranked among Ireland's professional criminals. Each year, the Irish judicial statistics showed that a considerably disproportionate amount of indictable offences such as burglary, house-breaking and breaking into shops and warehouses occurred in the capital;[87] although Belfast's share of these crimes rose significantly in the late nineteenth and early twentieth centuries,[88] the level of such offences remained greater in Dublin. In Belfast, burglars took advantage of many householders' fondness for holidays by the seaside, by robbing their homes while they were away; in 1895, this led to Commissioner T.F. Singleton urging householders to notify the police at their nearest RIC barracks of when they went on vacation, so that the constabulary could keep watch over their homes.[89] Although this system of police supervision was widened to cover all unoccupied dwellings in the city in the early years of the twentieth century,[90] a large number of break-ins still occurred each year, many of which consisted of robberies of money from gas meters in houses whose occupants had gone to work.[91] The RIC in Belfast were frequently criticised for what was perceived as their poor success rate in combating crime in the city. In this context, one constable astonished Belfast's summons court in December 1913 when he announced that he was bringing none other than Satan before the bench to be prosecuted. It turned out that 'Satan' was really one 'Seaton', whose surname the policeman pronounced as that of the greatest lawbreaker of all. Seaton's offence was 'obtaining liquor during prohibited hours by falsely representing himself to be a bona fide traveller'. On paying a small fine he left the court, 'leaving the Bench more easy in their minds than when his presence was announced according to the constable's description of him'.[92]

Counterfeiting coins was a crime that often involved greater organisation and sophistication than burglary. It was of particular concern to the authorities in Belfast and Dublin, especially because of its negative impact on small traders and people of low incomes.[93] In June 1868 Belfast recorder's court was told that passing base coin was 'a common occurrence' in the city; William Smith and his wife, who ran a small grocery shop in Winetavern Street, had an ideal outlet for passing the counterfeit coins that they manufactured on their premises in 1871.[94] In the early 1880s, it was believed that illegal betting establishments in High Street and Queen's Square were responsible for at least some of the counterfeit money circulating in Belfast.[95] In Dublin, many of the large number of counterfeit coins in circulation in the city from the 1870s to the 1890s were manufactured by a small number of well-organised families of coiners, such as the Carroll family of Upper Mecklenburgh Street, all of whose members served time in prison for the offence at one time or another,[96] and the Comerfords, usually of Francis Street, some of whom appear to have been related to the Carrolls.[97] In October 1896 a particularly well organised gang of coiners in Dublin, consisting of Patrick Bulger, William Brownrigg and Thomas Delaney, was sentenced to prison. The counterfeiters made use of *The Electroplaters' Handbook* when making base coin. In sentencing Bulger to prison, the Dublin recorder commented that 'There was a mythological personage called Proteus, who when he was caught in one form changed himself into something else, and when he was caught in that shape changed himself into some other form. Bulger was a Proteus in the way of law breaking, and that not in a small way, but in a wholesale manner.'[98]

Confidence tricksters and other swindlers constituted another small but active component of Ireland's professional criminals in this period. Begging-letter impostors preyed on the generosity and gullibility of their victims.[99] Henry Hensler of 61 Bridgefoot Street, who was aged sixty in 1880, was one of the most persistent and skilled practitioners of the begging-letter ruse in Dublin. In this year he was convicted of sending spurious begging letters to prominent individuals in Britain, including members of parliament, asking for money on behalf of non-existent destitute Irish women, including, in one case, the wife of a shipwrecked soldier. Hensler's letters were accompanied by forged references and supporting letters from prominent people in Irish society, including, in one instance, a fabricated letter from the magistrate who tried his case, J.W. O'Donell, which prompted the magistrate to remark that he 'never knew he [O'Donell] was so charitable until now'. Hensler had been obtaining money through fabricated begging letters since at least October 1848, the date of his first conviction for obtaining money by false pretences.[100] Other fraudsters pretended to be clergymen and travelled around the country conning money from dupes who believed that they were contributing to charitable causes.[101] Among the causes for which these alleged clergymen collected funds were the release of Archbishop Georges Darboy and other clergymen imprisoned by the Parisian communards in 1871, and the erection of a monument over St Patrick's grave in 1891.[102] The most notorious clerical impostor case was that of Theodore Oswald Keatinge, a ticket-of-leave convict who posed as a former Jesuit priest who had converted to Protestantism. Keatinge, who had numerous aliases, managed to secure a position as curate at St Philip's Church of Ireland parish, Milltown, in Dublin, in 1886, as well as receiving funds from the Priests' Protection Society and various Protestant well-wishers. Solving this particularly notorious case gave special satisfaction to Detective Inspector John Mallon of the DMP.[103] Not all criminals who obtained money on false pretences wrote spurious begging letters or pretended to be clergymen. For example, a native of New Jersey, who used various aliases, including Captain Launcelot Percival Mulpagone, Vane Tempest and F.B. Tucker, had a successful two-month spree posing as the son of a millionaire in 1914. He pretended to be on a walking tour of the world, carrying with him 'most elaborately-prepared diaries, containing, together with a description of his travels, minutes and letters of recommendation received from clergymen, magistrates, and other persons of note in nearly all the principal towns of Ireland'; by these means, he was able to build a successful persona of a millionaire's son on his travels, and 'succeeded in relieving hotel proprietors, restaurateurs, and lodging-house keepers of food, lodgings, and other classes of goods, up to and including, in some cases, fairly large sums of money', in various towns from Omagh to Nenagh.[104]

Child and juvenile offenders

Professional criminals were able to operate due to the ease with which they could pawn stolen goods.[105] Magistrates believed that many pawnbrokers, especially in Belfast and Dublin, were too ready to accept articles offered in pawn, and that they, in effect, encouraged crime because of their lack of curiosity about the provenance of the goods which were presented to them.[106] Similar claims were made regarding marine store dealers' eagerness to accept lead and other goods from customers.[107] Pawnbrokers' reluctance to enquire closely into the provenance of articles that they were offered in pawn meant that child and juvenile criminals had a ready outlet for their stolen goods. For instance, child-strippers in Dublin and Belfast – criminals who were often children or juveniles themselves – would entice children into secluded areas and rob them of some or most of their clothing and pawn the stolen items without being asked awkward questions by pawnbrokers.[108] It wasn't just illegally acquired clothes that children pawned: in 1870 a Kingstown pawnbroker was condemned by a magistrate for accepting a chair in pawn from twelve-year-old J. Holton and thirteen-year-old W. Holton, which was part of the furniture that they stole from their mother, who despaired that 'they led most abandoned lives, smoking, drinking, and staying out late at night'.[109] Whenever it emerged in evidence in court that a child offender also smoked, this was seen as further proof of his or her depravity.[110] The *Freeman's Journal* of 3 May 1897 lamented the baneful effects on young people of smoking, with boys as young as nine or ten regarding it as 'unmanly' not to smoke; according to the newspaper, smoking 'induced the utmost juvenile depravity'.[111] In April 1899, Resident Magistrate F.G. Hodder of Belfast claimed that half of the young boys and girls charged in his court with larcenies 'were made criminals by the conduct of pawnbrokers' who dishonestly accepted articles offered to them in pawn.[112]

Many children and juveniles, especially in Dublin, whose levels of poverty, deprivation and casual, poorly paid employment were much greater than those of any other Irish city,[113] had little option but to steal in order to survive. Homeless or abandoned children and youths were particularly vulnerable on Dublin's streets and, like the eponymous Flitters, Tatters and the Counsellor in May Laffan's short story,[114] sometimes combined in groups both for protection and to engage more efficiently in crime.[115] The most notorious example of such combinations was the 'Black Gang' in the 1880s. The prosecution of eight members of the gang, whose ages ranged from fourteen to twenty years, in November 1883 revealed that these 'juvenile outlaws' lived by various forms of plunder, either by committing burglaries or by accosting passers-by on the street and stealing their hats or rushing into shops and snatching items from the counters. Their abode was a house in Kennedy's Lane, off Christchurch Place, which had been condemned by Dublin Corporation.[116] The imprisonment of these eight youths, who were 'a terror in the district', meant that there were some fourteen members of the Black Gang in prison by the end of 1883, but this did not put an immediate stop to the gang's criminal activities. James Tobin, an eleven-year-old boy who was a member of the Black Gang, was admitted to hospital in an unconscious state, suffering from alcoholic poisoning, in February 1885. This was the result of drinking whiskey which he and two other boy members of the gang had stolen. His two companions in crime were arrested by the DMP.[117]

This was the fate of numerous other members of the Black Gang. For example, in January 1884 three older members of the gang – 'Spud' Murphy, 'Fogey Jar' Purcell and 'Jiggers' Brennan – were arrested after they forced another member, a 'little boy', to steal clothes from his employer's shop in Christchurch Place, threatening that 'he would get the knife' if he refused their orders. The boy received some of the money that the pawned stolen clothes fetched.[118] In October 1885 the alleged leader of the gang, nineteen-year-old Robert Ludlow, known as the 'King of the Kids', was arrested along with another gang member, after they stole a piece of bacon from a shop in Mary's Abbey and stabbed three shop assistants who tried to stop them.[119] It appears that the gang was suppressed partly as the result of evidence given against them in 1888 by Esther O'Brien of Belleview, off Thomas Street, in a case where the gang were accused of assaulting members of the DMP. O'Brien was given the nickname of 'Lagger' because she gave information in this case and she and her family were subjected to a campaign of assault and intimidation.[120]

The Black Gang represents an extreme example of the lengths to which some child and juvenile criminals went in order to survive in this period. Sensationalist reporting of the activities of gangs such as the Black Gang obscures the fact that there was an overall decline in the number of juvenile lawbreakers who came before the courts: this was mainly because actual or potential young offenders were taken off the streets for many years and incarcerated in either industrial schools or reformatories, thereby steadily reducing the overall number of crimes committed by youthful lawbreakers.[121] It was pointed out as early as 1872 that most Irish magistrates, who were initially sceptical of the benefits of the reformatory school system, were wont to sentence youthful offenders to lengthy terms in such institutions.[122] These schools tended towards reducing the amount of crime committed by children and juveniles, not necessarily by reforming young criminals into model citizens, although one cannot entirely discount this possibility,[123] but simply by taking them out of circulation for several years, and the growing number of industrial schools also contributed towards this.[124] Although most inmates of industrial schools were not guilty of committing any crime, a minority of the inmates were lawbreakers who were sent to these institutions by magistrates as an alternative to either prison or reformatory school, or were vulnerable children whose circumstances (such as homelessness or extreme destitution) magistrates regarded as likely to lead them into committing crimes in the future.[125] Institutional provision for young offenders in Ireland was extended with the introduction of the borstal system for offenders aged between sixteen and twenty-one: the country's only borstal institution in the period covered by this study was established at Clonmel in 1906.[126]

Not all youthful offenders were driven to commit crimes merely in order to survive. Some, it was claimed, broke the law in order to emulate real or imaginary criminals about whose exploits they read in 'penny dreadfuls' and other literature. Magistrates and others occasionally commented on how the corrupting effects of children's and youths' choice of reading matter led them into breaking the law. In August 1869 in Belfast, the trial of four young offenders – James Glover, William McMinn, Robert Graham and Arthur Deans – for robbing James Neill's jewellery shop at Donegall Place of a large quantity of jewellery and gold and silver watches revealed that at least some of the culprits were led astray by the perusal of 'low works of fiction'. According to one of their defence counsel, 'they have been led on to this by the perusal of those vile weekly publications which are now so numerous, and have such a demoralising effect upon youthful minds. The "Life of Dick Turpin", "Jack

Sheppard", and other works of a loose and sensational character, should not be allowed into the hands of young people. They have been the means of doing an incalculable amount of evil ...'.[127] In the following year, 'a young highwayman', a fourteen-year-old boy named Thomas Valentine, was found guilty of robbing people at gunpoint on Belfast's Holywood Road. According to the boy's father, Thomas was 'a good scholar' but had taken to reading 'bad books', which his mother burned when she found them. The books in question, *Dick Turpin* and *Robinson Crusoe*, were described by Resident Magistrate J.C. O'Donnell as 'Abominable trash'.[128] In October 1892, the burglary spree of two 'little boys', in which three houses in Belfast were broken into and '[a] good deal of property taken away', was blamed on the fact that 'they had been reading sensationalist literature of the "Black Avenger" type, and they had been led astray'.[129]

District Inspector P.A. Marrinan, a contributor to the *Royal Irish Constabulary Magazine* in May 1912, recorded how in the closing months of 1906 'Belfast was startled by a succession of the most daring and extensive house-breakings committed in the very heart of the city', which spawned various rumours that this was the work of either a 'gang of expert cross-Channel cracksmen', or that 'some famous American burglar was in our midst', or 'Continental safe-breakers' had 'left their usual haunts' and travelled to Belfast. The culprits turned out to be two 'young lads', both younger than fourteen years of age, 'of respectable parents', 'but fed up on the doings of Dick Turpin, Charlie Peace, and Spring-heeled Jack, and such like clever and daring gentlemen of crooked moral tendencies'. According to Marrinan, when the pair were eventually released from the reformatories to which they were sent, they committed more serious crimes, including the attempted murder of a policeman in the Antrim Road district. Not surprisingly, Marrinan called for a prohibition on the sale of 'those penny detective stories and nasty histories of Charlie Peace, Crippen, and such like sordid criminals'.

In April 1912, the *Royal Irish Constabulary Magazine* regaled its readers with the story of another crime spree in Belfast, which involved no less than sixty-six larcenies from houses in all parts of the city: 'The thief displayed the greatest impartiality in his wanderings. One day he enriched himself with the spoils of a villa in the suburbs; the next found him purloining the brass candlesticks and kitchen ornaments so dear to the heart of the factory girl.' In this instance, the culprit was a young man named Alfred McLaughlin, who, upon his arrest, told the RIC at the Cullingtree Road barracks that 'I was reading detective stories; I wanted to do Charles Peace'. The magazine's readers were informed:

That is the root cause of a good deal of crime. Foolish lads of an adventurous disposition read with avidity of the questionable doings of those sordid heroes of criminal history, and, in striving to imitate their exploits, fall themselves into the hands of the police, and go to swell the great army of social outcasts. From a social and humanitarian point of view, it would be a great matter if legislation made the sale of those idiotic penny dreadfuls impossible. At present, every city policeman has before him almost daily examples of criminality, induced and developed by such dangerous reading.

On 19 January 1916, also in Belfast, several members of the 'Black Lily Gang' were found guilty of theft. This gang, whose members were aged between eight and ten years, was formed 'with the object of systematically stealing from shops and private houses'. According to Acting Sergeant Madge, the 'reading of penny dreadfuls and viewing of exciting criminal film plays at the picture houses' was to blame for the boys' engaging in crime.[130]

The Exploits of Elaine, a film series which featured a villain known only as 'The Clutched Hand', was blamed for prompting young boys in Newry and Mullingar to form gangs known as 'The Clutched Hand Gang' who then went on shoplifting sprees in their native towns in February and March 1916.[131] As was the case in Belfast, Dublin was not free of child and juvenile lawbreakers whose criminal activity was perceived to be a result of reading 'sensationalist' literature. For instance, in December 1897 a 'lad' named Terence Kelly, of Mary's Lane, stabbed an acquaintance in the chest with a penknife; according to the prosecuting solicitor, 'this sort of thing was the result of reading the abominable "penny dreadfuls" sent over from London, such as "The Red Hand of Dick", and that sort of vile trash'. Three years later, during the trial of six boys who burgled a pawnbroker's shop in Blackrock, when evidence was given that they had a club house in the cellar of a house in Mabbot Street, the presiding magistrate remarked that 'Somebody must have been telling them some of Mark Twain's boys' stories'.[132]

The evidence suggests that there were some similarities between Irish child and juvenile criminality and lawbreaking by younger offenders in Britain. As in the case of Ireland, poverty was a principal reason why many youngsters in British cities turned to crime.[133] Other commentators in both countries often asserted that crime committed by children and juveniles was a mark of youthful depravity rather than poverty, with 'penny dreadfuls' and the cinema perceived as having a baneful effect on young people's lives and frequently influencing them to break the law in emulation of the criminals about whose exploits they read or whose deeds they watched on the cinema screen.[134] Notwithstanding the 'moral panic' regarding children and young people turning to crime as a result of their reading sensationalist literature or watching films with criminals as heroes, the reality was that reported youthful offending in both countries declined in the late nineteenth and early twentieth centuries.[135]

Crimes against 'morality'

Given the small size of Ireland's 'criminal classes', and the decline in the number of children who were imprisoned in the years after 1870, it is perhaps not surprising that Irish observers often regarded the relatively low level of crime in the country (with the main exception of the periodic outbreaks of agrarian crime) with satisfaction. Irish commentators took particular pride in the apparent absence in Ireland of what were deemed 'crimes against morality', particularly infanticide ('The Mode Anglais', according to the *Evening Telegraph* of 10 December 1875), domestic violence and rape, in stark contrast to the apparent prevalence of such offences in Britain.[136] Such a view was expressed well in a *Zozimus* cartoon that was published as early as 30 March 1872. Titled 'The Two Pandoras, or the Black Cap and the White Gloves', the cartoon shows one Pandora, Britannia, opening a large chest inscribed 'English Assizes' and out of which escape such evils as 'Profligacy', 'Murder', 'Poison', 'Wife Beating', 'Infanticide', 'Ruffianism' and 'Swindling', and over which floats a black cap, adorned by judges when they pronounced the death sentence in court; in contrast, the other Pandora, Hibernia, opens a small box inscribed 'Irish Assizes', out of which fly two white doves, one of which bears a pair of white gloves, traditionally awarded to judges at crime-free assizes (see Figure 2). Some Anglophobes such as Fr C.J. Herlihy were prepared to admit in 1904 that Dublin was an exception to the general rule of the absence of 'immorality' in Ireland, but offered an ingenious explanation for this apparent anomalous state of affairs:

But how shall we explain the exceptional wickedness of Dublin that renders it so much out of harmony with the rest of the country? The explanation is easy. Though situated in Ireland, in reality Dublin is not strictly speaking an Irish city at all. It was originally built by the Danes, and has long been a kind of cosmopolitan city, which, like other great sea-port towns, becomes a sink for the moral dregs of the world.

THE TWO PANDORAS,
OR
THE BLACK CAP AND THE WHITE GLOVES.

Figure 2: 'The Two Pandoras, or the Black Cap and the White Gloves', *Zozimus*, 30 March 1872. Reproduced by permission of the Librarian, Maynooth University, from the collections of St Patrick's College, Maynooth

He particularly stressed that it was 'the English garrison with its troops of vile camp-followers that debauched the capital of Ireland'.[137]

The view that Ireland was relatively free of such crimes as infanticide, domestic violence and rape was partly borne out by a sanguine reading of the returns of crime that were compiled annually by the RIC and DMP.[138] However, it would be unwise to regard such statistics as a comprehensive record of the incidence of such crimes, as they were under-reported for a variety of reasons. It is highly likely that, as in the case of Ireland today, many rape victims, particularly incest victims,[139] felt unable to inform the police that they had been assaulted. The hostility with which plaintiffs, including children, were often treated by defence counsel and judges in rape cases was hardly likely to have induced other rape victims to bring their cases forward.[140] The levity sometimes shown by the bench and defence counsel in cases of rape and indecent assault is also indicative of a lack of sympathy towards the complainants. For example, in 1884 Michael Morris, chief justice of the court of common pleas, made clear his lack of sympathy towards a married County Down woman who charged a neighbour with having indecently assaulted her, when in his charge to the jury he stated that 'The jury had seen the defendant, and certainly his appearance did not bear out the sort of character given of him. A gray headed elderly man he was, not one bit like a Don Juan.' In a similar case involving a married Jewish woman and a former RIC man at Dolphin's Barn, in Dublin, three years later, in which the plaintiff miscarried as a result of the assault upon her, the defending solicitor, Richard Adams, provoked laughter in court when he stated that 'unprotected' men would not travel in the company of women, even in railway carriages, for fear of being charged with indecent assault, a 'joke' in which Justice O'Brien joined. Adams cast doubt on the plaintiff's testimony by claiming that 'the daughters of Israel, although they had many virtues, had not very sweet tempers'.[141] The frequent leniency shown by judges when sentencing rapists, including men who were guilty of raping children, including their own daughters, was also unlikely to induce victims to bring charges against their attackers.[142]

The main reason why cases of husbands assaulting their wives were not fully represented in police returns of crime is that the victims were often reluctant to prosecute,[143] either out of fear of retribution or because a jail sentence for the assailants would mean financial hardship for their wives and families.[144] The police often refused to intervene in domestic violence cases.[145] Even when wives brought charges against their abusive husbands, they often subsequently changed their minds in court and pleaded for clemency or gave evidence that presented their husbands in a flattering light, often to the despair of the presiding magistrates.[146] Most cases of domestic violence that came before the courts involved working-class men assaulting their wives, usually when the men were drunk; domestic violence among the better-off classes was a crime that was largely hidden from the rest of Irish society, although occasionally incidents of domestic violence featured in divorce cases that were brought by Irish wives against their husbands.[147] As Diane Urquhart points out, the history of Irish divorce and domestic violence makes Lord Braye's boasts in the House of Lords in 1921, that 'even the enemies of Ireland are bound to confess that the purity of the Irish race is one of the lights of the world', ring hollow.[148] A similar claim may be made regarding the alleged Irish exceptionalism in the case of infanticide. As Dympna McLoughlin, Elaine Farrell and Clíona Rattigan show, the known cases of infanticide in Ireland suggest that this crime was more prevalent than some contemporaries acknowledged.[149] Furthermore, women who killed their babies were frequently treated with leniency by judges and jurors[150] and did not receive the intense degree of opprobrium in the courts that unmarried mothers received in Irish society more generally.[151]

Was Ireland unique?

The evidence detailed here would suggest that there were many similarities between crime committed in Ireland and the wider experience of crime in the western world in the period under discussion. For example, just as the authorities in Ireland often commented on there being a causal link between excessive alcohol consumption and crime, similar observations were also made elsewhere. It was frequently asserted in Britain and the USA that drunkenness, particularly among the urban lower classes, led to domestic violence and other violent crime, including disorderly behaviour in public. The fact that public drunkenness was made a crime in France in 1873 reflects the French authorities' concerns about the negative impact that people's excessive drinking was having on French society.[152] In its extreme form, anxiety about the damaging effects of excessive consumption of alcohol by people at the lower end of the social scale led to fears about the physical degeneration of the British and French 'races'.[153] In Britain, as in Ireland, women who were repeatedly imprisoned for public drunkenness or for drunkenness combined with other offences were regarded with greater disfavour than men in similar situations.[154] Another common feature between Ireland, Britain and other countries is that prostitutes figured disproportionately in criminal proceedings as a result of being arrested for public drunkenness, disorderly behaviour, assault or for stealing from their customers.[155] There was also a near universal fear of the perceived criminal disposition of the tramp, which was often fanned by sensationalist reports of violent crimes which were committed by a small number of individuals of the vagrant class.[156] It is likely that a more sustained transnational focus would reveal additional interesting examples of how Ireland's experience of crime in the late nineteenth and early twentieth centuries had much in common with that of Britain and other countries.

Conclusion

WHILE URBAN AREAS, and especially the cities, generally had higher crime levels than rural areas, the overall Irish crime level does not provide a sufficient explanation for the high numbers of police that were stationed in the country at the end of the nineteenth and the beginning of the twentieth centuries. This police presence was also partly a result of the wider expansion of state institutions which had occurred in Ireland throughout the nineteenth century.[1] The RIC's strength, which peaked at 14,559 in 1883, was gradually allowed to decline thereafter, to some 10,181 in 1914, which partly reflected the authorities' perception of the improved state of the country, but there were also financial and political considerations involved. That Ireland nevertheless remained the most heavily policed part of the United Kingdom was partly due to the fact that RIC men from what were usually relatively undisturbed or crime-free parts of the country were frequently needed as a reserve to reinforce the constabulary where large-scale agrarian or other disturbances occurred or were threatened; by the early twentieth century, this was most commonly the case with contentious twelfth of July parades in Ulster. From 1904 to 1913, the annual average of the force that served on detachment duty away from their permanent station was some ninety-one district inspectors, 108 head constables and 5,490 other ranks; in 1907, the year in which much of the Belfast RIC went on strike, some 136 district inspectors, 158 head constables and 8,296 other ranks – almost 84 per cent of the force – spent some time away from their barracks on detachment duty. According to Inspector-general Neville Chamberlain, this could only be accomplished by temporarily reducing many constabulary sub-districts to the bare minimum police strength, with some 161 sub-districts being policed by only two men, one of them a barrack orderly who could not leave his barracks, and some seventeen sub-districts being looked after by only one man.[2] Although the RIC serving on detachment duty did not always experience crowd violence – indeed, the largest single instance of detachment duty undertaken by the constabulary was the securing of the route of the Gordon Bennett race in Kildare, Carlow and Queen's County in July 1903[3] – the large-scale sectarian rioting that occurred in Belfast in 1872, 1880, 1886 and 1898 illustrates the dangers to which they could occasionally be exposed.[4] In the two years before the outbreak of the First World War, the RIC in Belfast had to face the additional danger of gun-toting rioters at sectarian clashes between supporters of Belfast Celtic and Linfield football clubs,[5] and they also struggled to combat the campaign of violence that was carried out by militant suffragists in Belfast from 1912 to 1914.[6]

Another reason why a relatively large constabulary presence was maintained in Ireland, despite the peaceful conditions that prevailed in most of the country most of the time, was because the RIC was an invaluable source of intelligence for the Dublin Castle authorities, due to the force's intimate knowledge of the communities that it policed; as Charles Townshend has pointed out, 'the whole force was in a sense a special branch'.[7] As events were to prove after 1914, a relatively large police presence was not enough in itself to enable the forces of law and order to grapple successfully with the familiar problems of non-political offences and sporadic agrarian crime on the one hand, and the simultaneous and novel problem of an armed guerilla campaign directed, to a considerable extent, against the RIC, on the other.[8] There was nothing in Irish policemen's experiences of combating crime in the pre-First World War decades that could have prepared them for the unique challenges of the IRA's onslaught during the War of Independence.

Notes

INTRODUCTION

1. It would require a separate tome to adequately survey the crimes of violence and other illegal acts that were committed by both sides during the War of Independence. There is a substantial scholarly literature covering these topics. Of particular importance are Peter Hart, *The I.R.A. and Its Enemies: Violence and community in Cork, 1916–1923* (Oxford: Clarendon Press, 1998); D.M. Leeson, *The Black and Tans: British police and auxiliaries in the Irish War of Independence, 1920–1921* (Oxford: Oxford University Press, 2011); Marie Coleman, 'Violence against Women during the Irish War of Independence, 1919–21', in Diarmaid Ferriter and Susannah Riordan (eds), *Years of Turbulence: The Irish revolution and its aftermath* (Dublin: UCD Press, 2015), pp. 137–55; John Crowley, Donal Ó Drisceoil and Mike Murphy (eds), *Atlas of the Irish Revolution* (New York: New York University Press, 2017).

2. L.P. Curtis, *Apes and Angels: The Irishman in Victorian caricature* (Newton Abbot: David & Charles, 1971); Michel de Nie, *The Eternal Paddy: Irish identity and the British press, 1798–1882* (Madison: University of Wisconsin Press, 2004); Niall Whelehan, 'Revolting Peasants: Southern Italy, Ireland, and cartoons in comparative perspective, 1860–1882', *International Review of Social History*, vol. 60, no. 1, 2015, pp. 1–35.

3. A.P.W. Malcomson, *Virtues of a Wicked Earl: The life and legend of William Sydney Clements, 3rd earl of Leitrim (1806–78)* (Dublin: Four Courts Press, 2009), pp. 186–91.

4. Tom Corfe, *The Phoenix Park Murders: Conflict, compromise and tragedy in Ireland, 1879–1882* (London: Hodder & Stoughton, 1968); Leon Ó Broin, 'The Invincibles', in T. Desmond Williams (ed.), *Secret Societies in Ireland* (Dublin: Gill & Macmillan, 1973), pp. 113–25; Senan Moloney, *The Phoenix Park Murders: Conspiracy, betrayal and retribution* (Cork: Mercier Press, 2006); Shane Kenna, *The Invincibles: The Phoenix Park murders and the conspiracy that shook an empire* (Dublin: O'Brien Press, 2019); Seán Ó Cuirreáin, *The Queen v. Patrick O'Donnell: The man who shot the informer James Carey* (Dublin: Four Courts Press, 2021); Julie Kavanagh, *The Irish Assassins: Conspiracy, revenge, and the Phoenix Park murders that stunned Victorian England* (New York: Atlantic Monthly Press, 2021).

5. Andrew Boyd, *Holy War in Belfast* (Tralee: Anvil Books, 1969); Catherine Hirst, *Religion, Politics and Violence in Nineteenth-Century Belfast: The Pound and Sandy Row* (Dublin: Four Courts Press, 2002); Mark Doyle, *Fighting Like the Devil for the Sake of God: Protestants, Catholics and the origins of sectarian violence in Victorian Belfast* (Manchester and New York: Manchester University Press, 2009); Mark Radford, *The Policing of Belfast 1870–1914* (London: Bloomsbury, 2015).

6. Radford, *Policing of Belfast*, pp. 99–121.

7. Virginia Crossman, *Politics, Law and Order in Nineteenth-Century Ireland* (Dublin: Gill & Macmillan, 1996).

8. Some of the more important contributions are Paul Bew, *Land and the National Question in Ireland 1858–82* (Dublin: Gill & Macmillan, 1982); Samuel Clark, *Social Origins of the Irish Land War* (Princeton: Princeton University Press, 1979); James S. Donnelly Jr, *The Land and the People of Nineteenth-Century Cork: The rural economy and the land question* (London and New York: Routledge & Kegan Paul, 1975); David Fitzpatrick, 'Class, Family and Rural Unrest in Nineteenth-Century Ireland', in P.J. Drury (ed.), *Ireland: Land, politics and people* (Cambridge: Cambridge University Press, 1982), pp. 31–75; Laurence Geary, *The Plan of Campaign, 1886–1891* (Cork: Cork University Press, 1986); David Seth Jones, 'The Cleavage between Graziers and Peasants in the Land Struggle, 1890–1910', in Samuel Clark and James S. Donnelly Jr (eds), *Irish Peasants: Violence and political unrest 1780–1914* (Dublin: Gill & Macmillan, 1983), pp. 374–417.

9. Despite its promising title, a recent collection of essays has little to say on the subject of 'ordinary' or non-agrarian crime at the end of the nineteenth century: Kyle Hughes and Donald M. MacRaild (eds), *Crime, Violence, and the Irish in the Nineteenth Century* (Liverpool: Liverpool University Press, 2017).

10. Mark Finnane, 'A Decline in Violence in Ireland? Crime, policing and social relations, 1860–1914', *Crime, Histoire et Sociétés*, vol. 1, no. 1, 1997, pp. 51–70; Carolyn Conley, *Melancholy Accidents: The meaning of violence in post-Famine Ireland* (Lanham: Lexington Books, 1999); Carolyn Conley, *Certain Other Countries: Homicide, gender, and national identity* (Columbus: Ohio State University Press, 2007).

11. Joanne Bourke, 'The Mocking of Margaret and the Misfortune of Mary: Sexual violence in Irish history, 1830s–1890s', *Canadian*

Journal of Irish Studies, vol. 43, 2020, pp. 16–36.

12. Clíona Rattigan, '"I Thought From Her Appearance that She was in the Family Way": Detecting infanticide cases in Ireland, 1900–1922', *Family and Community History*, vol. 11, no. 2, November 2008, pp. 134–51; Elaine Farrell, *'A Most Diabolical Deed': Infanticide and Irish society, 1850–1900* (Manchester: Manchester University Press, 2013).

13. Elizabeth Steiner-Scott, '"To Bounce a Boot Off Her Now & Then …": Domestic violence in post-Famine Ireland', in Maryann Gialanella Valiulis and Mary O'Dowd (eds), *Women and Irish History: Essays in honour of Margaret MacCurtain* (Dublin: Wolfhound Press, 1997), pp. 125–43; Diane Urquhart, 'Irish Divorce and Domestic Violence, 1857–1922', *Women's History Review*, vol. 22, no. 5, 2013, pp. 820–37.

14. Neal Garnham, 'The Survival of Popular Blood Sports in Victorian Ulster', *Proceedings of the Royal Irish Academy*, vol. 107C, 2007, pp. 107–26; Brian Ward, 'Cockfighting in Ireland, 1900 to 1925', *New Hibernia Review*, vol. 20, no. 3, Autumn 2016, pp. 97–111.

CHAPTER 1: AGRARIAN CRIME

1. Bew, *Land and the National Question in Ireland*, p. 149.

2. Geary, *The Plan of Campaign,* pp. 185–6. Further work is needed on rates at a county level.

3. Paul Bew, *Conflict and Conciliation in Ireland 1890–1910: Parnellites and radical agrarians* (Oxford: Oxford University Press, 1987), p. 142.

4. Fergus Campbell, *Land and Revolution: Nationalist politics in the west of Ireland 1891–1921* (Oxford: Oxford University Press, 2005), p. 247, n. 91. The sixteen counties were Galway, Mayo, Leitrim, Roscommon, Sligo, Carlow, Queen's County, Westmeath, Meath, Clare, Kerry, Tipperary, Waterford, Cavan, Tyrone and Donegal.

5. The principal authors are referred to at various points in this chapter. For an overview, see Terence Dooley, 'Irish Land Questions, 1879–1923', in Thomas Bartlett (ed.), *Cambridge History of Ireland: Volume 4, 1880 to the present* (Cambridge: Cambridge University Press, 2018), pp. 117–44.

6. Curtis, *Apes and Angels*; de Nie, *The Eternal Paddy*; Whelehan, 'Revolting Peasants'.

7. *Freeman's Journal*, 14 February 1870.

8. A.C. Murray, 'Agrarian Violence and Nationalism in Nineteenth-Century Ireland: The myth of Ribbonism', *Irish Economic and Social History*, vol. 13, 1986, p. 58. In 1869 and 1870, the RIC adopted a new system of recording agrarian outrages which meant that they were considerably inflated in the national crime statistics for those years. However, the returns of agrarian outrages that were submitted in evidence to the 1871 parliamentary committee into the Westmeath outbreak were not based on this inaccurate mode of recording agrarian crimes.

9. Murray, 'Myth of Ribbonism', p. 61.

10. *Report from the Select Committee on Westmeath, &c (Unlawful Combinations); Together with the Proceedings of the Committee, Minutes of Evidence, and Appendix* H.C. 1871 (147) xiii 547, pp. 164–71 (hereafter *1871 Westmeath Select Committee*). For an interesting textual analysis of the Westmeath threatening letters, see M. Van Hattum, 'The Language of "Ribbonmen": A CDA approach to identity construction in nineteenth-century Irish English threatening notices', *Journal of Historical Sociolinguistics*, vol. 3, no. 2, 2017, pp. 241–62.

11. Niall Whelehan, 'Labour and Agrarian Violence in the Irish Midlands, 1850–1870', *Saothar*, vol. 37, 2012, pp. 7–18.

12. W.E. Shepherd, 'Murder at Mullingar', *Journal of the Irish Railway Record Society*, vol. 18, 1992, pp. 80–8.

13. *Freeman's Journal*, 22 March 1870.

14. *1871 Westmeath Select Committee*, p. iii.

15. It must have been difficult for the members of the select committee to disregard the evidence of such witnesses as Captain George Talbot, a resident magistrate of some eighteen years' service, and Stephen Seed, who had served variously as crown solicitor and chief crown solicitor in Westmeath, Meath and Kildare since 1845, both of whom provided highly detailed descriptions of the alleged organisational structure and operational methods of the supposed Ribbon Society: *1871 Westmeath Select Committee*, pp. 9–11, 13–14, 89–93, 95–7, 162–3.

16. Murray, 'Myth of Ribbonism'.

17. According to W.E. Vaughan, threatening letters comprised around 45 per cent of agrarian outrages in Ireland between 1845 and 1880:

W.E. Vaughan, *Landlords and Tenants in Mid-Victorian Ireland* (Oxford: Oxford University Press, 1994), p. 142.

18. *1871 Westmeath Select Committee*, pp. 182–3, 186–8.

19. Murray, 'Myth of Ribbonism', p. 71. Some Ribbonmen participated in agrarian crime in some parts of pre-Famine Ireland. Kyle Hughes and Donald MacRaild write of pre-Famine Ribbonism that 'Ribbon societies engaged in Whiteboy-type agrarian activities in rural Ireland and there was little to distinguish the two on occasion'. They do not instance any Ribbon involvement in agrarian crime in the later nineteenth century, when the Ribbonmen were a secretive Catholic/nationalist counterpart to the Orange Order, especially in Ulster: Kyle Hughes and Donald MacRaild, *Ribbon Societies in Nineteenth-Century Ireland and Its Diaspora: The persistence of tradition* (Liverpool: Liverpool University Press, 2018), p. 8.

20. Murray, 'Myth of Ribbonism', pp. 67–8, 72.

21. Ibid., pp. 61, 68, 72.

22. Ibid., p. 64.

23. Vaughan, *Landlords and Tenants*, pp. 195–6.

24. Donald E. Jordan, *Land and Popular Politics in Ireland: County Mayo from the plantation to the Land War* (Cambridge: Cambridge University Press, 1994), pp. 183, 187.

25. For a recent discussion of the important role played by Fenians in organising the Land League in Mayo during the Land War, including their role in resisting evictions and their possible involvement in agrarian outrages, see Gerard Martin Mary Delaney, 'The Role of the Fenians in the Early Years of the Land War in Mayo', unpublished MA in Local History thesis, University of Limerick, 2022, pp. 31–50.

26. Pádraig G. Lane, 'Agricultural Labourers and Rural Violence, 1850–1914', *Studia Hibernica*, vol. 27, 1993, pp. 77–87.

27. Vaughan, *Landlords and Tenants*, p. 194. For a general discussion of threatening letters in nineteenth-century Ireland see Donal P. McCracken, *'You Will Dye at Midnight': Threatening letters in Victorian Ireland* (Dublin: Eastwood, 2021).

28. *Freeman's Journal*, 14 March 1871.

29. Ibid., 26 March 1870.

30. *Belfast News-Letter*, 15 March 1871, 20 July 1874. One gets a good sense of the dread in which 'Rory' was held by the authorities,

from the example of the prosecution in February 1870 of a ballad singer from Cork, a 'poor man named Duffy', who was arrested in Waterford 'for singing ballads of an inflammatory character against the landlords, and what it was considered, contained plain and direct incentive to his auditory to commit outrages'. Among the ballads that he sang was one titled 'Rory of the Hills'. Duffy was sentenced to two months in jail for this offence. Ballad-singers who sang seditious songs were frequently arrested by the police: *Freeman's Journal*, 15 February 1870; Maura Murphy, 'The Ballad Singer and the Role of the Seditious Ballad in Nineteenth-Century Ireland', *Ulster Folklife*, vol. 25, 1979, pp. 79–102.

31. *Belfast News-Letter*, 23 February 1874.

32. Ibid., 8 April 1875.

33. Hoax telephone callers were proving to be a nuisance to Dublin's fire brigade as early as the second decade of the twentieth century. The first of these cases occurred in 1910, when at least four people (two youths, a soldier and a colonial police inspector) were convicted of making nuisance calls to the fire brigade. In 1913 and 1919 the fire brigade had to respond to some twenty-six and forty-two false alarms, respectively: Tom Geraghty and Trevor Whitehead, *The Dublin Fire Brigade: A history of the brigade, the fires and the emergencies* (Dublin: Dublin City Council, 2004), pp. 135, 141, 161. For a brief discussion of 'crank' threatening letters see McCracken, *'You Will Dye at Midnight'*, pp. 112–13.

34. Stephen Ball (ed.), *A Policeman's Ireland: Recollections of Samuel Waters, RIC* (Cork: Cork University Press, 1999), pp. 44–6.

35. *Freeman's Journal*, 12 March 1870.

36. Ibid., 11 July 1879.

37. Quoted in ibid., 6 March 1872.

38. Ibid., 2 February 1881.

39. *Belfast News-Letter*, 6 August 1872; *Freeman's Journal*, 19 July 1881.

40. Alfred Turner, *Sixty Years of a Soldier's Life* (London: Methuen, 1912), p. 259.

41. W.E. Vaughan, 'Landlord and Tenant Relations in Ireland between the Famine and the Land War, 1850–1878', in L.M. Cullen and T.C. Smout (eds), *Comparative Aspects of Scottish and Irish Economic and Social History 1600–1900* (Edinburgh: John Donald, 1977),

pp. 216–26; Vaughan, *Landlords and Tenants*, passim.

42. McCracken, *'You Will Dye at Midnight'*, passim.

43. Vaughan, *Landlords and Tenants*, p. 209.

44. Geary, *Plan of Campaign*, p. 183.

45. Marc Mulholland, 'Land War Homicides', in Senia Paŝeta (ed.), *Uncertain Futures: Essays about the past for Roy Foster* (Oxford: Oxford University Press, 2016), pp. 81–96.

46. Vaughan, *Landlords and Tenants*, pp. 279–80.

47. J.W.H. Carter, *The Land War and Its Leaders in Queen's County, 1879–82* (Portlaoise: Leinster Express Newspapers, 1994), p. 311.

48. Vaughan, *Landlords and Tenants*, p. 280.

49. Donnelly, *Land and People of Nineteenth-Century Cork*; Bew, *Land and the National Question*; Clark, *Social Origins*; Thomas Nelson, *The Land War in County Kildare* (Maynooth: St Patrick's College Maynooth, 1985); Jordan, *Land and Popular Politics*; Carter, *Land War in Queen's County*; Edward Kennedy, *The Land Movement in Tullaroan, County Kilkenny, 1879–1891* (Dublin: Four Courts Press, 2004); Donncha Seán Lucey, *Land, Popular Politics and Agrarian Violence in Ireland: The case of County Kerry, 1872–86* (Dublin: UCD Press, 2011).

50. Terence Dooley, 'The Land War in Drumlish, 1879–82', in Martin Morris and Fergus O'Ferrall (eds), *Longford: History and society* (Dublin: Geography Publications, 2010), pp. 539–53.

51. Barbara Solow, *The Land Question and the Irish Economy, 1870–1903* (Cambridge, MA: Harvard University Press, 1971); Donnelly, *Land and People of Nineteenth-Century Cork*; Vaughan, 'Landlord and Tenant Relations'; Carter, *Land War in Queen's County*, pp. 1–27.

52. Bew, *Land and National Question*, p. 149. A recent study of agrarian offences committed in 1881 shows some distinctive regional patterns. Almost half of Ireland's cases of aggravated assault, injuries to property, and killing and maiming of cattle occurred in Connacht, while 65.4 per cent of assaults endangering life, 62.8 per cent of cases of firing at dwellings, 60.2 per cent of assaults on bailiffs and 53 per cent of cases of firing at persons occurred in Munster: William J. Smyth, 'Conflict, Reaction and Control in Nineteenth-Century Ireland: The archaeology of revolution', in Crowley et al. (eds), *Atlas of Revolution*, p. 40.

53. Pat Finnegan, *The Case of the Craughwell Prisoners during the Land War in Co. Galway, 1879–85: The law must take its course* (Dublin: Four Courts Press, 2012), p. 22.

54. The Plan of Campaign was adopted on some seventy-five estates in Munster, seventy-one in Connacht, thirty-three in Leinster and twenty-four in Ulster. Tenants who supported the campaign agreed to offer their landlords a reduced level of rent and, where this was refused, the money was paid instead into an estate fund to support tenants who were evicted for non-payment of rent: Geary, *Plan of Campaign*, p. 179.

55. Ibid., pp. 182–4.

56. John Baker Greene, *Notes on Ireland Made from Personal Observation of Its Political, Social and Economical Situation* (London: Samson Law, Marston, Searle & Rivington, 1886), p. 43.

57. In addition to enrolling hundreds of extra recruits for the hard-pressed constabulary in the early 1880s, the authorities also employed some 700 soldiers on protection duty in the areas most severely affected by the agrarian agitation, as well as raising a temporary force of 440 auxiliary policemen to perform protection duties. The latter force served from December 1881 to July 1883. Detachments of soldiers were frequently used to support the police on eviction duty throughout the 1880s: Richard Hawkins, 'An Army on Police Work, 1881–2: Ross of Bladensburg's memorandum', *Irish Sword*, vol. 11, 1973, pp. 75–115; Elizabeth A. Muenger, *The British Military Dilemma in Ireland: Occupation politics, 1886–1914* (Lawrence: University of Kansas Press, 1991).

58. Gerard Moran, 'The Origins and Development of Boycotting', *Journal of the Galway Archaeological and Historical Society*, vol. 40, 1985–6, pp. 49–64; Heather Laird, *Subversive Law in Ireland, 1879–1920: From "unwritten law" to the Dáil courts* (Dublin: Four Courts Press, 2005), pp. 28–36.

59. Domhnall Mac an Ghalloglaigh, 'The Land League in Leitrim 1879–1883', *Breifne*, vol. 6, no. 22, 1983–4, pp. 155–87; Stephen Ball, 'Crowd Activity during the Irish Land War, 1879–90', in Peter Jupp and Eoin Magennis (eds), *Crowds in Ireland, c. 1720–1920* (Basingstoke and New York: Macmillan, 2000), pp. 212–48; L.P. Curtis, *The Depiction of Eviction in Ireland 1845–1910* (Dublin: UCD Press, 2011).

60. William Feingold documents the widespread tenants' 'revolt' against landlord domination of the position of Poor Law guardian

in much of the country in the early 1880s. This 'revolt' was partly fuelled by hostility towards landlords, which was connected with the land agitation of the period: William Feingold, *The Revolt of the Tenantry: The transformation of local government in Ireland 1872–1886* (Boston: Northeastern University Press, 1984).

61. L.P. Curtis, 'Stopping the Hunt, 1881–1882: An aspect of the Irish Land War', in C.H.E. Philbin (ed.), *Nationalism and Popular Protest in Ireland* (Cambridge: Cambridge University Press, 1987), pp. 349–402; Carter, *Land War in Queen's County*, pp. 227–33; Laird, *Subversive Law*, pp. 78–102. Although this obstruction was usually peaceful, it sometimes involved criminal activity, such as assaulting hunters or poisoning their dogs. A similar campaign was orchestrated by Sinn Féin members and supporters in early 1919, in an effort to pressurise the British authorities into releasing republican detainees. While most of their anti-hunt actions were peaceful, a small number involved violence: William Murphy, 'Sport in a Time of Revolution: Sinn Féin and the hunt in Ireland, 1919', *Éire-Ireland*, vol. 48, nos 1 & 2, Spring–Summer 2013, pp. 79–102.

62. L.P. Curtis, *Coercion and Conciliation in Ireland 1880–1892: A study in conservative unionism* (Princeton: Princeton University Press, 1963), p. 9.

63. William O'Connor Morris, *Memories and Thoughts of a Life* (London: George Allen, 1895), pp. 259–60.

64. Clark, *Social Origins*; R.V. Comerford, 'The Land War and the Politics of Distress, 1877–82', in W.E. Vaughan (ed.), *A New History of Ireland. VI. Ireland under the Union, II: 1870–1921* (Oxford: Clarendon Press, 1996), pp. 26–52; Lucey, *Land, Popular Politics and Agrarian Violence*.

65. Richard Hawkins, 'Government Versus Secret Societies: The Parnell era', in T. Desmond Williams (ed.), *Secret Societies in Ireland* (Dublin: Gill & Macmillan, 1973), p. 105.

66. Ball (ed.), *Policeman's Ireland*, pp. 51, 55–6; Stephen Ball, 'Policing the Land War: Official responses to political protest and agrarian crime in Ireland, 1879–91', unpublished PhD dissertation, Goldsmith's College, University College London, 2000, pp. 27–8, 36, 119, 140–2, 144–5, 156–7, 161, 301, 312–15; Owen McGee, *The IRB: The Irish Republican Brotherhood from the Land League to Sinn Féin* (Dublin: Four Courts Press, 2005), pp. 79–80; Lucey, *Land, Popular Politics and Agrarian Violence*, pp. 99–100, 102, 109–12.

67. Clark, *Social Origins*; Jordan, *Land and Popular Politics*; McGee, *The IRB*; Frank Rynne, 'Permanent Revolutionaries: The IRB and the Land War in west Cork', in Fearghal McGarry and James McConnel (eds), *The Black Hand of Republicanism: Fenianism in modern Ireland* (Dublin: Four Courts Press, 2009), pp. 55–71; Frank Rynne, 'Redressing Historical Imbalance: The role of grassroots leaders Richard Hodnett and Henry O'Mahony in the Land League revolution in west Cork, 1879–82', in Brian Casey (ed.), *Defying the Law of the Land: Agrarian radicals in Irish history* (Dublin: History Press Ireland, 2013), pp. 133–53; Lucey, *Land, Popular Politics and Agrarian Violence*.

68. Ann Murtagh, *Portrait of a Westmeath Tenant Community, 1879–85: The Barbavilla murder* (Dublin: Irish Academic Press, 1999). This killing was allegedly perpetrated by a local 'Assassination Society' that was purportedly established in the area by three Dublin Invincibles with the purpose of killing local 'tyrants'. The intended target of the murderers was Mrs Smythe's brother-in-law, William Barlow Smythe, the owner of Barbavilla estate.

69. Jarlath Waldron, *Maamtrasna: The murders and the mystery* (Dublin: Edmund Burke Publisher, 1992); Margaret Kelleher, *The Maamtrasna Murders: Language, life and death in nineteenth-century Ireland* (Dublin: UCD Press, 2018). Maamtrasna, which is now in County Mayo, was in County Galway in 1882. Detective Inspector John Mallon of the Dublin Metropolitan Police was one of the officers who investigated the Maamtrasna murders. He remarked that 'At first it was reported that the murders were an act of agrarian or political character, but after I had investigated it I came to the conclusion that it had nothing to do with the agitation or with the organised revolt against landlordism or England'. Instead, in Mallon's view the murders 'were the result of a private quarrel' over the division of the proceeds of the sale of the locals' sheep, which grazed 'in one indistinguishable flock of huge dimensions' on the surrounding hills: Donal P. McCracken, *Inspector Mallon: Buying Irish patriotism for a five-pound note* (Dublin: Irish Academic Press, 2009), p. 98.

70. Kevin McMahon, 'The "Crossmaglen Conspiracy" Case. Part I', *Seanchas Ardmhacha*, vol. 6, no. 2, 1972, pp. 251–86; Kevin McMahon, 'The "Crossmaglen Conspiracy" Case. Part II', *Seanchas Ardmhacha*, vol. 7, no. 1, 1973, pp. 65–107; Kevin McMahon, 'The "Crossmaglen Conspiracy" Case. Part III', *Seanchas Ardmhacha*, vol. 7, no. 2, 1974, pp. 326–63.

71. Donnelly, *Land and People of Nineteenth-Century Cork*, pp. 287–8.

72. Lucey, *Land, Popular Politics and Agrarian Violence*, p. 110.

73. Margaret O'Callaghan, 'Parnellism and Crime: Constructing a conservative strategy of containment 1887–91', in Donal McCartney (ed.), *Parnell: The politics of power* (Dublin: Wolfhound Press, 1991), pp. 102–24.

74. Irish Loyal and Patriotic Union, *Verbatim Copy of the Parnell Commission Report, with Complete Index and Notes* (London: Irish Loyal and Patriotic Union, 1890), p. 103. Harris, a building contractor from Ballinasloe, was one of a coterie of Connacht Fenians (he became a member of the IRB Supreme Council in the late 1870s) who helped to launch the land agitation in the west in 1879: Brian Casey, 'Matt Harris and the Ballinasloe Tenant Defence Association, 1876–9', in Brian Casey (ed.), *Defying the Law of the Land: Agrarian radicals in Irish history* (Dublin: History Press Ireland, 2013), pp. 90–9; Gerard Moran, 'Matthew Harris, Fenianism and the Land Agitation in the West of Ireland', in Fergus Campbell and Tony Varley (eds), *Land Questions in Modern Ireland* (Manchester: Manchester University Press, 2013), pp. 218–37.

75. *Freeman's Journal*, 11 March 1887.

76. Ibid., 11 December 1880.

77. Crossman, *Politics, Law and Order*, pp. 222–7.

78. Vaughan, *Landlords and Tenants*, pp. 158–9.

79. This is discussed on p. 41 below.

80. *Freeman's Journal*, 28 May 1870.

81. Ibid., 18 August 1873; *The Times*, 20 August 1873.

82. *Belfast News-Letter*, 13 August 1873.

83. Fitzpatrick, 'Class, Family and Rural Unrest in Nineteenth-Century Ireland', pp. 31–75.

84. Clark, *Social Origins*, p. 325.

85. Joseph Lee, 'Patterns of Rural Unrest in Nineteenth-Century Ireland: A preliminary survey', in L.M. Cullen and F. Furet (eds), *Ireland and France, 17th–20th Centuries: Towards a comparative study of rural history* (Ann Arbor: UMI Publishing, 1980), p. 229.

86. Donald E. Jordan, 'The Irish National League and the "Unwritten Law": Rural protest and nation-building in Ireland 1882–1890',

Past and Present, no. 158, February 1998, pp. 146–71; Laird, *Subversive Law*.

87. Carter, *Land War in Queen's County*, p. 270.

88. *Freeman's Journal*, 2 August 1884, 11, 16 December 1884, 16, 17 January 1885; Dean Ruxton, *When the Hangman Came to Galway: A gruesome true story of murder in Victorian Ireland* (Dublin: Gill & Macmillan, 2018).

89. George Garrow Green, *In the Royal Irish Constabulary* (London: James Blackwood, 1905), p. 229.

90. Ibid., pp. 231–3.

91. Michael J.F. McCarthy, *Irish Land and Irish Liberty: A study of the new lords of the soil* (London: Robert Scott & Paternoster, 1911), p. 370; D.S. Greer and V.A. Mitchell, *Compensation for Criminal Damage to Property* (Belfast: S.L.S. Legal Publications (N.I.), 1982), pp. 11–14.

92. *Freeman's Journal*, 9 November 1898, 18 March 1899.

93. *Royal Irish Constabulary Magazine*, October 1914.

94. Edward MacLysaght, *Changing Times: Ireland since 1898* (Gerrards Cross: Colin Smythe, 1978), pp. 36–7. For some examples of rabbit-poaching see *Bray and South Dublin Herald*, 29 November 1884; *Leinster Reporter*, 15 January 1898; *Kerry Evening Star*, 24 November 1902; *Lisburn Standard*, 12 May 1906; *Drogheda Independent*, 13 June 1908; *Western People*, 25 November 1911.

95. Memoirs of District Inspector John M. Regan: PRONI/D.3160, p. 75.

96. Clare C. Murphy, 'Conflict in the West: The Ranch War continues, 1911–1912, Part I', *Cathair na Mart*, vol. 15, 1995, pp. 84–105; Clare C. Murphy, 'Conflict in the West: The Ranch War continues, 1911–1912, Part II', *Cathair na Mart*, vol. 16, 1997, pp. 112–39.

97. Sally Warwick-Haller, *William O'Brien and the Irish Land War* (Dublin: Irish Academic Press, 1990).

98. William O'Connor Morris, *Past Irish Questions* (London: Grant Richards, 1901), p. 29.

99. Jones, 'Cleavage between Graziers and Peasants', pp. 374–417; David Seth Jones, *Graziers, Land Reform, and Political Conflict in Ireland* (Washington: Catholic University of America Press, 1995); Campbell, *Land and Revolution*, pp. 106–7.

100. Irish Unionist Alliance, *Cattle-Driving in Ireland* (Dublin: Irish Unionist Alliance, 1908); Jones, *Graziers*, p. 189; Patrick Cosgrove, 'The Ranch War, *c.* 1906–09', in Crowley et al. (eds), *Atlas of Revolution*, pp. 81–4.

101. Jones, *Graziers*, pp. 187–90; Brendan Ó Cathaoir, 'Another Clare: Ranchers and moonlighters, 1700–1945', in Matthew Lynch and Patrick Nugent (eds), *Clare: History and society. Interdisciplinary essays on the history of an Irish county* (Dublin: Geography Publications, 2008), pp. 374–82. The RIC statistics can be somewhat misleading about the nature of cattle drives. For example, in June 1909, County Inspector Tyacke of Meath reported that of the five cattle drives that had taken place in his county in the previous month, one was an attempted drive by just one man who was caught in the act by the police, and another involved somebody breaking the locks on the gates on a grass farm – evidently the cattle in this case were supposed to stray onto the roads, rather than being forcibly driven away by a crowd: National Archives, CO 904/78: Meath RIC county inspector's monthly confidential report, 2 June 1909.

102. Miriam Moffitt, 'Protestant Tenant Farmers and the Land League in North Connacht', in Carla King and Conor McNamara (eds), *The West of Ireland: New perspectives* (Dublin: History Ireland Press, 2011), pp. 104–7, 109–12; Patrick Cosgrove, *The Ranch War in Riverstown, Co. Sligo, 1908* (Dublin: Four Courts Press, 2012), pp. 13–14.

103. Cosgrove, *Ranch War in Riverstown*.

104. Marie Coleman, *County Longford and the Irish Revolution 1910–1923* (Dublin: Irish Academic Press, 2003), p. 14; Campbell, *Land and Revolution*, p. 182; Ó Cathaoir, 'Ranchers and Moonlighters', pp. 378–80.

105. Breandán Mac Giolla Choille (ed.), *Chief Secretary's Office, Dublin Castle: Intelligence notes 1913–16 preserved in the State Paper Office* (Dublin: Oifig an tSoláthair, 1966), p. 249.

106. Mac Giolla Choille, *Intelligence Notes*, p. 192.

107. Fergus Campbell suggests that Kenny's secret society was a revival of a secret society that allegedly committed outrages in the Craughwell district in the early 1880s, but a close reading of the evidence that he advances for the existence of such a society some decades before Kenny's reveals that it is not compelling: Campbell, *Land and Revolution*, pp. 175–6.

108. Bureau of Military History, Witness Statement 347, p. 2 (hereafter BMH, WS); Fergus Campbell, '"Reign of Terror at Craughwell": Tom Kenny and the McGoldrick murder of 1909', *History Ireland*, vol. 18, no. 1, January–February 2010, pp. 26–9; Fergus Campbell, 'Land Purchase and Radicalisation in County Galway, *c.* 1881–1931', *Irish Studies Review*, vol. 28, no. 1, February 2020, pp. 32–5. This was not the only example of IRB members engaging in violence during the Ranch War. The Ó Maoileoin brothers of Tyrellspass, Séamas and Tomás, record that many of the IRB in their district were involved in the anti-grazier agitation. This was not entirely to the brothers' liking: Séamas was concerned that mere greed for land was what motivated this IRB involvement, and was convinced that some of his colleagues in the organisation were merely jealous that they themselves had not succeeded in buying a farm, but Tomás admitted that 'we would do anything to upset the constabulary and keep them busy'. IRB men often fired shots at the RIC during cattle drives, and on one occasion Tomás fired a shot into the window of Dalystown RIC barracks, 'which kept the Peelers busy for a week'. On another occasion, Séamas fired three or four grains of snipeshot into the behind of a man who was too friendly with the police, in order to frighten him: Séamas Ó Maoileoin, *B'Fhiú an Braon Fola* … (Dublin: Sáirséal & Dill, 1958), pp. 17–18; Uinseann Mac Eoin, *Survivors* (Dublin: Argenta, 1987), p. 77.

109. Cosgrove, *Ranch War in Riverstown*, pp. 23–5.

110. Robert Lynd, *Home Life in Ireland* (London: Mills & Boon, 1912), p. 28.

111. Mac Giolla Choille, *Intelligence Notes*, p. 246; Michael Farry, *Sligo 1914–1921: A chronicle of conflict* (Trim: Killoran Press, 1992), pp. 17–19; Pádraig G. Lane, 'Government Surveillance of Subversion in Laois, 1890–1916', in Pádraig G. Lane and William Nolan (eds), *Laois History and Society: Interdisciplinary essays on the history of an Irish county* (Dublin: Geography Publications, 1999), pp. 618–19; Coleman, *Longford*, p. 15; Michael Wheatley, *Nationalism and the Irish Party: Provincial Ireland 1910–1916* (Oxford: Oxford University Press, 2005), pp. 24–8, 30; Leigh-Ann Coffey, *The Planters of Luggancurran, County Laois: A Protestant community, 1879–1927* (Dublin: Four Courts Press, 2006), pp. 41–3; Joost Augusteijn (ed.), *The Memoirs of John M. Regan: A Catholic officer in the RIC and RUC, 1909–1948* (Dublin: Four Courts Press, 2007), pp. 47–9, 54–6, 61; Conor McNamara, *War and Revolution in the West of Ireland: Galway 1913–1922* (Dublin: Irish Academic Press, 2018), pp. 21–2, 25–6.

112. BMH, WS/983, p. 7; BMH, WS/1,048, p. 7; BMH, WS/1,068, p. 30; BMH, WS/1,075, p. 6; BMH, WS/1,288, pp. 6–7.

113. J. Anthony Gaughan (ed.), *The Memoirs of Constable Jeremiah Mee, RIC* (Dublin: Anvil, 1975), pp. 51–2; David Fitzpatrick, *Politics and Irish Life, 1913–1921: Provincial experience of war and revolution* (Dublin: Gill & Macmillan, 1977), pp. 131–2; Farry, *Sligo 1914–1921*, pp. 111–16; Ó Cathaoir, 'Ranchers and Moonlighters', pp. 392–3; Michael Farry, *The Irish Revolution, 1912–1923: Sligo* (Dublin: Four Courts Press, 2012), p. 38; Campbell, *Land and Revolution*, pp. 242–4; McNamara, *Galway 1913–1922*, p. 102.

114. Fitzpatrick, *Politics and Irish Life*, p. 264; McNamara, *Galway 1913–1922*, p. 100.

115. Fitzpatrick, *Politics and Irish Life*, p. 264.

116. *The Irish Times*, 21 July 1919.

117. Terence Dooley, *'The Land for the People': The land question in independent Ireland* (Dublin: UCD Press, 2004), p. 38.

118. Oliver Coogan, *Politics and War in Meath 1913–23* (Dublin: Folens, 1983), pp. 112–13.

119. Terence Dooley, *The Decline of the Big House in Ireland: A study of Irish landed families 1860–1960* (Dublin: Wolfhound Press, 2001), p. 182; Campbell, *Land and Revolution*, pp. 264–8; Ó Cathaoir, 'Ranchers and Moonlighters', p. 397; Farry, *Irish Revolution*, p. 53; Charles Townshend, *The Republic: The fight for Irish independence* (London: Allen Lane, 2013), pp. 27–8; Terry Dunne, '"Cattle Drivers, Marauders, Terrorists and Hooligans": The agrarian movement of 1920', *History Ireland*, vol. 28, no. 4, July–August 2020, pp. 30–3.

120. Coleman, *Longford*, p. 119.

121. Terence Dooley, *Burning the Big House: The story of the Irish country house in a time of war and revolution* (New Haven and London: Yale University Press, 2022), pp. 98–114, 144–50.

122. Campbell, *Land and Revolution*, pp. 264–6.

123. Dooley, *'The Land for the People'*, pp. 39–40.

124. Campbell, *Land and Revolution*, pp. 252, 266–7; McNamara, *Galway 1913–1922*, p. 172.

125. Perhaps unsurprisingly, the IRA in Meath took a keen interest in finding Clinton's killers. The republican police eventually arrested a dozen suspects, several of whom were ex-soldiers; the suspects were members of the 'Black Hand' gang of Cormeen, who attempted

to secure land for themselves by intimidating local farmers and landowners. It was claimed that some of the Clintons' neighbours paid for the attack. The alleged ring-leader was William Gordon of Killagriffe, Bailieboro, a former sniper in the British army, who was also reportedly the person who killed Clinton. Gordon, after two trials conducted by the IRA, was shot at Castlefarm, Dunboyne, and his body disposed of in a local quarry. The other prisoners received sentences of expulsion from Ireland for varying periods: the man who shot the horses was expelled from Ireland for life, while the others received sentences of expulsion for periods ranging from three to fifteen years, with their sentences to be reviewed 'when the occupying forces had left the country': Coogan, *Meath 1913–23*, p. 209; John F. Cogan, 'Michael Collins and the Cormeen Murder Case, 1920', *Ríocht na Midhe*, vol. 37, 2017, pp. 353–73; Myles Dungan, *Four Killings: Land hunger, murder and family in the Irish revolution* (London: Head of Zeus, 2021), pp. 40–105.

126. Tony Varley, 'Agrarian Crime and Social Control: Sinn Féin and the land question in the west of Ireland in 1920', in Mike Tomlinson, Tony Varley and Ciaran McCullagh (eds), *Whose Law and Order? Aspects of crime and social control in Irish society* (Belfast: Sociological Association of Ireland, 1988), pp. 54–75.

127. Ó Cathaoir, 'Ranchers and Moonlighters', p. 397.

128. Fergus Campbell and Kevin O'Shiel, 'The Last Land War? Kevin O'Shiel's memoir of the Irish revolution (1916–21)', *Archivium Hibernicum*, vol. 57, 2003, p. 199.

129. Campbell and O'Shiel, 'Memoir of the Irish Revolution', p. 196.

130. Paul Bew, 'Sinn Féin, Agrarian Radicalism and the War of Independence, 1919–1921', in D.G. Boyce (ed.), *The Revolution in Ireland, 1879–1923* (Dublin: Gill & Macmillan, 1988), pp. 229–30, 232; Varley, 'Agrarian Crime and Social Control'; Campbell and Shiel, 'Memoir of the Irish Revolution', p. 166.

131. BMH, WS/767, pp. 25–7; BMH, WS/1,072, pp. 7–8; BMH, WS/1,142, pp. 2–3; Varley, 'Agrarian Crime and Social Control'; Mary Kotsonouris, *Retreat from Revolution: The Dáil courts, 1920–24* (Dublin: Irish Academic Press, 1993); Campbell, *Land and Revolution*, pp. 280–1; McNamara, *Galway 1913–1922*, p. 174; Thomas Earls FitzGerald, *Combatants and Civilians in Revolutionary Ireland, 1918–1923* (London: Routledge, 2021), pp. 72, 77–8.

132. BMH, WS/1,064, p. 17; BMH, WS/1,072, pp. 8–9; Katharine Tynan, *The Wandering Years* (Boston and New York: Houghton

Mifflin, 1922), p. 207; Mossie Harnett, *Victory and Woe: The West Limerick Brigade in the War of Independence* (Dublin: UCD Press, 2002), pp. 42–3; Fearghal McGarry, *Eoin O'Duffy: A self-made hero* (Oxford: Oxford University Press, 2005), pp. 51–2; John Borgonovo, 'Republican Courts, Ordinary Crime, and the Irish Revolution, 1919–1921', in Margo de Koster, Hervé Leuwers, Dirk Luyten and Xavier Rousseaux (eds), *Justice in Wartime and Revolutions: Europe, 1795–1950* (Brussels: Algemeen Rijksarchief, 2012), pp. 49–65; Brian Hanley, *Republicanism, Crime and Parliamentary Policing in Ireland, 1916–2020* (Cork: Cork University Press, 2022).

133. J.P.D. Dunbabin (ed.), *Rural Discontent in Nineteenth-Century Britain* (New York: Holmes & Meier, 1974); Andrew Charlesworth (ed.), *An Atlas of Rural Protest in Britain 1548–1900* (London: Croom Helm, 1983); Ian Bradley, '"Having and Holding": The Highland Land War of the 1880s', *History Today*, vol. 37, no. 12, December 1987, pp. 23–8.

134. For a comparison between Ireland and Finland see Sami Suodenjoki, 'Mobilising for Land, Nation and Class Interests: Agrarian agitation in Finland and Ireland, 1879–1918', *Irish Historical Studies*, vol. 41, no. 160, November 2017, pp. 200–20.

135. Michael J. Winstanley, *Ireland and the Land Question 1800–1922* (London and New York: Methuen, 1984); W.E. Vaughan, *Landlords and Tenants in Ireland 1848–1904* (Dundalk: Dundalgan Press, 1984); Paul Bew, 'The National Question, Land, and "Revisionism": Some reflections', in D. George Boyce and Alan O'Day (eds), *The Making of Modern Irish History: Revisionism and the revisionist controversy* (London and New York: Routledge, 1996), pp. 90–9; Maura Cronin, *Agrarian Protest in Ireland 1750–1960* (Dundalk: Dundalgan Press, 2012).

CHAPTER 2: 'ORDINARY' CRIME AND ITS POLICING

1. Frank Thompson, 'The Land War in County Fermanagh', in Eileen M. Murphy and William J. Roulston (eds), *Fermanagh History and Society: Interdisciplinary essays on the history of an Irish county* (Dublin: Geography Publications, 2004), pp. 287–305.

2. Bernard H. Becker, *Disturbed Ireland: Being the letters written during the winter of 1880–81* (London: Macmillan, 1881), pp. 1–2.

3. The crimes committed by Ireland's 'criminal classes' will be discussed in Chapter 3.

4. For a general discussion see Brian Griffin, 'Prevention and Detection of Crime in Nineteenth-Century Ireland', in N.M. Dawson (ed.), *Reflections on Law and History* (Dublin: Four Courts Press, 2006), pp. 99–125.

5. Ian Robert Bridgeman, 'Policing Rural Ireland: A study of the origins, development and role of the Irish Constabulary, and its impact on crime prevention and detection in the nineteenth century', unpublished PhD dissertation, Open University, 1993, pp. 246, 252; Finnane, 'Decline in Violence'; S.J. Connolly, 'Unnatural Death in Four Nations: Contrasts and comparisons', in S.J. Connolly (ed.), *Kingdoms United? Great Britain and Ireland since 1500. Integration and diversity* (Dublin: Four Courts Press, 1999), pp. 200–14; Ian O'Donnell, 'Lethal Violence in Ireland, 1841 to 2003: Famine, celibacy and parental pacification', *British Journal of Criminology*, vol. 45, 2005, pp. 671–95; Ian O'Donnell, 'The Fall and Rise of Homicide in Ireland', in Sophie Body-Gendrot and Pieter Spierenburg (eds), *Violence in Europe: Historical and contemporary perspectives* (New York: Springer, 2008), pp. 79–92. According to Georgina Laragy, one side-effect of the decreasing incidence of murder was a rise in the rates of suicide and attempted suicide in the late nineteenth century, a phenomenon that some psychologists see as 'the inversion of the homicidal impulse'. As Irish people killed one another less frequently in the post-Famine period, they increasingly turned to killing themselves or attempting to do so. Of the 1,934 homicides (exclusive of infanticides) reported by the RIC between 1866 and 1892, some 42.3 per cent arose from brawls (what one historian refers to as 'recreational violence'), 22.7 per cent involved one family member killing another, 11.4 per cent had agrarian or political origins, 3.7 per cent of homicides were committed during the commission of another crime, such as burglary or rape, 2.6 per cent may be traced to sectarian disagreements, and 17.3 per cent were due to other causes: Georgina Laragy, 'Murder in Cavan, 1809–1891', *Breifne*, vol. 11, no. 44, 2008, p. 630; Conley, *Melancholy Accidents*, pp. 173–4.

6. V.A.C. Gatrell, 'The Decline of Theft and Violence in Victorian and Edwardian Britain', in V.A.C. Gatrell, Bruce Lenman and Geoffrey Parker (eds), *Crime and the Law: The social history of crime in western Europe since 1500* (London: Europa Publications, 1980), pp. 238–370; Clive Emsley, *Crime and Society in England 1750–1900*, 2nd edn (Harlow: Longman, 1996), p. 32; Barry Godfrey, *Crime in England 1880–1945: The rough and the criminal, the policed and the incarcerated* (London and New York: Routledge, 2014), pp. 31–4.

7. David Fitzpatrick, 'Unrest in Rural Ireland', *Irish Economic and Social History*, vol. 12, 1985, p. 100; Mark Finnane, 'Irish Crime without the Outrage: The statistics of criminal justice in the later nineteenth century', in Norma M. Dawson (ed.), *Reflections on Law and History* (Dublin: Four Courts Press, 2006), p. 207.

8. This cartoon was drawn by *Zozimus*' principal illustrator, the nationalist artist John Fergus O'Hea. From 1879 to 1883 O'Hea drew satirical cartoons for the pro-home rule illustrated weekly *Pat*, a publication which he co-founded with Edwin Hamilton, and he also produced cartoons for the *Weekly Freeman's Journal* in the 1880s: see Carmel Doyle's entry on O'Hea in the *Dictionary of Irish Biography*. For a discussion of the humorous magazine *Zozimus*, which was published from 1870 to 1872, see Emily Mark-FitzGerald, 'An Alien in Wexford: Harry Furniss, *Punch*, and *Zozimus* (The "Irish *Punch*")', *Visual Culture in Britain*, vol. 20, no. 2, 2019, pp. 135–51. I would like to thank Dr Ciara Molloy for bringing this source to my attention.

9. For a discussion of the annual judicial statistics, which the police began to collect from 1863, see Brian Griffin, *Sources for the Study of Crime in Ireland 1801–1921* (Dublin: Four Courts Press, 2005), pp. 61–2.

10. *Evening Telegraph*, 5 March 1872.

11. *Freeman's Journal*, 10 July 1879.

12. Christopher Lynch-Robinson, *The Last of the Irish RMs* (London: Cassell, 1951), p. 103.

13. Burton Egbert Stevenson, *The Charm of Ireland* (New York: Dodd & Mead, 1914), p. 329.

14. James J. Comerford, *My Kilkenny IRA Days 1916–22* (Kilkenny: James J. Comerford, 1978), pp. 144, 147.

15. Finnane, 'Decline in Violence', pp. 59–60. Ian Bridgeman's analysis of police returns of assaults against the person (such as causing bodily harm, attacks on police officers, common assault and wounding) shows that 'From the 1870s it can be said with certainty that violence in Ireland was declining, and continued to decline until the First [World] War': Bridgeman, 'Policing Rural Ireland', p. 252.

16. O'Donnell, 'Lethal Violence in Ireland', p. 677. Neal Garnham has documented regional variations in the incidence of homicides in the late nineteenth century: see Neal Garnham, 'Crime, Policing, and the Law, 1600–1900', in Liam Kennedy and Philip Ollerenshaw

(eds), *Ulster since 1600: Politics, economy, society* (Oxford: Oxford University Press, 2013), p. 98.

17. Máire Lohan, *An 'Antiquarian Craze': The life, times and work in archaeology of Patrick Lyons RIC (1861–1954)* (Dublin: Edmund Burke Publisher, 2008).

18. Stephen Crane, *Last Words* (London: Digby & Long, 1902), p. 207.

19. Tom Kettle, *The Open Secret of Ireland* (London: W.J. Ham-Smith, 1912), p. 143.

20. The evidence of J.J. McConnell, who joined the RIC in October 1907, eventually rising to the rank of district inspector, supports this picture of a relatively easy existence for Irish policemen. He records that 'Those were carefree, peaceful days in Ireland and a policeman's life was then a happy one. Duty consisted of maintaining peace at fairs and race-meetings, supervising licensed premises, and generally preventing and detecting ordinary crime.' The ex-RIC men whom John Brewer interviewed also presented positive accounts of life in the constabulary before the political violence of the First World War and War of Independence years: BMH, WS/509, p. 1; John D. Brewer, *The Royal Irish Constabulary: An oral history* (Belfast: Queen's University of Belfast, 1990).

21. Clive Emsley, *The Great British Bobby: A history of British policing from the 18th century to the present* (London: Quercus, 2009), pp. 135–8.

22. 50 & 51 Vic., c. 25.

23. *Belfast News-Letter*, 1 June 1899.

24. Ibid., 1 August 1891, 10 August 1891.

25. Ibid., 2 April 1892, 30 October 1893. For an in-depth discussion of the Probation Act see Gerry McNally, 'Probation in Ireland: A brief history of the early years', *Irish Probation Journal*, vol. 4, no. 1, 2007, pp. 5–24. I would like to thank Dr Ciara Molloy for bringing this source to my attention.

26. O'Donnell, 'Fall and Rise in Homicide', p. 90.

27. *Freeman's Journal*, 30 July 1873.

28. Ibid., 30 August 1884, 6 October 1884, 16 December 1885, 19 January 1886; Maurice Healy, *The Old Munster Circuit: A book of memories and traditions* (London: Michael Joseph, 1939), pp. 19–21.

29. *The Times*, 7 March 1904, 5 December 1904; *Royal Irish Constabulary Magazine*, April 1912.

30. *Royal Irish Constabulary Magazine*, April 1912.

31. K. Theodore Hoppen, *Elections, Politics, and Society in Ireland 1832–1885* (Oxford: Clarendon Press, 1984), pp. 388–407.

32. Joseph V. O'Brien, *'Dear, Dirty Dublin': A city in distress, 1899–1916* (Berkeley and London: University of California Press, 1982), p. 188. The fall in arrests for drunkenness and disorderly behaviour might also have been partly the result of greater police circumspection when encountering drunks in Ireland's two largest cities in the period, Dublin and Belfast, rather than reflecting better decorum in public on the part of these cities' drinkers. In 1881, Baron Richard Dowse, of the Irish court of exchequer, expressed his scepticism that the recorded figures of arrests carried out by the DMP for drunkenness reflected the actual number of such cases, as the police 'did not take up anyone whom they could help taking; they generally allowed them to go away, giving them the benefit of the doubt'. In Belfast, following the extensive riots in Protestant areas of the city in 1886, the constabulary changed what was regarded as its over-officious approach towards suppressing summary offences. The result was a marked decline in the rate of arrests for non-indictable offences (which included drunkenness) in the city; this less rigorous approach on the part of the RIC was also linked with a decline in the number and rate of assaults on the police: *Freeman's Journal*, 25 October 1881; Mark Radford, 'A Trial of Strength: The policing of Belfast 1870–1914', unpublished PhD dissertation, University of Liverpool, 2002, pp. 84–7.

33. Elizabeth Malcolm, *'Ireland Sober, Ireland Free': Drink and temperance in nineteenth-century Ireland* (Dublin: Gill & Macmillan, 1986), p. 249.

34. Ibid., p. 275.

35. Norma N. Dawson, 'Illicit Distillation and the Revenue Police in Ireland in the Eighteenth and Nineteenth Centuries', *Irish Jurist*, vol. 12, no. 2, 1977, p. 292, n. 48; K.H. Connell, 'Illicit Distillation', in K.H. Connell, *Irish Peasant Society: Four historical essays* (Dublin: Irish Academic Press, 1968), pp. 1–50.

36. K.H. Connell, 'Ether Drinking in Ulster', in *Irish Peasant Society*, pp. 87–111.

37. Stanley H. Palmer, *Police and Protest in England and Ireland 1780–1850* (Cambridge: Cambridge University Press, 1988), pp. 559–61; O'Brien, *'Dear, Dirty Dublin'*, p. 180.

38. Desmond McCabe, 'Open Court: Law and the expansion of magisterial jurisdiction at petty sessions in nineteenth-century Ireland', in Norma M. Dawson (ed.), *Reflections on Law and History* (Dublin: Four Courts Press, 2006), p. 156.

39. V.A.C. Gatrell and T.B. Hadden, 'Criminal Statistics and Their Interpretation', in E.A. Wrigley (ed.), *Nineteenth-Century Society: Essays in the use of quantitative methods for the study of social data* (London: Cambridge University Press, 1972), pp. 336–96; R.S. Sindall, 'The Criminal Statistics of Nineteenth-Century Cities: A new approach', *Urban History Yearbook*, 1986, pp. 28–36; Emsley, *Crime and Society in England*, pp. 23–32; Howard Taylor, 'Rationing Crime: The political economy of crime statistics since the 1850s', *Economic History Review*, new series, vol. 51, no. 3, August 1998, pp. 569–90; Robert K. Morris, '"Lies, Damned Lies, and Criminal Statistics": Reinterpreting the criminal statistics of England and Wales', *Crime, Histoire et Sociétés*, vol. 5, no. 1, 2001, pp. 111–27; Barry Godfrey, Chris A. Williams and Paul Lawrence, *History and Crime* (Los Angeles, London, New Delhi and Singapore: SAGE Publications, 2007), pp. 26–48; Godfrey, *Crime in England*, pp. 18–29.

40. Garnham, 'Crime, Policing, and the Law, 1600–1900', pp. 90–105.

41. Lynd, *Home Life in Ireland*, p. 1.

42. Bridgeman, 'Policing of Rural Ireland', pp. 191–6.

43. Neal Garnham, 'How Violent was Eighteenth-Century Ireland?', in Ian O'Donnell and Finbarr McAuley (eds), *Criminal Justice History: Themes and controversies from pre-independence Ireland* (Dublin: Four Courts Press, 2003), pp. 20–1.

44. *Irish Judicial Statistics*, 1872, p. 26.

45. Taylor, 'Rationing Crime', p. 205. For a critique of Taylor's argument see Morris, '"Lies, Damned Lies, and Statistics"'.

46. Connolly, 'Unnatural Death', p. 205.

47. Garnham, 'Crime, Policing, and the Law', pp. 98–9.

48. *Irish Judicial Statistics*, 1870–1919; O'Brien, *'Dear, Dirty Dublin'*, pp. 184–187; Pádraig Partridge, 'Crime in the Dublin Metropolitan Police District, 1894–1914', *Retrospect*, vol. 2, 1982, pp. 36–43; Anastasia Dukova, *A History of the Dublin Metropolitan Police and Its Colonial Legacy* (London: Palgrave Macmillan, 2016), p. 117.

49. *Irish Judicial Statistics*, 1885–94.

50. John McKenna, *A Beleaguered Station: The memoirs of Head Constable John McKenna, 1891–1921* (Belfast: Ulster Historical Foundation, 2009), pp. 17–18.

51. Bridgeman, 'Policing Rural Ireland', p. 257.

52. Eric Dunning, Patrick Murphy and John Williams, *The Roots of Football Hooliganism: An historical and sociological study* (London and New York: Routledge, 1988), pp. 154–5, 163, 226–31.

53. Kevin C. Kearns, *Dublin Tenement Life: An oral history* (Harmondsworth: Penguin, 1994); Dukova, *Dublin Metropolitan Police*, pp. 69–83.

54. *Freeman's Journal*, 12 September 1871, 26 September 1871, 6 December 1871, 21 August 1872, 15 October 1872, 29 October 1872, 20 December 1872, 24 April 1873, 27 December 1873, 9 March 1874, 6 June 1874.

55. Ibid., 9 June 1873.

56. Ibid., 19 June 1875, 21 June 1875.

57. Brian Griffin, '"Such Varmint": The Dublin police and the public, 1838–1913', *Irish Studies Review*, vol. 4, no. 13, Winter 1995, pp. 21–5.

58. *Freeman's Journal*, 21 June 1880.

59. Ibid., 24 July 1880, 2 August 1880.

60. For a detailed account see Pádraig Yeates, *Lockout: Dublin, 1913* (Dublin: Gill & Macmillan, 2000).

61. *Dublin Disturbances Commission. Appendix to Report of the Dublin Disturbances Commission. Minutes of Evidence and Appendix*, H.C. 1914 (Cd. 7272) xviii 533, p. 134.

62. Bertram R. Carter, *Another Part of the Platform* (London: Houghton, 1931), pp. 28–9.

63. BMH, WS/1,280, p. 50. For a general discussion of the looting and looters see Pádraig Yeates, 'Who Were Dublin's Looters in 1916? Crime and society in Dublin during the Great War', *Saothar*, vol. 41, 2016, pp. 111–23.

64. Alasdair Lindsay Goldsmith, 'The Development of the City of Glasgow Police, *c.* 1800 – *c.* 1939', unpublished PhD dissertation, University of Strathclyde, 2002; David Taylor, *Policing the Victorian Community: The development of the police in Middlesbrough, c. 1840–1914* (Basingstoke: Palgrave Macmillan, 2002); Emsley, *Great*

British Bobby, pp. 144–59; Joanne Klein, *Invisible Men: The secret lives of police constables in Liverpool, Manchester and Birmingham, 1900–1939* (Liverpool: Liverpool University Press, 2010).

65. For the supposed decline in urban violence and murder, see Eric A. Johnson and Eric H. Monkkonen (eds), *The Civilization of Crime: Violence in town and city since the Middle Ages* (Urbana: University of Chicago Press, 1996); Manuel Eisner, 'Modernization, Self-Control and Lethal Violence: The long-term dynamics of European homicidal rates in theoretical perspective', *British Journal of Criminology*, vol. 41, no. 4, September 2001, pp. 618–38; Manuel Eisner, 'Long-Term Historical Trends in Violent Crime', *Crime and Justice*, vol. 30, 2003, pp. 83–142; Pieter Spierenburg, *A History of Murder: Personal violence in Europe from the Middle Ages to the present* (Cambridge: Polity, 2008). For a critique, see Peter King, 'Exploring the Geography of Homicide: Patterns of lethal violence in Britain and Europe, 1805–1990', *European Review of History*, vol. 2, no. 6, 2013, pp. 967–87. For a review of the debate see Richard Mc Mahon, 'Urbanisation and Interpersonal Violence in Europe and North America', *Informationen zur modernen Stadtgeschichte*, vol. 2, 2013, pp. 21–30.

66. James Macaulay, *Ireland in 1872: A tour of observation* (London: Henry S. King, 1873), p. 291; William Hemstreet, *The Economical European Tourist* (New York: S.W. Green, 1875), p. 44; C.D.H. Howard (ed.), 'Select Documents XXVI: "The Man on a Tricycle". W.H. Duignan and Ireland, 1881–85', *Irish Historical Studies*, vol. 14, no. 55, March 1965, p. 258; Stevenson, *Charm*, pp. 327–8.

67. Jack B. Yeats captured the observant RIC presence in country districts in his evocative drawing 'The Police Sergeant', which was first published in 1913: George Bermingham, *Irishmen All*, 2nd edn (London and Edinburgh: T.N. Foulis, 1914), between pp. 40 and 41.

68. Tim Carey, *Mountjoy: The story of a prison* (Cork: Collins Press, 2000), p. 120.

69. *Report of the General Prisons Board, Ireland, 1896–97*, p. 14.

70. Randal McDonnel, *Cushendun in the Glens of Antrim* (Cushendun: Randal McDonnel, n.d.), pp. 109–44.

71. *Belfast News-Letter*, 17 February 1871, 22 October 1879; *Daily Express*, 2 October 1885; *Kildare Observer*, 19 February 1887; *Wexford People*, 7 May 1887; *Constabulary Gazette*, 10 April 1897, 22 October 1898, 15 November 1902, 13 April 1918; *Derry Journal*, 22 January 1909; *Royal Irish Constabulary Magazine*, March 1914, April 1914, October 1914, April 1915. For a recent discussion

of the *Hue and Cry* see Elaine Farrell and Eliza McKee, 'Captured in the Clothing: Ireland, 1850s–1890s', *Dress: The journal of the Costume Society of America*, published online 7 April 2022, DOI: 10.1080/03612112.2022.2039484

72. *Clare Advertiser and Kilrush Gazette*, 30 April 1870; *Cork Daily Herald*, 5 August 1870; *Belfast Telegraph*, 26 October 1875, 23 November 1898; *Hansard's Parliamentary Debates*, third series, vol. CCCXLVI, 7 July 1890, col. 932; *Belfast Weekly News*, 29 August 1891; *Waterford Standard*, 3 January 1891; *Drogheda Conservative*, 1 July 1893; *Constabulary Gazette*, 4 May 1901, 10 July 1915.

73. *Clarion*, 3 October 1896.

74. From the 1870s RIC officers were also stationed at Holyhead port 'to deal with wrongdoers absconding from Ireland': Daniel Mulhall, *A New Day Dawning: A portrait of Ireland in 1900* (Cork: Collins Press, 1999), p. 30.

75. *The Irish Times*, 28 May 1875.

76. George Bidwell, *Forging His Chains: The autobiography of George Bidwell* (Hartford: S.S. Scranton, 1888), pp. 248–74.

77. Derrick Westenra (Lord Rossmore), *Things I Can Tell* (London: Eveleigh Nash, 1912), p. 255.

78. *Freeman's Journal*, 7 June 1877.

79. Alexander Innes Shand, *Letters from the West of Ireland, 1884* (Edinburgh and London: W. Blackwood, 1885), pp. 14–15.

80. *1898 Commission on Liquor Licensing Laws*, p. 30.

81. Dawson, 'Illicit Distillation'; Jim Herlihy, *The Irish Revenue Police* (Dublin: Four Courts Press, 2018), p. 39; Elizabeth Malcolm, *The Irish Policeman 1822–1922: A life* (Dublin: Four Courts Press, 2006), pp. 116–19.

82. *Freeman's Journal*, 23 September 1873; Edward McCarron, *Life in Donegal 1850–1900* (Dublin and Cork: Mercier Press, 1981), pp. 92–3, 113–21.

83. Ball (ed.), *A Policeman's Ireland*, pp. 34–5; Gaughan (ed.), *Jeremiah Mee, RIC*, pp. 55–9.

84. *1898 Commission on Liquor Licensing Laws*, pp. 30–1.

85. *Freeman's Journal*, 3 October 1883.

86. *Thirtieth Report of Inland Revenue Commissioners, 1887*, p. 9; *Thirty-first Report of Inland Revenue Commissioners, 1888*, p. 9; Anonymous ('A Guardian of the Poor'), *The Irish Peasant: A*

sociological study (London: S. Sonnenschein, 1892), p. 19. The high taxes on 'government whiskey' were another reason why poteen-making remained a tempting venture for some illicit distillers. It was pointed out in 1902 that 'the temptation to carry on illicit distillation is much greater now, when the tax is 11*s*. per gallon, than it was fifty years ago, when the tax was less than one-third of this amount': William P. Coyne (ed.), *Ireland: Industrial and agricultural* (Dublin, Cork and Belfast: Browne & Nolan, 1902), p. 500.

87. *Freeman's Journal*, 28 February 1872.

88. A.B.R. Young, *Reminiscences of an Irish Priest* (Dundalk: Dundalgan Press, n.d.), pp. 110–11. I would like to record my gratitude to the late Reverend Professor Monsignor Patrick J. Corish for allowing me to read this rare publication.

89. William O'Malley, *Glancing Back: 70 years' experiences and reminiscences of press man, sportsman and member of parliament* (London: Wright & Brown, 1933), p. 19.

90. Vere T.R. Gregory, *The House of Gregory* (Dublin: Browne & Nolan, 1943), pp. 185–6.

91. Katharine Tynan, *The Years of the Shadow* (London: Constable, 1919), p. 172.

92. E.B. McGuire, *Irish Whiskey: A history of distilling, the spirit trade and excise controls in Ireland* (Dublin: Gill & Macmillan, 1973), pp. 428–9.

93. Gregory, *House of Gregory*, pp. 186–7.

94. *Belfast News-Letter*, 16 May 1895.

95. Malcolm, 'Ireland Sober, Ireland Free', p. 275.

96. Tom Garvin, *1922: The birth of Irish democracy* (Dublin: Gill & Macmillan, 1996), p. 113.

97. BMH, WS/366; Fearghal McGarry, *Eoin O'Duffy: A self-made hero* (Oxford: Oxford University Press, 2005), pp. 51–2. For a recent overview see Caoimhín de Barra, '"This Abominable Evil is the Source of Fetid Corruption": The IRA's 1920 war on poitín', *Éire-Ireland*, vol. 57, nos 3 & 4, Autumn–Winter 2022, pp. 283–310. For the IRA's policing role see Brian Hanley, *Republicanism, Crime and Paramilitary Policing in Ireland, 1916–2020* (Cork: Cork University Press, 2022), pp. 13–33.

98. BMH, WS/519, p. 3; BMH, WS/528, p. 2; BMH, WS/530, p. 5; BMH, WS/609, p. 7; BMH, WS/693, p. 4; BMH, WS/762,

p. 18; BMH, WS/820, pp. 19–22; BMH, WS/911, pp. 6–7; BMH, WS/1313, p. 9; BMH, WS/1554, pp. 10–11; BMH, WS/1668, p. 52; Arthur Mitchell, *Revolutionary Government in Ireland: Dáil Éireann, 1919–22* (Dublin: Gill & Macmillan, 1995), p. 153. Volunteers did not always take a dim view of the poteen trade. James McCaffrey records that during the 1918 general election he secured the position of poll clerk at a polling booth in Creeslough, County Donegal, in the hope of being able to 'enhance the chances of the Sinn Féin nominee', Joe Sweeney. McCaffrey managed to secure a bottle of poteen from Termon parish, which 'was then rife with poteen', and persuaded the presiding officer to drink it. McCaffrey relates that 'by degrees, we got him so muddled that I was able to record what must have been a record poll for the Sinn Féin candidate': BMH, WS/1484, pp. 3–5.

99. BMH, WS/911, pp. 6–7; Fergal McCluskey, *The Irish Revolution, 1912–23: Tyrone* (Dublin: Four Courts Press, 2014), p. 82.

100. Griffin, 'Prevention and Detection of Crime', pp. 104–6.

101. BMH, WS/1280, pp. 33–4.

102. John Keogh, 'The Royal Irish Constabulary', *Carloviana*, vol. 4, no. 32, 1984–5, pp. 16–17.

103. Farrell, *'A Most Diabolical Deed'*, p. 122.

104. P.S. O'Hegarty, *A History of Ireland under the Union 1801 to 1922* (London: Methuen, 1922), pp. 403–4.

105. *Freeman's Journal*, 12 May 1875, 2 July 1875, 26 June 1879, 11 July 1888; *Royal Irish Constabulary Magazine*, July 1913, August 1915; Garnham, 'Popular Blood Sports in Ulster'; Paul Rouse, *Sport and Ireland: A history* (Oxford: Oxford University Press, 2015), p. 218; Ward, 'Cockfighting in Ireland'.

106. *Freeman's Journal*, 31 January 1881, 11 May 1881, 18 December 1893, 23 September 1896, 26 November 1896; Garnham, 'Blood Sports'.

107. *Belfast News-Letter*, 25 June 1872; *Freeman's Journal*, 6 April 1876, 20 December 1876, 30 January 1877, 26 June 1877, 29 January 1878, 22 June 1880, 5 October 1887, 23 August 1889.

108. *Belfast News-Letter*, 21 April 1870, 26 April 1871, 25 January 1872, 10 April 1873, 9 April 1875, 16 April 1875, 26 October 1877, 10 November 1881, 12 May 1894; Fintan Lane, *Long Bullets: A history of road bowling in Ireland* (Cork: Galley Head Press, 2005), p. 18; John Gray, 'Bullet-Throwing in Belfast', *History Ireland*, vol. 23, no. 2, March–April 2015, pp. 30–2.

109. *Belfast News-Letter*, 17 March 1894.

110. Despite the improvements in technology and forensic techniques that were available in the early twentieth century, the DMP were still unable to solve what was perhaps the most famous case of theft in Irish history, the theft of the Irish 'crown jewels' from Dublin Castle in 1907. The fact that Dublin Castle was the headquarters of both the DMP and its detective branch, the G Division, heightened the embarrassment caused to the DMP by its failure to solve this high-profile crime. For accounts of the theft and its aftermath see Francis Bamford, *Vicious Circle: The case of the missing Irish crown jewels* (London: Parrish, 1965); Tomás O'Riordan, 'The Theft of the Irish Crown Jewels, 1907', *History Ireland*, vol. 9, no. 4, Winter 2001, pp. 23–8; John Cafferky and Kevin Hannafin, *Scandal and Betrayal: Shackleton and the Irish crown jewels* (Cork: Collins Press, 2002); Myles Dungan, *The Stealing of the Irish Crown Jewels: An unsolved crime* (Dublin: Town House, 2003).

111. Martin was killed by a mob during an ill-advised attempt to arrest Fr James McFadden of Gweedore, one of the leaders of the Plan of Campaign on the Olphert estate, as McFadden emerged from his church after saying Mass on 3 February 1889. The costs (£51) of producing the photographic evidence in this case were one of the factors that led to the RIC's Special Branch establishing its own photographic department in the following year. The DMP also set up a similar department in 1890: Desmond Murphy, 'The Land War in Donegal 1879–1891', *Donegal Annual*, vol. 32, 1980, pp. 483–4; Breandán Mac Suibhne and Amy Martin, 'Fenians in the Frame: Photographing Irish political prisoners, 1865–68', *Field Day Review*, 2005, pp. 111–12; Gail Baylis, 'Metropolitan Surveillance and Rural Opacity: Secret photography in nineteenth-century Ireland', *History of Photography*, vol. 33, no. 1, 2009, p. 30.

112. *Weekly Irish Times*, 2 January 1904; *Royal Irish Constabulary Magazine*, April 1912; Angela Bourke, *The Burning of Bridget Cleary: A true story* (London: Pimlico, 1999), pp. 51, 133; W.E. Vaughan, *Murder Trials in Ireland, 1836–1914* (Dublin: Four Courts Press, 2009), p. 38. At the Cavan spring assizes in 1912, when a case of murder in Ballybay and attempted murder in Castleblayney were being tried, 'much interest was taken in the splendid photographs of the different scenes of the outrages'. These were taken by Sergeant Charles Berry of Belfast's detective department, 'where the Sergeant served a long apprenticeship'. According to the *Royal Irish Constabulary Magazine*,

'It was the unanimous opinion of all that he deserved the greatest credit for his skill and artistic taste'. Berry was a man of many talents: 'As a model maker in criminal cases, he has no rival', and he was also an accomplished maker and sailor of model yachts, 'carrying off prize after prize in public competitions', as well as winning 'numerous certificates of proficiency' in engineering: *Royal Irish Constabulary Magazine*, April 1912.

113. *Belfast News-Letter*, 20 August 1890, 10 January 1896.

114. *Cork Examiner*, 24 September 1870; *Freeman's Journal*, 24 November 1871; *Belfast News-Letter*, 7 June 1883, 14 February 1893, 8 February 1895; *Constabulary Gazette*, 9 July 1898, 2 September 1899, 16 September 1905; *Royal Irish Constabulary Magazine*, November 1911, December 1911, April 1912, February 1914, May 1914, January 1915, August 1915. Over 400 towns and villages had telegraph offices by the early 1870s, and by the end of the nineteenth century the post office 'operated a comprehensive telegraph system throughout the country': R.V. Comerford, 'Ireland 1850–70: Post-Famine and mid-Victorian', in W.E. Vaughan (ed.), *A New History of Ireland. V. Ireland under the Union, I: 1801–70* (Oxford: Clarendon Press, 1989), p. 376. H.D. Gribbon, 'Economic and Social History, 1850–1921', in W.E. Vaughan (ed.), *A New History of Ireland. VI. Ireland under the Union, II: 1870–1921* (Oxford: Clarendon Press, 1996), p. 341.

115. *Freeman's Journal*, 13 January 1882.

116. *Northern Whig*, 2 October 1890.

117. *Londonderry Sentinel*, 14 June 1900.

118. *Belfast News-Letter*, 8 February 1909.

119. Brewer, *Royal Irish Constabulary*, p. 25.

120. Brian Griffin, *Cycling in Victorian Ireland* (Dublin: Nonsuch, 2006), pp. 75–83; *Royal Irish Constabulary Magazine*, January 1912, April 1912, May 1912. The increasing popularity of cycling in the 1890s also presented welcome opportunities for thieves to steal bicycles and to sell or pawn the purloined machines: *Belfast News-Letter*, 13 August 1890, 29 June 1898, 3 July 1900; *Irish Cyclist*, 11 May 1892; *Rathmines News*, 4 January 1896; Irish National Archives, Criminal Index Files C-131-1896: case of William Currie of Belfast, a serial bicycle thief; *Cyclists' Touring Club Gazette*, July 1904. The editor of one newspaper in 1899 had little sympathy for Dublin cyclists whose machines were stolen, when he wrote that:

'Cycling thieves are, I am sorry to say, busier than ever. Still, when one looks around Dublin, and views the way in which valuable machines are left about, this larceny cannot be wondered at. Costly bicycles are left about in the most reckless fashion, all over town, and poor, hungry, impecunious, desperate, and careless men are not so scarce as well-to-do folk think they are. Really, some people deserve to lose their machines for spreading temptation about in the way they do': *Irish Wheelman*, 4 July 1899.

121. BMH, WS/1280, pp. 32–3.

122. *The Irish Times*, 3 January 1905.

123. *Royal Irish Constabulary Magazine*, December 1911.

124. Palmer, *Police and Protest*, p. 533.

125. Ian Bridgeman, 'The Constabulary and the Criminal Justice System in Nineteenth-Century Ireland', in Ian O'Donnell and Finbarr McAuley (eds), *Criminal Justice History: Themes and controversies from pre-independence Ireland* (Dublin: Four Courts Press, 2003), pp. 137–8; J.W.H. Carter, *Murder in the Midlands 1862–1915* ([n.p.]: J.W.H. Carter, 2005), pp. 359–77.

126. Fingerprinting was introduced into Ireland in 1903. The warders at Mountjoy jail were the first Irish personnel to be trained in how to take prisoners' fingerprints: *Royal Irish Constabulary Magazine*, November 1911; Carey, *Mountjoy*, p. 120. For a brief discussion of references to fingerprint evidence in popular crime fiction see Stephanie Rains, 'Reading the Hand: Palmistry, graphology and alternative literacies', in Rebecca Anne Barr, Sarah-Anne Buckley and Muireann O'Cinneide (eds), *Literacy, Language and Reading in Nineteenth-Century Ireland* (Liverpool: Liverpool University Press, 2019), p. 178.

127. *Royal Irish Constabulary Magazine*, December 1911. This issue of the magazine listed a variety of items upon which fingerprints had been left by burglars and were afterwards used as evidence in criminal trials in Ireland. These consisted of 'Window glass, drinking glasses, bottles, candles, cash boxes, silver or plated ware, tin, the glass side of a photographic negative, and (only in one instance) wood'.

128. *Royal Irish Constabulary Magazine*, December 1911.

129. Ibid.

130. Ibid.

131. British members of the 'swell mob' – professional pickpockets, who were often flashily dressed – often plied their trade in Dublin,

occasionally in tandem with Dublin pickpockets: *Freeman's Journal*, 13 May 1870, 24 November 1871, 1 May 1877, 28 August 1877, 13 July 1882, 21 March 1884, 28 August 1888, 24 May 1898, 20 July 1903; *Daily Express*, 19 July 1907, 10 July 1911.

132. *Royal Irish Constabulary Magazine*, November 1911.

133. Ibid., December 1911, January 1912.

134. Elizabeth Malcolm and W.J. Lowe, 'The Domestication of the Royal Irish Constabulary, 1836–1922', *Irish Economic and Social History*, vol. 19, 1992, pp. 27–48.

CHAPTER 3: FREQUENT OFFENDERS, THE 'CRIMINAL CLASSES' AND THE POLICE

1. Clive Emsley, *Crime and Society*, pp. 68–77, 168–75; Barry S. Godfrey and Paul Lawrence, *Crime and Justice 1750–1950* (Cullompton: Willan Publishing, 2005), pp. 113–15; Barry S. Godfrey, Chris A. Williams and Paul Lawrence, *History and Crime* (London: Sage, 2007), pp. 83–5.

2. Victor Bailey, 'The Fabrication of Deviance: "Dangerous classes" and "criminal classes" in Victorian England', in John Rule and Robert Malcolmson (eds), *Protest and Survival: The historical experience. Essays for E.P. Thompson* (London: Merlin, 1993), pp. 221–56; David Taylor, 'Beyond the Bounds of Respectable Society: The "dangerous classes" in Victorian and Edwardian England', in Julia Rowbotham and Kim Stevenson (eds), *Criminal Conversations: Victorian crimes, social panic, and moral outrage* (Columbus: Ohio State University Press, 2005), pp. 3–22.

3. For discussions of contemporaries' belief in the existence of criminal classes in Britain, and the development of the policing and criminal justice instruments used to target and control them, see S.J. Stevenson, 'The "Habitual Criminal" in Nineteenth-Century England: Some observations on the figures', *Urban History Yearbook*, vol. 13, 1986, pp. 37–60; Terence George Stanford, 'The Metropolitan Police, 1850–1914: Targeting, harassment and the creation of a criminal class', unpublished PhD dissertation, University of Huddersfield, 2007; George Pavlich, 'The Emergence of Habitual Criminals in 19th-Century Britain: Implications for criminology', *Journal of Theoretical and Philosophical Criminology*, vol. 2, no. 1, 2010, pp. 1–62; Helen Johnston, *Crime in England 1815–1880: Experiencing the criminal justice system* (London and New York: Routledge, 2015), pp. 26–42;

Matthew Bach, *Combating London's Criminal Class: A state divided, 1869–95* (London: Bloomsbury Academic, 2020).

4. In 1899 the County Clare prison in Ennis, which had closed in 1880, was reopened as a state inebriate reformatory. In addition to the Ennis institution, which was administered by the Irish General Prisons Board, a number of certified inebriate reformatories, which were licensed by the state but operated and largely funded by county and borough councils, religious and philanthropic bodies or private individuals, were also established in various parts of the country in the early twentieth century: George Bretherton, 'Irish Inebriate Reformatories, 1899–1920: A small experiment in coercion', *Contemporary Drug Problems*, vol. 13, no. 3, Autumn 1986, pp. 473–502; Beverly A. Smith, 'Ireland's Ennis Inebriates' Reformatory: A 19th century example of failed institutional reform', *Federal Probation*, vol. LIII, no. 1, March 1989, pp. 53–64; Elizabeth Malcolm, 'Between Habitual Drunkards and Alcoholics: Inebriate women and reformatories in Ireland, 1899–1919', in Margaret H. Preston and Margaret Ó hÓgartaigh (eds), *Gender and Medicine in Ireland 1700–1950* (Syracuse: Syracuse University Press, 2012), pp. 108–22.

5. Soldiers were another group who committed a disproportionate amount of crime, although they were not categorised as belonging to Ireland's 'criminal classes'. For example, soldiers were frequent offenders in County Kildare. Head Constable Robert Dunlop, who served in Newbridge from 1867 to 1875, found that soldiers often committed larcenies purely as a means of ensuring that they would be discharged from the army once they had served their sentence. Rickard Deasy, baron of the exchequer, informed the Kildare summer assizes in July 1877 that most of the county's crimes emanated from the Curragh camp, but that the overall number was still surprisingly small, 'when it is considered that the number of troops concentrated there, including camp followers, far exceeds the population of all the large towns in the county put together'. Two years later, Deasy told the same assizes that cases of indecent assault 'must prevail in this county as long as we have a large military camp'. From 1866 to 1892, Kildare had an abnormally high incidence of sexual assault, with some 11 per cent of recorded serious crimes consisting of this offence. Soldiers were the accused in some 26 per cent of the indictments: Memoirs of Head Constable Robert Dunlop, Public Record of Northern Ireland T.2815/1; *Freeman's Journal*, 17 July 1877, 19 July 1879; Conley, *Melancholy Accidents*, p. 98.

6. *Belfast News-Letter*, 4 March 1870, 4 April 1871, 22 July 1871.

7. Ibid., 6 February 1873. He was also prosecuted some seventeen times for using 'party expressions' – in his case, cursing the pope – by December 1870: *Belfast News-Letter*, 29 December 1870.

8. *Belfast News-Letter*, 26 March 1872.

9. Ibid., 27 January 1871.

10. Ibid., 24 November 1876.

11. Ibid., 28 August 1882.

12. Ibid., 1 August 1891, 30 October 1893, 17 August 1899. A number of Belfast women also chalked up more than 100 convictions each for drunkenness in the first decade of the twentieth century. These included Maggie McLaughlin, Lizzie Caughey, Mary Lappin, Annie McCrudden, Bella Fisher and Lizzie Porter with 102, 119, 121, 133, 192 and 238 convictions, respectively: Michael Boyle, 'Women and Crime in Belfast, 1900–13', unpublished PhD dissertation, Queen's University of Belfast, 1997, p. 174.

13. *Freeman's Journal*, 30 March 1898.

14. Geraldine Curtin, *The Women of Galway Jail: Female criminality in nineteenth-century Galway* (Galway: Arlen House, 2001), p. 71.

15. *Larne Times*, 18 March 1905.

16. *Cork Examiner*, 17 September 1873.

17. *Freeman's Journal*, 9 September 1875.

18. Ibid., 30 October 1878.

19. Ibid., 13 November 1883.

20. *Kildare Observer*, 8 October 1887.

21. Conor Reidy, 'Inebriate Women in Early Twentieth-Century Ireland', *History Ireland*, vol. 22, no. 6, November–December 2014, pp. 26–9; Holly Dunbar, 'Women and Alcohol during the First World War in Ireland', *Women's History Review*, vol. 27, no. 23, 2018, pp. 379-96; Elaine Farrell, 'Crime, Punishment and Gender', in Jyoti Atwal, Ciara Breathnach and Sarah-Anne Buckley (eds), *Gender and History: Ireland, 1852–1922* (London and New York: Routledge, 2023), pp. 143–4.

22. *Waterford News*, 11 March 1893.

23. *Freeman's Journal*, 30 March 1898; Maria Luddy, 'The Early Years of the NSPCC in Ireland', *Éire-Ireland*, vol. 44, nos 1 & 2, Spring–Summer 2009, p. 80.

24. Caitriona Clear, *Social Change and Everyday Life in Ireland, 1850–1922* (Manchester: Manchester University Press, 2007), p. 135.

25. *Freeman's Journal*, 16 January 1875, 14 January 1876.

26. Maria Luddy, *Prostitution and Irish Society, 1800–1940* (Cambridge: Cambridge University Press, 2007), pp. 153–4.

27. Joseph V. O'Brien, *'Dear, Dirty Dublin': A city in distress, 1899–1916* (Berkeley and London: University of California Press, 1982), pp. 193–4; Gary A. Boyd, *Dublin 1745–1922: Hospitals, spectacle and vice* (Dublin: Four Courts Press, 2006), pp. 179–80; Luddy, *Prostitution*, pp. 158–9, 167–9.

28. Boyle, 'Women and Crime', pp. 199–201; Curtin, *Women of Galway Jail*, pp. 82–5.

29. Luddy, *Prostitution*, p. 153.

30. Frances Finnegan, *Poverty and Prostitution: A study of Victorian prostitutes in York* (Cambridge: Cambridge University Press, 1979); Louise Settle, *Sex for Sale in Scotland: Prostitution in Edinburgh and Glasgow, 1900–1939* (Edinburgh: Edinburgh University Press, 2016).

31. *Fiftieth Report of the Inspectors-General on the General State of the Prisons of Ireland 1871: with Appendix* H.C. (C.535), xxxii, 1, p. xv. The inspectors-generals noted that of the 6,362 female prisoners, some 3,571, or 56 per cent of the total, had been in jail before; in contrast, only 34 per cent of male prisoners had been jailed before. Five women had more than 200 convictions, while one had more than 300.

32. *Freeman's Journal*, 8 July 1876.

33. Frances Finnegan, *Do Penance or Perish: A study of Magdalen asylums in Ireland* (Piltown: Congrave Press, 2001), passim; Maria Luddy, *Women and Philanthropy in Nineteenth-Century Ireland* (Cambridge: Cambridge University Press, 1995), pp. 125–8; Colman O'Mahony, *In the Shadows: Life in Cork 1750–1930* (Ballincollig: Tower Books, 1997), pp. 248–50, 252–4; Luddy, *Prostitution*, pp. 77–90.

34. Margaret H. Preston, *Charitable Words: Women, philanthropy, and the language of charity in nineteenth-century Dublin* (Westport, CT: Praeger, 2004), pp. 113–16.

35. Luddy, *Prostitution*, pp. 246–8.

36. *Freeman's Journal*, 13 April 1870.

37. Luddy, *Prostitution*, pp. 61–70.

38. Elizabeth Malcolm, '"Troops of Largely Diseased Women": The Contagious Diseases Acts and moral policing in late nineteenth-century Ireland', *Irish Economic and Social History*, vol. 26, 1999, pp. 1–14.

39. O'Brien, *'Dear, Dirty Dublin'*, p. 117. A visitor to Dublin in 1916 was struck by the numerous 'creatures' in the city whose faces bore the terrible scars of syphilis, which they contracted from diseased parents: Carter, *Another Part*, p. 41.

40. *Freeman's Journal*, 21 March 1884, 6 April 1896, 18 January 1898.

41. Ibid., 18 June 1870.

42. Ibid., 19 September 1871.

43. Ibid., 24 October 1878, 31 October 1878.

44. Ibid., 4 October 1875.

45. Ibid., 22 November 1876.

46. Ibid., 19 October 1878.

47. *Belfast News-Letter*, 11 April 1871, 9 May 1871, 12 May 1871.

48. Brian Lacey, *Terrible Queer Creatures: Homosexuality in Irish history* (Dublin: Wordwell, 2008), p. 141.

49. Drew D. Gray, *London's Shadows: The dark side of the Victorian city* (London: Continuum, 2010), pp. 154–7; Alyson Brown and David Barrett, *Knowledge of Evil: Child prostitution and sexual abuse in twentieth-century England* (Cullompton: Willan Publishing, 2002); Jeffrey Weeks, 'Inverts, Perverts and Mary Annes: Male prostitution and the regulation of homosexuality in England in the nineteenth and early twentieth centuries', *Journal of Homosexuality*, vol. 6, nos 1–2, 1981, pp. 113–34.

50. Finnegan, *Poverty and Prostitution*; Settle, *Sex for Sale in Scotland*; Emsley, *Crime and Society*, pp. 153–4; Paula Bartley, *Prostitution: Prevention and reform in England, 1860–1914* (London: Routledge, 1999); Mick Macilwee, *The Liverpool Underworld: Crime in the city, 1750–1900* (Liverpool: Liverpool University Press, 2011), pp. 270–1.

51. Caitriona Clear, 'Crime, Punishment and Poor Relief in Galway 1850–1914: An introduction', *Journal of the Galway Archaeological and Historical Society*, vol. 50, 1998, pp. 118–34; Clear, *Social Change*, pp. 127–35.

52. Virginia Crossman, *Poverty and the Poor Law in Ireland, 1850–1914* (Liverpool: Liverpool University Press, 2013), pp. 204–6, 211–14, 216.

53. *Freeman's Journal*, 22 December 1870, 23 December 1870, 24 September 1873, 15 July 1874, 21 November 1895, 28 August 1899; *Belfast News-Letter*, 4 October 1899. In the period from March 1885 to March 1886, the largest number of 'night lodgers' or 'casuals' relieved in any one week in Ireland was 3,802, and the smallest number was 2,944: C.J. Ribton-Turner, *A History of Vagrants and Vagrancy, and Beggars and Begging* (London: Chapman & Hall, 1887), p. 427.

54. *Freeman's Journal*, 2 February 1875, 1 March 1875, 28 August 1899; *Belfast News-Letter*, 17 August 1886, 9 February 1894; *Waterford News*, 4 February 1893. The notion of a 'moral panic' – fear created by scaremongering reports concerning distinctive groups who are perceived or portrayed as posing a threat to social norms – is taken from Stanley Cohen's influential study of media portrayals of 'mods' and 'rockers' in Britain in the 1960s: Stanley Cohen, *Folk Devils and Moral Panics: The creation of the mods and rockers* (London: MacGibbon & McKee, 1972).

55. *Freeman's Journal*, 17 December 1878; *Belfast News-Letter*, 9 March 1893.

56. Clear, *Social Change*, p. 130.

57. A perusal of the accounts of the murders that were committed in one county, Wicklow, provides interesting anecdotal examples to suggest that there was perhaps some evidence to support this perception. Tramps were the culprits or the suspected culprits in three of the twelve murders that were committed in Wicklow between 1870 and 1899: Ken Hannigan, 'A Miscellany of Murder: Violent murder in 19th century Wicklow', *Wicklow Historical Society*, vol. 1, no. 7, 1994, pp. 22–34.

58. *Freeman's Journal*, 2 February 1875.

59. Ibid., 2 March 1875.

60. *Belfast News-Letter*, 24 January 1884.

61. *The Irish Times*, 12 July 1919.

62. *Freeman's Journal*, 18 March 1875, 20 March 1875.

63. Ibid., 7 October 1881.

64. Conley, *Melancholy Accidents*, pp. 103–4; J.W.H. Carter, *Murder in the Midlands 1862–1915* ([n.p.]: J.W.H. Carter, 2005), pp. 213–17.

65. Pauline M. Prior, *Madness and Murder: Gender, crime and mental disorder in nineteenth-century Ireland* (Dublin: Irish Academic Press, 2008). Some 8 per cent of defendants in murder trials from 1866 to

1875 were acquitted as insane: Vaughan, *Murder Trials*, pp. 277, 282. Perhaps the most shocking instances of murders committed by an insane person were the brutal killing of Sergeant Michael Rogan of the RIC, his wife, Rebecca, and three of their seven children by a deranged policeman, Constable John Pilkington, in Ballinadrimna RIC barracks, in County Kildare, on the night of 31 October 1892. Pilkington shot the adult Rogans and battered their children's heads with his truncheon, before committing suicide by shooting himself: Ciaran McCabe, '"Are You Mad Also?": The murder of Sergeant Michael Rogan and his family in Ballinadrimna, Co. Kildare in 1892', *Journal of the Kildare Archaeological Society*, vol. 20, no. 2, 2010–11, pp. 159–72.

66. Joseph Matthew Sullivan, 'Irish Police Gleanings', *Journal of the American Institute of Criminal Law and Criminology*, vol. 4, no. 6, March 1914, p. 882.

67. Niamh O'Sullivan, *Every Dark Hour: A history of Kilmainham jail* (Dublin: Liberties Press, 2007), p. 199.

68. *Royal Irish Constabulary Magazine*, August 1914.

69. Augusteijn (ed.), *John M. Regan*, pp. 41–2.

70. Rosemary Fennell (ed.), *The Royal Irish Constabulary: A history and personal memoir. Thomas Fennell (RIC No. 41310)* (Dublin: UCD Press, 2003), pp. 136–7.

71. Robert Lynd, *Rambles in Ireland* (London: Mills & Boon, 1912), pp. 258–9.

72. Peter Hart, *The IRA and Its Enemies: Violence and community in Cork, 1916–1923* (Oxford: Clarendon Press, 1998), pp. 303–4; Joost Augusteijn, *From Public Defiance to Guerilla Warfare: The experience of ordinary Volunteers in the War of Independence* (London: Irish Academic Press, 1998), pp. 293–4; Townshend, *The Republic*, p. 264; FitzGerald, *Combatants and Civilians*, pp. 83–4.

73. Comerford, *Kilkenny IRA*, p. 143.

74. BMH, WS/1585, statement of Timothy Dinneen, Co. Cork, p. 9.

75. BMH, WS/1595, statement of Seamus Babington, Co. Tipperary, pp. 96–7.

76. BMH, WS/451, statement of George Power, Co. Cork, pp. 15–16; BMH, WS/1130, statement of Edmond Power, Co. Waterford, p. 24; BMH, WS/1335, statement of James Leahy, Co. Kilkenny, pp. 37–8; BMH, WS/1572, statement of Padraig Kane, Co. Carlow, p. 16.

77. Mary Carpenter, *Reformatory Prison Discipline, as Developed by the Rt. Hon. Sir Walter Crofton, via the Irish Convict Prisons* (London: Longman, Longman, Green & Longman, 1872), pp. 48–56; Patrick Carroll-Burke, *Colonial Discipline: The making of the Irish convict system* (Dublin: Four Courts Press, 2000), pp. 125–6.

78. *Freeman's Journal*, 17 July 1878, 18 July 1878, 13 January 1882.

79. *Royal Commission on Prisons in Ireland. Vol. I. Reports, with Digest of Evidence, Appendices, &c* H.C. 1884–5 [C.4233] [C.4233-1] xxxviii.1, 259, p. 204.

80. *Freeman's Journal*, 15 January 1900.

81. Ibid., 24 November 1871, 30 November 1874; *Daily Express*, 12 May 1885, 10 July 1911; *Warder*, 29 July 1899; *Dublin Evening Mail*, 29 November 1901.

82. *Freeman's Journal*, 9 August 1881, 4 August 1893; *Evening Herald*, 25 February 1895; *Daily Express*, 19 July 1907.

83. *Freeman's Journal*, 31 July 1874.

84. Ibid., 2 December 1874, 18 January 1898.

85. *Carlow Sentinel*, 31 July 1875; *Midland Counties Advertiser*, 2 February 1888; *Waterford Standard*, 21 August 1889; *Waterford Star*, 26 June 1897; *Constabulary Gazette*, 17 July 1897, 1 January 1898, 19 March 1898, 14 October 1899, 20 April 1901, 4 August 1906, 24 August 1912; *Royal Irish Constabulary Magazine*, August 1915; Tom Hunt, 'The Knife, the Card and the Trick-of-the-Loop: Crime and sport in County Westmeath', in Liam Clare and Máire Ní Chearbhaill (eds), *Trouble with the Law: Crimes and trials from Ireland's past* (Dublin: Woodfield Press, 2007), p. 28; McCracken, *Inspector Mallon*, p. 164.

86. *Daily Mirror*, 13 February 1912.

87. Partridge, 'Crime in the DMP District'; O'Brien, *'Dear, Dirty Dublin'*, pp. 185–6.

88. Radford, 'Trial of Strength', pp. 101–2.

89. *Ulster Saturday Night*, 15 June 1895.

90. Radford, 'Trial of Strength', p. 104.

91. Boyle, 'Women and Crime', p. 98; *Royal Irish Constabulary Magazine*, February 1914.

92. *Belfast News-Letter*, 1 January 1914.

93. Ibid., 4 December 1867, 3 April 1868, 5 December 1871; *Freeman's Journal*, 13 April 1878.

94. *Belfast News-Letter*, 17 June 1868, 17 October 1871.

95. Ibid., 3 December 1884.

96. *Freeman's Journal*, 13 April 1878, 4 April 1879, 13 July 1879, 16 July 1879, 26 November 1887, 31 January 1888, 21 December 1894; Elaine Farrell, *Women, Crime and Punishment in Ireland: Life in the nineteenth-century convict prison* (Cambridge: Cambridge University Press, 2020), pp. 81–91.

97. *Freeman's Journal*, 17 November 1880, 15 January 1881, 10 April 1882, 13 January 1888, 21 April 1898, 27 July 1900. For families of coiners in London, see Heather Shore, *London's Criminal Underworlds, c. 1720–1930: A social and cultural history* (Basingstoke: Palgrave Macmillan, 2015).

98. *Freeman's Journal*, 9 October 1896.

99. Ibid., 22 December 1871; *Belfast News-Letter*, 6 October 1888, 12 October 1888.

100. *Freeman's Journal*, 19 October 1880, 21 October 1880.

101. Ibid., 1 November 1886, 2 April 1888, 5 June 1896, 14 January 1899.

102. Ibid., 24 July 1871, 30 May 1891.

103. McCracken, *Inspector Mallon*, p. 164.

104. *Royal Irish Constabulary Magazine*, March 1914, May 1914.

105. *Belfast News-Letter*, 1 June 1872, 13 August 1890, 2 September 1895; *Freeman's Journal*, 11 August 1873.

106. *Freeman's Journal*, 10 March 1870, 26 August 1898; *Belfast News-Letter*, 9 December 1870, 28 August 1882, 15 February 1899, 15 May 1899. There were some sixty pawnbrokers in Dublin in 1870, who owned seventy-six pawnshops. According to Raymond James Raymond, 'The highly competitive nature of the business encouraged pawnbrokers to increase to reckless proportions the sums advanced on pledges', which helps to explain why pickpockets and other purloiners of property were attracted to these outlets with their ill-gotten spoils. No doubt a similar state of affairs existed in Belfast, where there were more than 100 pawnbroker shops in the early years of the twentieth century: Raymond James Raymond, 'Pawnbrokers and Pawnbroking in Dublin: 1830–1870', *Dublin Historical Record*, vol. 32, no. 1, December 1978, p. 21; Boyle, 'Women and Crime', p. 157.

107. *Freeman's Journal*, 26 October 1871, 9 June 1886; *Belfast News-Letter*, 1 June 1872.

108. *Belfast News-Letter*, 28 September 1870, 10 February 1874; *Freeman's Journal*, 29 July 1874, 5 June 1875, 22 October 1881; Donald M. MacRaild and Frank Neal, 'Child Stripping in the Victorian City', *Urban History*, vol. 39, no. 3, 2012, pp. 431–52.

109. *Freeman's Journal*, 10 March 1870.

110. Ibid., 8 July 1873, 17 November 1880, 27 June 1882.

111. The perceived link between smoking and juvenile criminality in Irish towns mirrored similar fears in Britain, where alarmists believed that the smoking 'man child ... overwhelmed by the feverish anxiety to become a man' would be drawn into a precocious and delinquent sub-culture: Matthew Hilton, *Smoking in British Popular Culture 1800–2000: Perfect pleasures* (Manchester: Manchester University Press, 2000), pp. 162–4, 168, 170.

112. *Belfast News-Letter*, 21 April 1899.

113. O'Brien, *'Dear, Dirty Dublin'*, pp. 21–2, 28, 31, 132–3; Mary E. Daly, *Dublin: The deposed capital. A social and economic history 1860–1914* (Cork: Cork University Press, 1984), pp. 77, 79–80; Jacinta Prunty, *Dublin Slums 1800–1925: A study in urban geography* (Dublin: Four Courts Press, 1998).

114. Laffan's tale tells the story of eleven-year-old Flitters, a barefoot 'street arab' who looks after the younger Tatters and the Counsellor. Tatters was 'about six years old, small and infantine of looks but with a world of guile in his far-apart blue eyes. He could chew, drink and steal, and was altogether a finished young reprobate'. The Counsellor was aged about nine, 'but might have been ninety, for the *Weltkunst* his wrinkled, pock-marked countenance portrayed'. They were all orphans or abandoned children: Flitters' mother was dead and her father abandoned her when he emigrated to the United States; Tatters was a foundling, whose nurse abandoned him when she ceased getting paid for nursing him; and the Counsellor's 'antecedents were wrapped in complete obscurity', although he had a vague idea that his grandmother lived in the notorious Bull Lane, which, along with Greek Street, was considered by the *Freeman's Journal* of 19 September 1871 to be one of 'the two great head-quarters of crime in the city'. The three children maintained a precarious existence by begging from foreign visitors to Dublin, running messages for workmen, singing and playing music in the streets, stealing coal from the city's wharves or sifting cinders in waste land around Dublin's outskirts and selling them: their money went on food, cheap lodgings and porter. Their world collapsed when Flitters was killed as a result of intervening in

a fight between two drunken draymen; as she lay dying in hospital, Flitters refused to identify the man who hit her, as she knew that this would mean prison for him and 'starvation and ruin to the man's wife and little children': May Laffan, *Flitters, Tatters and the Counsellor and Other Tales* (London: Macmillan, 1882).

115. *Freeman's Journal*, 10 June 1882, 7 January 1884.

116. Ibid., 6 November 1883, 15 October 1885.

117. Ibid., 6 February 1885.

118. Ibid., 12 January 1884.

119. Ibid., 15 October 1885.

120. Ibid., 10 September 1888, 26 October 1892, 2 November 1892, 8 November 1892, 21 March 1893.

121. Jane Barnes, *Irish Industrial Schools, 1868–1908: Origins and development* (Dublin: Irish Academic Press, 1989).

122. *Freeman's Journal*, 23 January 1872. Some young offenders continued to be sentenced to jail terms, however. For example, in April 1873 Resident Magistrate J.C. O'Donnell sentenced fourteen-year-old Catherine Staunton of Belfast, who already had several convictions against her, to one month in prison for being drunk and disorderly and using party expressions in public. O'Donnell viewed Staunton as 'the most terrible instance of moral depravity I have come across in all my experience', and believed that, because she was 'past reformation' and tried to 'contaminate' any person with whom she came into contact, no reformatory school governor would agree to accept her as an inmate. In 1880 there were still some 1,000 children incarcerated in Ireland's prisons; approximately 150 of these prisoners were younger than twelve years of age: *Belfast News-Letter*, 7 April 1873; Conor Reidy, *Ireland's 'Moral Hospital': The Irish borstal system 1906–1956* (Dublin: Irish Academic Press, 2010), p. 1; Geraldine Curtin, '"The Child Condemned": The imprisonment of children in Ireland, 1850–1908', *Irish Economic and Social History*, vol. 47, 2020, pp. 78–96.

123. *Belfast News-Letter*, 28 January 1870, 4 January 1893; *Freeman's Journal*, 28 August 1874, 11 July 1877, 28 November 1877, 14 July 1882, 18 July 1884; Thomas Molony, 'The Prevention and Punishment of Crime', in Ian O'Donnell and Finbarr McAuley (eds), *Criminal Justice History: Themes and controversies from pre-independence Ireland* (Dublin: Four Courts Press, 2003), pp. 87–8.

124. *Freeman's Journal*, 26 October 1880, 19 November 1888; *Belfast News-Letter*, 29 November 1899; Molony, 'Prevention and

Punishment', pp. 87–8. Cardinal Michael Logue believed that 'the deserted and needy children of the country' who were not criminals, but who were 'thrown amongst the criminal classes' and were in danger of resorting to crime in order to survive, would be much safer in industrial schools than in workhouses. He argued in 1899 that 'every child who is brought up in an Irish workhouse is a "potential criminal"', as he 'never yet knew of a boy or a girl brought up in a workhouse coming to any good afterwards'. Contemporary sources are silent on whether the children in industrial schools in the period under study were victims of a similar regime of physical and sexual abuse as existed in industrial schools in the independent Irish state: *Freeman's Journal*, 8 June 1899; Mary Raftery and Eoin O'Sullivan, *Suffer the Little Children: The inside story of Ireland's industrial schools* (Dublin: New Island, 1999).

125. *Freeman's Journal*, 5 February 1872, 28 February 1877.

126. Nial Osborough, *Borstal in Ireland: Custodial provision for the young adult offender 1906–1974* (Dublin: Institute of Public Administration, 1975). Reidy's findings show that the Clonmel inmates came overwhelmingly from Ireland's largest urban centres. Of the 516 inmates incarcerated at Clonmel between 1910 and 1921, some 31 per cent came from 'Antrim/Belfast' and 29.1 per cent came from Dublin. Cork provided the next largest proportion of prisoners, but Cork prisoners constituted a mere 5 per cent of the total number of borstal inmates. Larceny was by far the most common reason for borstal detention, with 352 convictions for this offence registered at Clonmel; the next most common recorded offence was breaking and entering, with some 114 recorded convictions for this crime: Reidy, *Ireland's 'Moral Hospital'*, pp. 64, 68–9.

127. *Belfast News-Letter*, 23 August 1869.

128. Ibid., 26 February 1870.

129. *Freeman's Journal*, 22 October 1892.

130. *Royal Irish Constabulary Magazine*, February 1916.

131. *Portadown News*, 12 February 1916; *Daily Express*, 8 March 1916.

132. *Freeman's Journal*, 24 December 1897, 20 January 1900.

133. Macilwee, *Liverpool Underworld*, pp. 228–9; Heather Shore, *Artful Dodgers: Youth and crime in early nineteenth-century London* (Woodbridge: Boydell Press, 1999); Emma Watkins and Barry Godfrey, *Criminal Children: Researching juvenile offenders, 1820–1920* (Barnsley: Pen & Sword, 2018).

134. John Springhall, *Coming of Age: Adolescence in Britain 1860–1960* (Dublin: Gill & Macmillan, 1986), pp. 128–9, 136–8; Kate Summerscale, *The Wicked Boy: An infamous murder in Victorian London* (London: Penguin, 2017); Macilwee, *Liverpool Underworld*, pp. 240–1.

135. For England, see Emsley, *Crime and Society*, pp. 275–6.

136. *Freeman's Journal*, 22 March 1870, 24 August 1872, 21 November 1872; Cornelius Joseph Herlihy, *The Celt above the Saxon or a Comparative Sketch of the Irish and English People in War, in Peace and in Character* (Boston: Angel Guardian Press, 1904), pp. 182–3, 189–95; Henry Bellingham, *Irish and English Crime* (Dublin: Catholic Truth Society of Ireland, 1909), pp. 10, 15; Stephen Gwynn, *The Case for Home Rule* (Dublin: Maunsel, 1911), pp. 115, 117; Maria Luddy and Mary O'Dowd, *Marriage in Ireland, 1660–1925* (Cambridge: Cambridge University Press, 2020), pp. 313–14.

137. Herlihy, *Celt above the Saxon*, p. 184.

138. Steiner-Scott, '"To Bounce a Boot Off Her"'; Conley, *Melancholy Accidents*; Conley, *Certain Other Countries*; Farrell, 'A Most Diabolical Deed'. Assaults by husbands on their wives were not recorded as crimes in their own right, but were subsumed into the general category of aggravated assaults against women and children.

139. Eoin O'Sullivan, '"This Otherwise Delicate Subject": Child sexual abuse in early twentieth-century Ireland', in Paul O'Mahony (ed.), *Criminal Justice in Ireland* (Dublin: Institute of Public Administration, 2002), pp. 176–201.

140. *Freeman's Journal*, 10 November 1885, 24 October 1887, 16 March 1888, 20 June 1896; Healy, *Old Munster Circuit*, p. 228; Bourke, 'Sexual Violence', pp. 29–30. For a discussion of the hostile courtroom cross-examination of child and juvenile plaintiffs in rape and sexual assault cases in England, see Victoria Bates, *Sexual Forensics in Victorian and Edwardian Britain: Age, crime and consent in the courts* (Basingstoke: Palgrave Macmillan, 2016).

141. *Freeman's Journal*, 20 January 1884, 21 February 1887.

142. Ibid., 11 August 1873, 9 September 1875, 15 July 1878, 3 July 1884, 7 October 1886; *Belfast News- Letter*, 17 October 1890, 23 July 1895; Louise Ryan, 'Publicising the Private: Suffragists' critique of sexual abuse and domestic violence', in Louise Ryan and Margaret Ward (eds), *Irish Women and the Vote: Becoming citizens* (Dublin: Irish Academic Press, 2007), pp. 78–80; Sandra McAvoy, 'Sexual

Crime and Irish Women's Campaign for a Criminal Law Amendment Act, 1912–35', in Maryann Gialanella Valiulis (ed.), *Gender and Power in Irish History* (Dublin: Irish Academic Press, 2009), p. 91; Diarmaid Ferriter, *Occasions of Sin: Sex and society in modern Ireland* (London: Profile, 2009), pp. 52–3; Sarah-Anne Buckley, 'Family and Power: Incest in Ireland, 1880–1950', in Anthony McElligott, Liam Chambers, Ciara Breathnach and Catherine Lawless (eds), *Power in History: From medieval Ireland to the post-modern world* (Dublin: Irish Academic Press, 2011), p. 199.

143. *Freeman's Journal*, 4 February 1876, 18 May 1882, 23 June 1882, 19 July 1882, 3 August 1882.

144. *Belfast News-Letter*, 17 October 1890; Steiner-Scott, '"To Bounce a Boot Off Her"', pp. 131–3; Ryan, 'Publicising the Private', p. 85. For the similar situation in Britain, see A. James Hannerton, *Cruelty and Companionship: Conflict in nineteenth-century married life* (London: Routledge, 1992).

145. Joan Hoff and Marian Yeates, *The Cooper's Wife Is Missing* (New York: Basic Books, 2000), p. 161.

146. *Belfast News-Letter*, 9 August 1870, 27 September 1870; *Freeman's Journal*, 7 March 1871, 12 July 1882, 30 April 1886.

147. Diane Urquhart, 'Irish Divorce and Domestic Violence, 1857–1922', *Women's History Review*, vol. 22, no. 5, 2013, pp. 820–37; Luddy and O'Dowd, *Marriage in Ireland*, p. 322.

148. Urquhart, 'Irish Divorce and Domestic Violence', p. 833.

149. Dympna McLoughlin, 'Infanticide in Nineteenth-Century Ireland', in Angela Bourke, Siobhán Kilfeather, Maria Luddy, Margaret MacCurtain, Gerardine Meaney, Máirín Ní Dhonnchadha, Mary O'Dowd and Clair Wills (eds), *Field Day Anthology of Irish Writing* (Cork: Cork University Press, 2005), vol. IV, pp. 915–22; Rattigan, '"I Thought From Her Appearance"'; Elaine Farrell (ed.), *Infanticide in the Irish Crown Files at Assizes, 1883–1900* (Dublin: Irish Manuscripts Commission, 2012); Farrell, *'A Most Diabolical Deed'*.

150. Ferriter, *Occasions of Sin*, p. 58; Farrell, *'A Most Diabolical Deed'*, pp. 74–5, 78–9, 90–1, 95–7, 110–11. Irish juries were not unique in frequently showing sympathy to the accused in infanticide cases. In nineteenth-century Britain, juries were reluctant to convict the accused of the capital offence of infanticide. In Carmarthenshire, prosecuting was a form of shaming ritual in itself and the low number of convictions reflects the fact that the public airing of these cases was

regarded as sufficient punishment in most instances: Emsley, *Crime and Society*, p. 157; R.W. Ireland, '"Perhaps My Mother Murdered Me": Child death and the law in Victorian Carmarthenshire', in Christopher Brooks and Michael Lobban, *Communities and Courts in Britain 1150–1900* (London: Hambledon Press, 1997), pp. 229–44. With thanks to Dr Richard Mc Mahon for bringing the latter source to my attention.

151. Mary Carbery, *The Farm by Lough Gur* (Cork and Dublin: Mercier Press, 1986), pp. 49–50; Paul O'Dwyer, *Counsel for the Defense: The autobiography of Paul O'Dwyer* (New York: Simon & Schuster, 1979), pp. 33–4; Mulhall, *New Day Dawning*, pp. 34–5; Finnegan, *Do Penance or Perish*.

152. William Rhys Lambert, *Drink and Sobriety in Victorian Wales* (Cardiff: University of Wales Press, 1983), p. 169; Robert A. Nye, *Crime, Madness and Politics in Modern France: The medical concept of national decline* (Princeton: Princeton University Press, 1984), p. 19; Thomas F. Babor and Barbara G. Rosenkrantz, 'Public Health, Public Morals, and Public Order: Social science and liquor control in Massachusetts, 1880–1916', in Susanna Barrows and Robin Room (eds), *Drinking: Behavior and belief in modern history* (Berkeley: University of California Press, 1991), pp. 265–85; David J. Cox, Kim Stevenson, Candida Harris and Judith Rowbotham, *Public Indecency in England 1857–1960: 'A serious and growing evil'* (London: Routledge, 2015); Thora Hands, *Drinking in Victorian and Edwardian Britain: Beyond the spectacle of the drunkard* (Cham: Springer International Publishing, 2018), pp. 17, 29.

153. Nye, *Crime, Madness and Politics*; Paul Jennings, *A History of Drink and the English, 1500–2000* (Abingdon: Routledge, 2016), p. 160.

154. Hands, *Drinking*, pp. 42–3.

155. Mary Gibson, *Prostitution and the State in Italy, 1860–1915* (New Brunswick: Rutgers University Press, 1986); Alain Corbin, *Women for Hire: Prostitution and society in France after 1850* (Cambridge, MA: Harvard University Press, 1990), pp. 106–7; Anne M. Hayes, *Female Prostitution in Costa Rica: Historical perspectives, 1880–1930* (New York: Routledge, 2006); Cynthia M. Blair, *I've Got to Make My Livin': Black women's sex work in turn-of-the-century Chicago* (Chicago: University of Chicago Press, 2010); Nancy Meriwether Wingfield, *The World of Prostitution in Late Imperial Austria* (Oxford: Oxford University Press, 2017).

156. Emsley, *Crime and Society*, pp. 172–3; Lionel Rose, *'Rogues and Vagabonds': Vagrant underworld in Britain 1815–1985* (Abingdon: Routledge, 1988); Paul Lawrence, 'Policing the Poor in England and France, 1850–1900', in Clive Emsley, Eric Johnson and Pieter Spierenburg (eds), *Social Control in Europe: Vol 2, 1800–2000* (Columbus: Ohio State University Press, 2004), pp. 213–17; Frank Tobias Higbie, 'Between Romance and Degradation: Navigating the meanings of vagrancy in North America, 1870–1940', in A.L. Beier and Paul Ocobock (eds), *Cast Out: Vagrancy and homelessness in global and historical perspective* (Athens, OH: Ohio University Press, 2008), pp. 256–69; Douglas Starr, *The Killer of Little Shepherds: The case of the French Ripper and the birth of forensic science* (London: Simon Schuster, 2011).

CONCLUSION

1. R.B. McDowell, *The Irish Administration 1801–1914* (London: Routledge & Kegan Paul, 1964), pp. 135–145; Virginia Crossman, 'The Growth of the State in the Nineteenth Century', in James Kelly (ed.), *The Cambridge History of Ireland: Volume III, 1730–1880* (Cambridge: Cambridge University Press, 2018), pp. 542–66.

2. *Royal Irish Constabulary and Dublin Metropolitan Police. Appendix to the Report of the Committee of Enquiry, 1914. Containing Minutes of Evidence with Appendices* H.C. 1914–16 7637 xxxii 359, pp. 15, 194.

3. Donal J. O'Sullivan, *The Irish Constabularies 1822–1922: A century of policing in Ireland* (Dingle: Brandon, 1999), pp. 217–19.

4. Boyd, *Holy War in Belfast*; Hirst, *Religion, Politics and Violence in Nineteenth-Century Belfast*; Doyle, *Sectarian Violence in Victorian Belfast*; Radford, *Policing of Belfast 1870–1914*.

5. Neal Garnham, *Association Football in Pre-Partition Ireland* (Belfast: Ulster Historical Foundation, 2004), pp. 125–8.

6. For the militant suffragists' campaign of violence in Dublin, Belfast and other places in Ulster see *Royal Irish Constabulary Magazine*, May 1914, July 1914, September 1914, July 1915; Rosemary Cullen Owens, *Did Your Granny Have a Hammer? A history of the Irish suffrage movement, 1867–1922* (Dublin: Attic Press, 1985); Diane Urquhart, *Women in Ulster Politics 1890–1940: A history not yet told* (Dublin: Irish Academic Press, 2000), pp. 30, 35–9; Rosemary Cullen Owens, *A Social History of Women in Ireland 1870–1970* (Dublin:

Gill & Macmillan, 2005), pp. 90–1, 101; Ciaran Toal, '"The Brutes": Mrs Metge and the Lisburn Cathedral Bomb, 1914', *History Ireland*, vol. 22, no. 6, November–December 2014, pp. 30–3.

7. Charles Townshend, *The British Campaign in Ireland 1919–1921: The development of political and military strategies* (Oxford: Oxford University Press, 1975), p. 41.

8. John Abbott, *Police Casualties in Ireland, 1919–1922* (Cork and Dublin: Mercier Press, 2000); W.J. Lowe, 'The War against the R.I.C., 1919–21', *Éire-Ireland*, vol. 37 nos 3 & 4, Autumn–Winter 2002, pp. 79–117; John Reynolds, *46 Men Dead: The Royal Irish Constabulary in County Tipperary, 1919–22* (Cork: Collins Press, 2016).

Bibliography

PRIMARY SOURCES

Unpublished manuscripts

National Archives, Dublin: Criminal index files

Bureau of Military History, Dublin: Witness Statements: WS/347 Patrick Callanan; WS/366 Alice M. Cashel; WS/509 J.J. McConnell; WS/519 Thomas Donnelly; WS/528 John McAnerney; WS/530 P.V. Hoey; WS/609 Felim McGuill; WS/693 Patrick Maguire; WS/762 Liam McMullen; WS/767 Patrick Moylett; WS/820 Francis Tummon; WS/911 Patrick McKenna; WS/983 Thomas Tuohy; WS/1,048 Sean Murnane; WS/1,064 Michael Healy; WS/1,068 Michael Brennan; WS/1,072 Sean McNamara; WS/1,075 Thomas Shalloe; WS/1,142 Joseph O'Byrne; WS/1,288 Michael Gleeson; WS/1,280 and WS/1,285 Ned Broy; WS/1,313 Charles Gildea; WS/1,484 James McCaffrey; WS/1,554 William J. O'Hora; WS/1,572 Padraig Kane; WS/1,585 Timothy Dinneen; WS/1,595 Seamus Babington; WS/1,668 Thomas Hevey; WS/1,729 Joseph J. Togher

Public Record Office of Northern Ireland: D.3160: Memoirs of District Inspector John M. Regan; T.2815/1 Memoirs of Head Constable Robert Dunlop

National Archives, Kew Gardens, London: Colonial Office CO904 papers (Royal Irish Constabulary monthly confidential reports)

Parliamentary papers

(a) Criminal and Judicial Statistics

Criminal and Judicial Statistics for Ireland 1870 H.C. 1871 (C.433) lxiv 231

Criminal and Judicial Statistics for Ireland 1871 H.C. 1872 (C.674) lxv 235

Criminal and Judicial Statistics for Ireland 1872 H.C. 1873 (C.851) lxx 247

Criminal and Judicial Statistics for Ireland 1873 H.C. 1874 (C.291) liv 513

Criminal and Judicial Statistics for Ireland 1874 H.C. 1875 (C.1295) lxxxi 259

Criminal and Judicial Statistics for Ireland 1875 H.C. 1876 (C.1563) lxxix 273

Criminal and Judicial Statistics for Ireland 1876 H.C. 1877 (C.1822) lxxxvi 261

Criminal and Judicial Statistics for Ireland 1877 H.C. 1878 (C.2152) lxxix 265

Criminal and Judicial Statistics for Ireland 1878 H.C. 1878–9 (C.2389) lxxvi 279

Criminal and Judicial Statistics for Ireland 1879 H.C. 1880 (C.2698) lxxvii 251

Criminal and Judicial Statistics for Ireland 1880 H.C. 1881 (C.3028) xcv 243

Criminal and Judicial Statistics for Ireland 1881 H.C. 1882 (C.3355) lxxv 243

Criminal and Judicial Statistics for Ireland 1882 H.C. 1883 (C.3808) lxxvii 243

Criminal and Judicial Statistics for Ireland 1883 H.C. 1884 (C.4181) lxxxvi 243

Criminal and Judicial Statistics for Ireland 1884 H.C. 1884–5 (C.4554) lxxxvi 243

Criminal and Judicial Statistics for Ireland 1885 H.C. 1886 (C.4796) lxxii 233

Criminal and Judicial Statistics for Ireland 1886 H.C. 1887 (C.5177) xc 241

Criminal and Judicial Statistics for Ireland 1887 H.C. 1888 (C.5495) cviii 241

Criminal and Judicial Statistics for Ireland 1888 H.C. 1889 (C.5795) lxxxv 241

Criminal and Judicial Statistics for Ireland 1889 H.C. 1890 (C.6122) lxxx 253

Criminal and Judicial Statistics for Ireland 1890 H.C. 1890–1 (C.6511) xciii 251

Criminal and Judicial Statistics for Ireland 1891 H.C. 1892 (C.6782) lxxxix 253

Criminal and Judicial Statistics for Ireland 1892 H.C. 1893–4 (C.7189) ciii 279

Criminal and Judicial Statistics for Ireland 1893 H.C. 1894 (C.7534) xcv 105

Criminal and Judicial Statistics for Ireland 1894 H.C. 1895 (C.7799) cviii 323

Criminal and Judicial Statistics for Ireland 1895 H.C. 1896 (C.8207) xciv 521

Criminal and Judicial Statistics for Ireland 1896 H.C. 1899 (C.9492) cviii Part I

Criminal and Judicial Statistics for Ireland 1897 H.C. 1899 (C.9493) cviii Part II.175

Criminal and Judicial Statistics for Ireland 1898 H.C. 1900 (Cd. 225) civ 1

Criminal and Judicial Statistics for Ireland 1899 H.C. 1900 (Cd. 313) civ 177

Criminal and Judicial Statistics for Ireland 1900 H.C. 1901 (Cd. 725, 682) lxxxix 463

Criminal and Judicial Statistics for Ireland 1901 H.C. 1902 (Cd. 1208, 1187) cxvii 395

Criminal and Judicial Statistics for Ireland 1902 H.C. 1903 (Cd. 1746, 1676) lxxxiii 403

Criminal and Judicial Statistics for Ireland 1903 H.C. 1904 (Cd. 2218, 2149) cvii 431

Criminal and Judicial Statistics for Ireland 1904 H.C. 1905 (Cd. 2632, 2593) xcix 417

Criminal and Judicial Statistics for Ireland 1905 H.C. 1906 (Cd. 3112, 3050) cxxxv 405

Criminal and Judicial Statistics for Ireland 1906 H.C. 1907 (Cd. 3654, 3616) xcviii 447

Criminal and Judicial Statistics for Ireland 1907 H.C. 1908 (Cd. 4200, 3050) cxxiii 619

Criminal and Judicial Statistics for Ireland 1908 H.C. 1909 (Cd. 4793, 4747) civ 207

Criminal and Judicial Statistics for Ireland 1909 H.C. 1910 (Cd. 5320, 5264) cxi 359

Criminal and Judicial Statistics for Ireland 1910 H.C. 1911 (Cd. 5866, 5848) cii 367

Criminal and Judicial Statistics for Ireland 1911 H.C. 1912–13 (Cd. 6419, 6329) cx 703

Criminal and Judicial Statistics for Ireland 1912 H.C. 1914 (Cd. 7064) c 349

Criminal and Judicial Statistics for Ireland 1913 H.C. 1914 (Cd. 7536, 7600) c 519

Criminal and Judicial Statistics for Ireland 1914 H.C. 1914–16 (Cd.

8077, 8006) lxxxii 451

Criminal and Judicial Statistics for Ireland 1915 H.C. 1917–18 (Cd. 8636) xxxvii 283

Criminal and Judicial Statistics for Ireland 1916 H.C. 1918 (Cd. 9066) xxv 29

Criminal and Judicial Statistics for Ireland 1917 H.C. 1919 (Cmd. 43, 438) ii 1

Criminal and Judicial Statistics for Ireland 1919 H.C. 1921 (Cmd. 1431) xli 591

(b) Inland Revenue Commissioners' and Customs and Excise Commissioners' Reports

Fourteenth Report of the Commissioners of Her Majesty's Inland Revenue on the Inland Revenue, for the Years ended 31st March 1870 and 1871 H.C. 1871 (C.370) (C.370-1) xvii 647, 743

Fifteenth Report of the Commissioners of Her Majesty's Inland Revenue on the Inland Revenue, for the Year ended 31st March 1872 H.C. 1872 (C.646) xviii 259

Sixteenth Report of the Commissioners of Her Majesty's Inland Revenue on the Inland Revenue, for the Year ended 31st March 1873 H.C. 1873 (C.844) xxi 651

Seventeenth Report of the Commissioners of Her Majesty's Inland Revenue on the Inland Revenue, for the Year ended 31st March 1874 H.C. 1874 (C.1098) xv 673

Eighteenth Report of the Commissioners of Her Majesty's Inland Revenue on the Inland Revenue, for the Year ended 31st March 1875 H.C. 1875 (C. 1329) xx 513

Nineteenth Report of the Commissioners of Her Majesty's Inland Revenue on the Inland Revenue, for the Year ended 31st March 1876 H.C. 1876 (C.1607) xx 457

Twentieth Report of the Commissioners of Her Majesty's Inland Revenue on the Inland Revenue, for the Year ended 31st March 1877 H.C. 1877 (C.1896) xxvi 593

Twenty-First Report of the Commissioners of Her Majesty's Inland Revenue on the Inland Revenue, for the Year ended 31st March 1878 H.C. 1878 (C.2158) xxvi 717

Twenty-Second Report of the Commissioners of Her Majesty's Inland Revenue on the Inland Revenue, for the Year ended 31st March 1879 H.C. 1878–9 (C.2406) xx 635

Twenty-Third Report of the Commissioners of Her Majesty's Inland Revenue on the Inland Revenue, for the Year ended 31st March 1880 H.C. 1881 (C.2770) xxix 89

Twenty-Fourth Report of the Commissioners of Her Majesty's Inland Revenue on the Inland Revenue, for the Year ended 31st March 1881 H.C. 1881 (C.2967) xxix 181

Twenty-Fifth Report of the Commissioners of Her Majesty's Inland Revenue on the Inland Revenue, for the Year ended 31st March 1882 H.C. 1882 (C.3325) xxi 275

Twenty-Sixth Report of the Commissioners of Her Majesty's Inland Revenue on the Inland Revenue, for the Year ended 31st March 1883 H.C. 1883 (C.3718) xxii 1

Twenty-Seventh Report of the Commissioners of Her Majesty's Inland Revenue on the Inland Revenue, for the Year ended 31st March 1884 H.C. 1884 (C.4088) xxiii 45

Twenty-Eighth Report of the Commissioners of Her Majesty's Inland Revenue on the Duties under their Management, for the Year ended 31st March 1885 H.C. 1884–5 (C.4474)

Twenty-Ninth Report of the Commissioners of Her Majesty's Inland Revenue, for the Year ended 31st March 1886 H.C. 1886 (C.4816) xx 279

Thirtieth Report of the Commissioners of Her Majesty's Inland Revenue, for the Year ended 31st March 1887 H.C. 1887 (C.5154) xxvii 331

Thirty-First Report of the Commissioners of Her Majesty's Inland Revenue, for the Year ended 31st March 1888 H.C. 1888 (C.5541) xxxiv 349

Thirty-Second Report of the Commissioners of Her Majesty's Inland Revenue, for the Year ended 31st March 1889 H.C. 1889 (C.5843) xxviii 379

Thirty-Third Report of the Commissioners of Her Majesty's Inland Revenue, for the Year ended 31st March 1890 H.C. 1890 (C.6187) xxvi 397

Thirty-Fourth Report of the Commissioners of Her Majesty's Inland Revenue, for the Year ended 31st March 1891 H.C. 1890–1 (C.6537) xxvi 307

Thirty-Fifth Report of the Commissioners of Her Majesty's Inland Revenue, for the Year ended 31st March 1892 H.C. 1892 (C.6731) xxvii 487

Thirty-Sixth Report of the Commissioners of Her Majesty's Inland

Revenue, for the Year ended 31st March 1893 H.C. 1893–4 (C.7141) xxv 437

Thirty-Seventh Report of the Commissioners of Her Majesty's Inland Revenue, for the Year ended 31st March 1894 H.C. 1894 (C.7557) xxviii 289

Thirty-Eighth Report of the Commissioners of Her Majesty's Inland Revenue, for the Year ended 31st March 1895 H.C. 1895 (C.7854) xxvi 443

Thirty-Ninth Report of the Commissioners of Her Majesty's Inland Revenue, for the Year ended 31st March 1896 H.C. 1896 (C.8226) xxv 329

Fortieth Report of the Commissioners of Her Majesty's Inland Revenue, for the Year ended 31st March 1897 H.C. 1897 (C.8548) xxiv 353

Forty-First Report of the Commissioners of Her Majesty's Inland Revenue, for the Year ended 31st March 1898 H.C. 1898 (C.9020) xxi 345

Forty-Second Report of the Commissioners of Her Majesty's Inland Revenue H.C. 1899 (C.9461) xix 345

Forty-Third Report of the Commissioners of Her Majesty's Inland Revenue H.C. 1900 (Cd. 347) xviii 363

Forty-Fourth Report of the Commissioners of His Majesty's Inland Revenue H.C. 1901 (Cd. 647) xviii 427

Forty-Fifth Report of the Commissioners of His Majesty's Inland Revenue H.C. 1902 (Cd. 1216) xxii 365

Forty-Sixth Report of the Commissioners of His Majesty's Inland Revenue H.C. 1903 (Cd. 1717) xix 387

Forty-Seventh Report of the Commissioners of His Majesty's Inland Revenue H.C. 1904 (Cd. 2228) xviii 401

Forty-Eighth Report of the Commissioners of His Majesty's Inland Revenue H.C. 1905 (Cd. 2633) xxiv 1

Forty-Ninth Report of the Commissioners of His Majesty's Inland Revenue H.C. 1906 (Cd. 3110) xxvi 419

Fiftieth Report of the Commissioners of His Majesty's Inland Revenue H.C. 1907 (Cd. 3686) xx 409

Fifty-First Report of the Commissioners of His Majesty's Inland Revenue H.C. 1908 (Cd. 4226) xxiv 369

Fifty-Second Report of the Commissioners of His Majesty's Inland Revenue H.C. 1909 (Cd. 4868) xxvii 1

First Report of the Commissioners of His Majesty's Customs and Excise H.C. 1910 (Cd. 5302) xxii 1

Second Report of the Commissioners of His Majesty's Customs and Excise H.C. 1911 (Cd. 5827) xv 187

Third Report of the Commissioners of His Majesty's Customs and Excise H.C. 1912–13 (Cd. 6462) xvii 547

Fourth Report of the Commissioners of His Majesty's Customs and Excise H.C. 1913 (Cd. 6993) xix 497

Fifth Report of the Commissioners of His Majesty's Customs and Excise H.C. 1914 (Cd. 7574) xvii 1

Sixth Report of the Commissioners of His Majesty's Customs and Excise H.C. 1914–16 (Cd. 7621) xiii 161

Seventh Report of the Commissioners of His Majesty's Customs and Excise H.C. 1916 (Cd. 8428) vi 605

Eighth Report of the Commissioners of His Majesty's Customs and Excise H.C. 1917–18 (Cd. 8938) x 297

Ninth Report of the Commissioners of His Majesty's Customs and Excise H.C. 1918 (Cd. 9215) vii 865

Tenth Report of the Commissioners of His Majesty's Customs and Excise H.C. 1919 (Cmd. 503) xiii 597

Eleventh Report of the Commissioners of His Majesty's Customs and Excise H.C. 1920 (Cmd. 1082) xiii 399

Twelfth Report of the Commissioners of His Majesty's Customs and Excise H.C. 1921 (Cmd. 1435) x 19

Thirteenth Report of the Commissioners of His Majesty's Customs and Excise H.C. 1922 (Cmd. 17767) ii 143

(c) Other Parliamentary Papers

Report from the Select Committee on Westmeath, &c (Unlawful Combinations); Together with the Proceedings of the Committee, Minutes of Evidence, and Appendix H.C. 1871 (147) xiii 547

Fiftieth Report of the Inspectors-General on the General State of the Prisons of Ireland 1871; with Appendix H.C. 1872 (C.535) xxxii 1

Royal Commission on Prisons in Ireland. Vol. I. Reports, with Digest of Evidence, Appendices, &c H.C. 1884–5 [C.4233][C.4233-1] xxxviii.1, 259

Nineteenth Report of the General Prisons Board, Ireland, 1896–97; with an Appendix H.C. 1897 [C.8589] xl 545

Minutes of Evidence taken before the Royal Commission on Liquor Licensing Laws, with Appendices and Index H.C. 1898 (C.8980) xxxviii 527

Dublin Disturbances Commission. Appendix to Report of the Dublin Disturbances Commission. Minutes of Evidence and Appendix H.C. 1914 (Cd. 7272) xviii 533

Royal Irish Constabulary and Dublin Metropolitan Police. Appendix to Report of the Committee of Enquiry, 1914. Containing Minutes of Evidence with Appendices H.C. 1914–16 [Cd. 7637] xxxii 359

Parliamentary debates

Hansard's Parliamentary Debates, third series, vol. cccxlvi, 26 June 1890 – 16 July 1890

Newspapers and periodicals

Belfast News-Letter
Belfast Telegraph
Belfast Weekly News
Bray and South Dublin Herald
Clare Advertiser and Kilrush Gazette
Clarion
Constabulary Gazette
Cork Daily Herald
Cork Examiner
Cyclists' Touring Club Gazette
Daily Express
Daily Mirror
Derry Journal
Drogheda Conservative
Drogheda Independent
Evening Telegraph
Freeman's Journal
Irish Cyclist
Irish Wheelman
Kerry Evening Star
Kildare Observer
Larne Times

Leinster Reporter
Lisburn Standard
Portadown News
Rathmines News
Royal Irish Constabulary Magazine
The Irish Times
Times (London)
Ulster Saturday Night
Warder
Waterford News
Waterford Standard
Western People
Wexford People
Zozimus

Published reminiscences and other writings by contemporaries

Anonymous ('A Guardian of the Poor'), *The Irish Peasant: A sociological study* (London: S. Sonnenschein, 1892)

Augusteijn, Joost (ed.), *The Memoirs of John M. Regan: A Catholic officer in the RIC and RUC, 1909–48* (Dublin: Four Courts Press, 2007)

Ball, Stephen (ed.), *A Policeman's Ireland: Recollections of Samuel Waters, RIC* (Cork: Cork University Press, 1999)

Becker, Bernard H., *Disturbed Ireland: Being the letters written during the winter of 1880–81* (London: Macmillan, 1881)

Bellingham, Henry, *Irish and English Crime* (Dublin: Catholic Truth Society of Ireland, 1909)

Bermingham, George A. (James Owen Hannay), *Irishmen All*, 2nd edn (London and Edinburgh: T.N. Foulis, 1914)

Bidwell, George, *Forging His Chains: The autobiography of George Bidwell* (Hartford: S.S. Scranton, 1888)

Campbell, Fergus and Kevin O'Shiel, 'The Last Land War? Kevin O'Shiel's memoir of the Irish revolution (1916–21)', *Archivium Hibernicum*, vol. 57, 2003, pp. 155–200

Carbery, Mary, *The Farm by Lough Gur* (Cork and Dublin: Mercier Press, 1986)

Carpenter, Mary, *Reformatory Prison Discipline, as Developed by the Rt. Hon. Sir Walter Crofton, via the Irish Convict Prisons* (London: Longman, Longman, Green & Longman, 1872)

Carter, Bertram R., *Another Part of the Platform* (London: Houghton, 1931)

Comerford, James J., *My Kilkenny IRA Days 1916–22* (Kilkenny: James J. Comerford, 1978)

Coyne, William P. (ed.), *Ireland: Industrial and agricultural* (Dublin, Cork and Belfast: Browne & Nolan, 1902)

Crane, Stephen, *Last Words* (London: Digby & Long, 1902)

Farrell, Elaine (ed.), *Infanticide in the Irish Crown Files at Assizes, 1883–1900* (Dublin: Irish Manuscripts Commission, 2012)

Fennell, Rosemary (ed.), *The Royal Irish Constabulary: A history and personal memoir. Thomas Fennell (RIC No. 41310)* (Dublin: UCD Press, 2003)

Garrow Green, George, *In the Royal Irish Constabulary* (London: James Blackwood, 1905)

Gaughan, J. Anthony (ed.), *Memoirs of Constable Jeremiah Mee, RIC* (Dublin: Anvil, 1975)

George, Henry, 'England and Ireland: An American view', *Fortnightly Review*, 1 June 1882, pp. 780–94

Greene, John Baker, *Notes on Ireland Made from Personal Observation of Its Political, Social, and Economical Situation* (London: Samson Law, Marston, Searle & Rivington, 1886)

Gregory, Vere T.R., *The House of Gregory* (Dublin: Browne & Nolan, 1943)

Gwynn, Stephen, *The Case for Home Rule* (Dublin: Maunsel, 1911)

Harnett, Mossie, *Victory and Woe: The West Limerick Brigade in the War of Independence* (ed. James H. Joy) (Dublin: UCD Press, 2002)

Healy, Maurice, *The Old Munster Circuit: A book of memories and traditions* (London: Michael Joseph, 1939)

Hemstreet, William, *The Economical European Tourist* (New York: S.W. Green, 1875)

Herlihy, Cornelius Joseph, *The Celt above the Saxon or a Comparative Sketch of the Irish and English People in War, in Peace and in Character* (Boston: Angel Guardian Press, 1904)

Howard, C.H.D. (ed.), 'Select Documents XXVI: "The Man on a Tricycle": W.H. Duignan and Ireland, 1881–85', *Irish Historical Studies*, vol. 14, no. 55, March 1965, pp. 246–60

Irish Loyal and Patriotic Union, *Verbatim Copy of the Parnell Commission Report, with Complete Index and Notes* (London: Irish Loyal and Patriotic Union, 1890)

Irish Unionist Alliance, *Cattle-Driving in Ireland* (Dublin: Irish Unionist Alliance, 1908)

Joynes, James Leigh, *The Adventures of a Tourist in Ireland* (London: Kegan Paul & Trench, 1882)

Kearns, Kevin C., *Dublin Tenement Life: An oral history* (Harmondsworth: Penguin, 1994)

Kettle, Tom, *The Open Secret of Ireland* (London: W.J. Ham-Smith, 1912)

Laffan, May, *Flitters, Tatters and the Counsellor and Other Sketches* (London: Macmillan, 1882)

Lynch-Robinson, Christopher, *The Last of the Irish RMs* (London: Cassell, 1951)

Lynd, Robert, *Home Life in Ireland* (London: Mills & Boon, 1909)

———, *Rambles in Ireland* (London: Mills & Boon, 1912)

Macaulay, James, *Ireland in 1872: A tour of observation* (London: Henry S. King, 1873)

Mac Eoin, Uinseann (ed.), *Survivors* (Dublin: Argenta, 1987)

Mac Giolla Choille, Breandán (ed.), *Chief Secretary's Office, Dublin Castle: Intelligence notes 1913–16 preserved in the State Paper Office* (Dublin: Oifig an tSoláthair, 1966)

MacLysaght, Edward, *Changing Times: Ireland since 1898* (Gerrards Cross: Colin Smythe, 1978)

McCarron, Edward, *Life in Donegal 1850–1900* (Dublin and Cork: Mercier Press, 1981)

McCarthy, Michael J.F., *Irish Land and Irish Liberty: A study of the new lords of the soil* (London: Robert Scott & Paternoster, 1911)

McKenna, John, *A Beleaguered Station: The memoirs of Head Constable John McKenna, 1891–1921* (Belfast: Ulster Historical Foundation, 2009)

O'Connor Morris, William, *Memories and Thoughts of a Life* (London: George Allen, 1895)

———, *Past Irish Questions* (London: Grant Richards, 1901)

O'Dwyer, Paul, *Counsel for the Defense: The autobiography of Paul O'Dwyer* (New York: Simon & Schuster, 1979)

O'Malley, William, *Glancing Back: 70 Years' experiences and reminiscences of press man, sportsman and member of parliament* (London: Wright & Brown, 1933)

Ó Maoileoin, Séamas, *B'fhiú an Braon Fola …* (Dublin: Sáirséal & Dill, 1958)

Ribton-Turner, C.J., *A History of Vagrants and Vagrancy, and Beggars and Begging* (London: Chapman & Hall, 1887)

Shand, Alexander Innes, *Letters from the West of Ireland, 1884* (Edinburgh and London: W. Blackwood, 1885)

Stevenson, Burton Egbert, *The Charm of Ireland* (New York: Dodd & Mead, 1914)

Sullivan, Joseph Matthew, 'Irish Police Gleanings', *Journal of the American Institute of Criminal Law and Criminology*, vol. 4, no. 6, March 1914, pp. 876–87

Turner, Alfred, *Sixty Years of a Soldier's Life* (London: Methuen, 1912)

Tynan, Katharine, *The Years of the Shadow* (London: Constable, 1919)

———, *The Wandering Years* (Boston and New York: Houghton Mifflin, 1922)

Westenra, Derrick (Lord Rossmore), *Things I Can Tell* (London: Eveleigh Nash, 1912)

Young, A.B.R., *Reminiscences of an Irish Priest* (Dundalk: Dundalgan Press, 1931)

SECONDARY SOURCES: BOOKS AND ARTICLES

Abbott, Richard, *Police Casualties in Ireland, 1919–1922* (Cork and Dublin: Mercier Press, 2000)

Augusteijn, Joost, *From Public Defiance to Guerilla Warfare: The experience of ordinary Volunteers in the Irish War of Independence 1916–1921* (London: Irish Academic Press, 1998)

Babor, Thomas F. and Barbara G. Rosenkrantz, 'Public Health, Public Morals, and Public Order: Social science and liquor control in Massachusetts, 1880–1916', in Susanna Barrows and Robin Room (eds), *Drinking: Behavior and belief in modern history* (Berkeley: University of California Press, 1991), pp. 265–85

Bach, Matthew, *Combating London's Criminal Class: A state divided, 1869–95* (London: Bloomsbury Academic, 2020)

Bailey, Victor, 'The Fabrication of Deviance: "Dangerous classes" and "criminal classes" in Victorian England', in John Rule and Robert Malcolmson (eds), *Protest and Survival: The historical experience. Essays for E.P. Thompson* (London: Merlin, 1993), pp. 221–56

Ball, Stephen, 'Crowd Activity during the Irish Land War, 1879–90', in Peter Jupp and Eoin Magennis (eds), *Crowds in Ireland, c. 1720–1920* (Basingstoke and New York: Macmillan, 2000), pp. 212–48

Bamford, Francis, *Vicious Circle: The case of the missing Irish crown jewels* (London: Parrish, 1965)

Barnes, Jane, *Irish Industrial Schools, 1868–1908: Origins and development* (Dublin: Irish Academic Press, 1989)

Bartley, Paula, *Prostitution: Prevention and reform in England, 1860–1914* (London: Routledge, 1999)

Bates, Victoria, *Sexual Forensics in Victorian and Edwardian Britain: Age, crime and consent in the courts* (Basingstoke: Palgrave Macmillan, 2016)

Baylis, Gail, 'Metropolitan Surveillance and Rural Opacity: Secret photography in nineteenth-century Ireland', *History of Photography*, vol. 33, no. 1, 2009, pp. 26–38

Bew, Paul, *Land and the National Question in Ireland 1858–82* (Dublin: Gill & Macmillan, 1978)

———, *Conflict and Conciliation in Ireland 1890–1910: Parnellites and radical agrarians* (Oxford: Oxford University Press, 1987)

———, 'Sinn Féin, Agrarian Radicalism and the War of Independence, 1919–1921', in D.G. Boyce (ed.), *The Revolution in Ireland, 1879–1923* (Dublin: Gill & Macmillan, 1988), pp. 217–34

———, 'The National Question, Land, and "Revisionism": Some reflections', in D. George Boyce and Alan O'Day (eds), *The Making of Modern Irish History: Revisionism and the revisionist controversy* (London and New York: Routledge, 1996), pp. 90–9

Blair, Cynthia M., *'I've Got to Make My Livin': Black women's sex work in turn-of-the-century Chicago* (Chicago: University of Chicago Press, 2010)

Borgonovo, John, 'Republican Courts, Ordinary Crime, and the Irish Revolution, 1919–1921', in Margo de Koster, Hervé Leuwers, Dirk Luyten and Xavier Rousseaux (eds), *Justice in Wartime and Revolutions: Europe, 1795–1950* (Brussels: Algemeen Rijksarchief, 2012), pp. 49–65

Bourke, Angela, *The Burning of Bridget Cleary: A true story* (London: Pimlico, 1999)

Bourke, Joanna, 'The Mocking of Margaret and the Misfortune of Mary: Sexual violence in Irish history, 1830s–1890s', *Canadian Journal of Irish Studies*, vol. 43, 2020, pp. 16–36

Boyd, Andrew, *Holy War in Belfast* (Tralee: Anvil Books, 1969)

Boyd, Gary A., *Dublin 1745–1922: Hospitals, spectacle and vice* (Dublin: Four Courts Press, 2006)

Bradley, Ian, '"Having and Holding": The Highland Land War of the 1880s', *History Today*, vol. 37, no. 12, December 1987, pp. 23–8

Bretherton, George, 'Irish Inebriate Reformatories, 1899–1920: A small experiment in coercion', *Contemporary Drug Problems*, vol. 13, no. 3, Autumn 1986, pp. 473–502

Brewer, John D., *The Royal Irish Constabulary: An oral history* (Belfast: Queen's University of Belfast, 1990)

Bridgeman, Ian Robert, 'The Constabulary and the Criminal Justice System in Nineteenth-Century Ireland', in Ian O'Donnell and Finbarr McAuley (eds), *Criminal Justice History: Themes and controversies from pre-independence Ireland* (Dublin: Four Courts Press, 2003), pp. 113–41

Brown, Alyson and David Barrett, *Knowledge of Evil: Child prostitution and child sexual abuse in twentieth-century England* (Cullompton: Willan Publishing, 2002)

Buckley, Sarah-Anne, 'Family and Power: Incest in Ireland, 1880–1950', in Anthony McElligott, Liam Chambers, Ciara Breathnach and Catherine Lawless (eds), *Power in History: From medieval Ireland to the post-modern world* (Dublin: Irish Academic Press, 2011), pp. 185–206

Cafferky, John and Kevin Hannafin, *Scandal and Betrayal: Shackleton and the Irish crown jewels* (Cork: Collins Press, 2002)

Campbell, Fergus, *Land and Revolution: Nationalist politics in the west of Ireland 1891–1921* (Oxford: Oxford University Press, 2005)

———, '"Reign of Terror at Craughwell": Tom Kenny and the McGoldrick murder of 1909', *History Ireland*, vol. 18, no. 1, January–February 2010, pp. 26–9

———, 'Land Purchase and Radicalisation in County Galway, c. 1881–1931', *Irish Studies Review*, vol. 28, no. 1, February 2020, pp. 20–42

Carey, Tim, *Mountjoy: The story of a prison* (Cork: Collins Press, 2000)

Carroll-Burke, Patrick, *Colonial Discipline: The making of the Irish convict system* (Dublin: Four Courts Press, 2000)

Carter, J.W.H., *The Land War and Its Leaders in Queen's County, 1879–82* (Portlaoise: Leinster Express Newspapers, 1994)

———, *Murder in the Midlands 1862–1915* ([n.p.]: J.W.H. Carter, 2005)

Casey, Brian, 'Matt Harris and the Ballinasloe Tenant Defence Association, 1876–9', in Brian Casey (ed.), *Defying the Law of the*

Land: Agrarian radicals in Irish history (Dublin: History Press Ireland, 2013), pp. 90–9

Charlesworth, Andrew (ed.), *An Atlas of Rural Protest in Britain 1548–1900* (London: Croom Helm, 1983)

Clark, Samuel, *Social Origins of the Irish Land War* (Princeton: Princeton University Press, 1979)

Clear, Caitriona, 'Crime, Punishment and Poor Relief in Galway 1850–1914: An introduction', *Journal of the Galway Archaeological and Historical Society*, vol. 50, 1998, pp. 118–34

———, *Social Change and Everyday Life in Ireland, 1850–1922* (Manchester: Manchester University Press, 2007)

Coffey, Leigh-Ann, *The Planters of Luggancurran, County Laois: A Protestant community, 1879–1927* (Dublin: Four Courts Press, 2006)

Cogan, John F., 'Michael Collins and the Cormeen Murder Case, 1920', *Ríocht na Midhe*, vol. 27, 2017, pp. 353–73

Cohen, Stanley, *Folk Devils and Moral Panics: The creation of the mods and rockers* (London: MacGibbon & Kee, 1972)

Coleman, Marie, *County Longford and the Irish Revolution 1910–1923* (Dublin: Irish Academic Press, 2003)

———, 'Violence against Women during the Irish War of Independence, 1919–21', in Diarmaid Ferriter and Susannah Riordan (eds), *Years of Turbulence: The Irish revolution and its aftermath* (Dublin: UCD Press, 2015), pp. 137–55

Comerford, R.V., 'Ireland 1850–70: Post-Famine and mid-Victorian', in W.E. Vaughan (ed.), *A New History of Ireland. V. Ireland under the Union, I: 1801–70* (Oxford: Clarendon Press, 1989), pp. 372–95

———, 'The Land War and the Politics of Distress, 1877–82', in W.E. Vaughan (ed.), *A New History of Ireland. VI. Ireland under the Union, II: 1870–1921* (Oxford: Clarendon Press, 1996), pp. 26–52

Conley, Carolyn, *Melancholy Accidents: The meaning of violence in post-Famine Ireland* (Lanham: Lexington Books, 1999)

———, *Certain Other Countries: Homicide, gender, and national identity in late nineteenth-century England, Ireland, Scotland and Wales* (Columbus: Ohio State University Press, 2007)

Connell, K.H., *Irish Peasant Society: Four historical essays* (Dublin: Irish Academic Press, 1968)

Connolly, S.J., 'Unnatural Death in Four Nations: Contrasts and comparisons', in S.J. Connolly (ed.), *Kingdoms United? Great Britain and Ireland since 1500: Integration and diversity* (Dublin: Four Courts Press, 1999), pp. 200–14

Coogan, Oliver, *Politics and War in Meath 1913–23* (Dublin: Folens, 1983)

Corbin, Alain, *Women for Hire: Prostitution and society in France after 1850* (Cambridge, MA: Harvard University Press, 1990)

Corfe, Tom, *The Phoenix Park Murders: Conflict, compromise and tragedy in Ireland, 1879–1882* (London: Hodder & Stoughton, 1968)

Cosgrove, Patrick, *The Ranch War in Riverstown, Co. Sligo, 1908* (Dublin: Four Courts Press, 2012)

———, 'The Ranch War, *c.* 1906–09', in John Crowley, Donal Ó Drisceoil and Mike Murphy (eds), *Atlas of the Irish Revolution* (New York: New York University Press, 2017), pp. 81–4

Cox, David J., Kim Stevenson, Candida Harris and Judith Rowbotham, *Public Indecency in England 1857–1960: 'A serious and growing evil'* (London: Routledge, 2015)

Cronin, Maura, *Agrarian Protest in Ireland 1750–1960* (Dundalk: Dundalgan Press, 2012)

Crossman, Virginia, *Politics, Law and Order in Nineteenth-Century Ireland* (Dublin: Gill & Macmillan, 1996)

———, *Poverty and the Poor Law in Ireland, 1850–1914* (Liverpool: Liverpool University Press, 2013)

———, 'The Growth of the State in the Nineteenth Century', in James Kelly (ed.), *The Cambridge History of Ireland: Volume III, 1730–1880* (Cambridge: Cambridge University Press, 2018), pp. 542–66

Crowley, John, Donal Ó Drisceoil and Mike Murphy (eds), *Atlas of the Irish Revolution* (New York: New York University Press, 2017)

Cullen Owens, Rosemary, *Did Your Granny Have a Hammer? A history of the Irish suffrage movement, 1867–1922* (Dublin: Attic Press, 1985)

———, *A Social History of Women in Ireland, 1870–1920* (Dublin: Gill & Macmillan, 2005)

Curtin, Geraldine, *The Women of Galway Jail: Female criminality in nineteenth-century Ireland* (Galway: Arlen House, 2001)

———, '"The Child Condemned": The imprisonment of children in Ireland, 1850–1908', *Irish Economic and Social History*, vol. 47, 2020, pp. 78–96

Curtis, L.P., *Coercion and Conciliation in Ireland 1880–1892: A study in conservative unionism* (Princeton: Princeton University Press, 1963)

———, *Apes and Angels: The Irishman in Victorian caricature*

(Newton Abbot: David & Charles, 1971)

———, 'Stopping the Hunt, 1881–1882: An aspect of the Irish Land War', in C.H.E. Philbin (ed.), *Nationalism and Popular Protest in Ireland* (Cambridge: Cambridge University Press, 1987), pp. 349–402

———, *The Depiction of Eviction in Ireland 1845–1910* (Dublin: UCD Press, 2011)

Daly, Mary, *Dublin: The deposed capital. A social and economic history 1860–1914* (Cork: Cork University Press, 1984)

Dawson, Norma M., 'Illicit Distillation and the Revenue Police in Ireland in the Eighteenth and Nineteenth Centuries', *Irish Jurist*, vol. 12, no. 2, 1977, pp. 282–94

de Barra, Caoimhín, '"This Abominable Evil is the Source of Fetid Corruption": The IRA's 1920 war on poitín', *Éire-Ireland*, vol. 57, nos 3 & 4 (Autumn–Winter 2022), pp. 283–310

de Nie, Michael, *The Eternal Paddy: Irish identity and the British press, 1798–1882* (Madison: University of Wisconsin Press, 2004)

Donnelly, James S. Jr, *The Land and the People of Nineteenth-Century Cork: The rural economy and the land question* (London and New York: Routledge & Kegan Paul, 1975)

Dooley, Terence, *The Decline of the Big House in Ireland: A study of Irish landed families 1860–1960* (Dublin: Wolfhound Press, 2001)

———, *'The Land for the People': The land question in independent Ireland* (Dublin: UCD Press, 2004)

———, 'The Land War in Drumlish, 1879–82', in Martin Morris and Fergus O'Ferrall (eds), *Longford: History and society* (Dublin: Geography Publications, 2010), pp. 539–53

———, 'Irish Land Questions, 1879–1923', in Thomas Bartlett (ed.), *Cambridge History of Ireland: Volume 4, 1880 to the present* (Cambridge: Cambridge University Press 2018), pp. 117–44

———, *Burning the Big House: The story of the Irish country house in a time of war and revolution* (New Haven and London: Yale University Press, 2022)

Doyle, Mark, *Fighting Like the Devil for the Sake of God: Protestants, Catholics and the origins of sectarian violence in Victorian Belfast* (Manchester and New York: Manchester University Press, 2009)

Dukova, Anastasia, *A History of the Dublin Metropolitan Police and Its Colonial Legacy* (London: Palgrave Macmillan, 2016)

Dunbabin, J.P.D. (ed.), *Rural Discontent in Nineteenth-Century Britain* (New York: Holmes & Meier, 1974)

Dunbar, Holly, 'Women and Alcohol during the First World War in Ireland', *Women's History Review*, vol. 27, no. 23, 2018, pp. 379–96

Dungan, Myles, *The Stealing of the Irish Crown Jewels: An unsolved crime* (Dublin: Town House, 2003)

——, *Four Killings: Land hunger, murder and family in the Irish revolution* (London: Head of Zeus, 2021)

Dunne, Terry, '"Cattle Drivers, Marauders, Terrorists and Hooligans": The agrarian movement of 1920', *History Ireland*, vol. 28, no. 4, July–August 2020, pp. 30–3

Dunning, Eric, Patrick Murphy and John Williams, *The Roots of Football Hooliganism: A historical and sociological study* (London and New York: Routledge, 1988)

Eisner, Manuel, 'Modernization, Self-Control and Lethal Violence: The long-term dynamics of European homicide rates in theoretical perspective', *British Journal of Criminology*, vol. 41, no. 4, September 2001, pp. 618–38

——, 'Long-Term Historical Trends in Violent Crime', *Crime and Justice*, vol. 30, 2003, pp. 83–142

Emsley, Clive, *Crime and Society in England, 1750–1900*, 2nd edn (London and New York: Longman, 1996)

——, *The Great British Bobby: A history of British policing from the 18th century to the present* (London: Quercus, 2009)

Farrell, Elaine, *'A Most Diabolical Deed': Infanticide and Irish society, 1850–1900* (Manchester: Manchester University Press, 2013)

——, 'Crime, Punishment and Gender', in Jyoti Atwal, Ciara Breathnach and Sarah-Anne Buckley (eds), *Gender and History: Ireland, 1852–1922* (London and New York: Routledge, 2023), pp. 143–54

—— and Eliza McKee, 'Captured in the Clothing: Ireland, 1850s–1890s', *Dress: The journal of the Costume Society of America*, published online 7 April 2022, DOI: 10.1080/03612112.2022.2039484

Farry, Michael, *Sligo 1914–1921: A chronicle of conflict* (Trim: Killoran Press, 1992)

——, *The Irish Revolution, 1912–23: Sligo* (Dublin: Four Courts Press, 2012)

Feingold, William, *The Revolt of the Tenantry: The transformation of local government in Ireland 1872–1886* (Boston: Northeastern University Press, 1984)

Ferriter, Diarmaid, *Occasions of Sin: Sex and society in modern*

Ireland (London: Profile, 2009)

Finnane, Mark, 'A Decline in Violence in Ireland? Crime, policing and social relations, 1860–1914', *Crime, Histoire et Sociétés*, vol. 1, no. 1, 1997, pp. 51–70

———, 'Irish Crime without the Outrage: The statistics of criminal justice in the later nineteenth century', in Norma M. Dawson (ed.), *Reflections on Law and History* (Dublin: Four Courts Press, 2006), pp. 203–22

Finnegan, Frances, *Poverty and Prostitution: A study of Victorian prostitutes in York* (Cambridge: Cambridge University Press, 1979)

———, *Do Penance or Perish: A study of magdalen asylums in Ireland* (Piltown: Congrave Press, 2001)

Finnegan, Pat, *The Case of the Craughwell Prisoners during the Land War in Co. Galway, 1879–85: The law must take its course* (Dublin: Four Courts Press, 2012)

FitzGerald, Thomas Earls, *Combatants and Civilians in Revolutionary Ireland, 1918–1923* (London: Routledge, 2021)

Fitzpatrick, David, *Politics and Irish Life, 1913–1921: Provincial experience of war and revolution* (Dublin: Gill & Macmillan, 1977)

———, 'The Disappearance of the Irish Agricultural Labourer, 1841–1913', *Irish Economic and Social History*, vol. 7, 1980, pp. 66–92

———, 'Class, Family and Rural Unrest in Nineteenth-Century Ireland', in P.J. Drury (ed.), *Ireland: Land, politics and people* (Cambridge: Cambridge University Press, 1982), pp. 31–75

———, 'Unrest in Rural Ireland', *Irish Economic and Social History*, vol. 12, 1985, pp. 98–105

Garnham, Neal, 'How Violent was Eighteenth-Century Ireland?', in Ian O'Donnell and Finbarr McAuley (eds), *Criminal Justice History: Themes and controversies from pre-independence Ireland* (Dublin: Four Courts Press, 2003), pp. 19–34

———, *Association Football in Pre-Partition Ireland* (Belfast: Ulster Historical Foundation, 2004)

———, 'The Survival of Popular Blood Sports in Victorian Ulster', *Proceedings of the Royal Irish Academy*, vol. 107C, 2007, pp. 107–26

———, 'Crime, Policing, and the Law, 1600–1900', in Liam Kennedy and Philip Ollerenshaw (eds), *Ulster since 1600: Politics, economy, society* (Oxford: Oxford University Press, 2013), pp. 90–105

Garvin, Tom, *1922: The birth of Irish democracy* (Dublin: Gill & Macmillan, 1996)

Gatrell, V.A.C. and T.B. Hadden, 'Criminal Statistics and Their Interpretation', in E.A. Wrigley (ed.), *Nineteenth-Century Society: Essays in the use of quantitative methods for the study of social data* (London: Cambridge University Press, 1972), pp. 336–96

———, 'The Decline of Theft and Violence in Victorian and Edwardian England', in V.A.C. Gatrell, Bruce Lenman and Geoffrey Parker (eds), *Crime and the Law: The social history of crime in western Europe since 1500* (London: Europa Publications, 1980), pp. 238–370

Geary, Laurence, *The Plan of Campaign, 1886–1891* (Cork: Cork University Press, 1986)

Geraghty, Tom and Trevor Whitehead, *The Dublin Fire Brigade: A history of the brigade, the fires and the emergencies* (Dublin: Dublin City Council, 2004)

Gibson, Mary, *Prostitution and the State in Italy, 1860–1915* (New Brunswick: Rutgers University Press, 1986)

Godfrey, Barry S. and Paul Lawrence, *Crime and Justice 1750–1950* (Cullompton: Willan Publishing, 2005)

———, Chris A. Williams and Paul Lawrence, *History and Crime* (Los Angeles, London, New Delhi and Singapore: SAGE Publications, 2007)

———, *Crime in England, 1880–1945: The rough and the criminal, the policed and the incarcerated* (London and New York: Routledge, 2014)

Gray, Drew, *London's Shadows: The dark side of the Victorian city* (London: Continuum, 2010)

Gray, John, 'Bullet-Throwing in Belfast', *History Ireland*, vol. 23, no. 2, March–April 2015, pp. 30–3

Greer, D.S. and V.A. Mitchell, *Compensation for Criminal Damage to Property* (Belfast: S.L.S. Legal Publications (N.I.), 1982)

Gribbon, H.D., 'Economic and Social History, 1850–1921', in W.E. Vaughan (ed.), *A New History of Ireland. VI. Ireland under the Union, II: 1870–1921* (Oxford: Clarendon Press, 1996), pp. 260–356

Griffin, Brian, '"Such Varmint": The Dublin police and the public, 1838–1913', *Irish Studies Review*, vol. 4, no. 13, Winter 1995, pp. 21–5

———, *Sources for the Study of Crime in Ireland, 1800–1921* (Dublin: Four Courts Press, 2005)

———, 'Prevention and Detection of Crime in Nineteenth-Century Ireland', in N.M. Dawson (ed.), *Reflections on Law and History* (Dublin: Four Courts Press, 2006), pp. 99–125

————, *Cycling in Victorian Ireland* (Dublin: Nonsuch Press, 2006)

Hands, Thora, *Drinking in Victorian and Edwardian Britain: Beyond the spectacle of the drunkard* (Cham: Springer International Publishing, 2018)

Hanley, Brian, *Republicanism, Crime and Parliamentary Policing in Ireland, 1916–2020* (Cork: Cork University Press, 2022)

Hannerton, A. James, *Cruelty and Companionship: Conflict in nineteenth-century married life* (London: Routledge, 1992)

Hannigan, Ken, 'A Miscellany of Murder: Violent murder in 19th century Wicklow', *Wicklow Historical Society*, vol. 1, no. 7, 1994, pp. 22–34

Hart, Peter, *The IRA and Its Enemies: Violence and community in Cork, 1916–1923* (Oxford: Clarendon Press, 1998)

Hawkins, Richard, 'Government Versus Secret Societies: The Parnell era', in T. Desmond Williams (ed.), *Secret Societies in Ireland* (Dublin: Gill & Macmillan, 1973), pp. 100–12

————, 'An Army on Police Work, 1881–2: Ross of Bladensburg's memorandum', *Irish Sword*, vol. 11, 1973, pp. 75–117

Hayes, Anne M., *Female Prostitution in Costa Rica: Historical perspectives, 1880–1930* (New York: Routledge, 2006)

Herlihy, Jim, *The Irish Revenue Police* (Dublin: Four Courts Press, 2018)

Higbine, Frank Thomas, 'Between Romance and Degradation: Navigating the meanings of vagrancy in North America, 1870–1914', in A.L. Beier and Paul Ocobock (eds), *Cast Out: Vagrancy and homelessness in global and historical perspective* (Athens, OH: Ohio State University Press, 2008), pp. 256–69

Hilton, Matthew, *Smoking in British Popular Culture 1800–2000: Perfect pleasures* (Manchester: Manchester University Press, 2000)

Hirst, Catherine, *Religion, Politics and Violence in Nineteenth-Century Belfast: The Pound and Sandy Row* (Dublin: Four Courts Press, 2002)

Hoff, Joan and Marian Yeates, *The Cooper's Wife Is Missing* (New York: Basic Books, 2000)

Hoppen, K. Theodore, *Elections, Politics, and Society in Ireland 1832–1885* (Oxford: Clarendon Press, 1984)

Hughes, Kyle and Donald MacRaild, *Ribbon Societies in Nineteenth-Century Ireland and Its Diaspora: The persistence of tradition* (Liverpool: Liverpool University Press, 2018)

Hunt, Tom, 'The Knife, the Card and the Trick-of-the-Loop: Crime and sport in County Westmeath', in Liam Clare and Máire Ní Chearbhaill, *Trouble with the Law: Crimes and trials from Ireland's past* (Dublin: Woodfield Press, 2007), pp. 21–35

Ireland, R.W., '"Perhaps My Mother Murdered Me": Child death and the law in Victorian Carmarthenshire', in Christopher Brooks and Michael Lobban, *Communities and Courts in Britain 1150–1900* (London: Hambledon Press, 1997), pp. 229–44

Jennings, Paul, *A History of Drink and the English, 1500–2000* (Abingdon: Routledge, 2016)

Johnson, Eric A. and Eric H. Monkkonen (eds), *The Civilization of Crime: Violence in town and city since the Middle Ages* (Urbana: University of Illinois Press, 1996)

Johnston, Helen, *Crime in England 1815–1880: Experiencing the criminal justice system* (London and New York: Routledge, 2015)

Jones, David Seth, 'The Cleavage between Graziers and Peasants in the Land Struggle, 1890–1910', in Samuel Clark and James S. Donnelly Jr (eds), *Irish Peasants: Violence and political unrest 1780–1914* (Dublin: Gill & Macmillan, 1983), pp. 374–417

———, *Graziers, Land Reform, and Political Conflict in Ireland* (Washington: Catholic University of America Press, 1995)

Jordan, Donald E., *Land and Popular Politics in Ireland: County Mayo from the plantation to the Land War* (Cambridge: Cambridge University Press, 1994)

———, 'The Irish National League and the "Unwritten Law": Rural protest and nation-building in Ireland 1882–1890', *Past and Present*, no. 158, February 1998, pp. 146–71

Kavanagh, Julie, *The Irish Assassins: Conspiracy, revenge, and the Phoenix Park murders that stunned Victorian England* (New York: Atlantic Monthly Press, 2021)

Kelleher, Margaret, *The Maamtrasna Murders: Language, life and death in nineteenth-century Ireland* (Dublin: UCD Press, 2018)

Kenna, Shane, *The Invincibles: The Phoenix Park assassinations and the conspiracy that shook an empire* (Dublin: O'Brien Press, 2019)

Kennedy, Edward, *The Land Movement in Tullaroan, County Kilkenny, 1879–1891* (Dublin: Four Courts Press, 2004)

Keogh, John, 'The Royal Irish Constabulary', *Carloviana*, vol. 4, no. 32, 1984–5, pp. 16–18

King, Peter, 'Exploring and Explaining the Geography of Homicide: Patterns of lethal violence in Britain and Europe, 1805–1900',

European Review of History, vol. 20, no. 6, 2013, pp. 967–87

Klein, Joanne, *Invisible Men: The secret lives of police constables in Liverpool, Manchester and Birmingham, 1900–1939* (Liverpool: Liverpool University Press, 2010)

Kotsonouris, Mary, *Retreat from Revolution: The Dáil courts, 1920–24* (Dublin: Irish Academic Press, 1993)

Lacey, Brian, *Terrible Queer Creatures: Homosexuality in Irish history* (Dublin: Wordwell, 2008)

Laird, Heather, *Subversive Law in Ireland, 1879–1920: From "unwritten law" to the Dáil courts* (Dublin: Four Courts Press, 2005)

Lambert, William Rhys, *Drink and Society in Victorian Wales* (Cardiff: University of Wales Press, 1983)

Lane, Fintan, *Long Bullets: A history of road bowling in Ireland* (Cork: Galley Head Press, 2005)

Lane, Pádraig G., 'Agricultural Labourers and Rural Violence, 1850–1914', *Studia Hibernica*, vol. 27, 1993, pp. 77–87

———, 'Government Surveillance of Subversion in Laois, 1890–1916', in Pádraig G. Lane and William Nolan (eds), *Laois History and Society: Interdisciplinary essays on the history of an Irish county* (Dublin: Geography Publications, 1999), pp. 601–25

Laragy, Georgina, 'Murder in Cavan, 1809–1891', *Breifne*, vol. 11, no. 44, 2008, pp. 611–30

Lawrence, Paul, 'Policing the Poor in England and France, 1850–1900', in Clive Emsley, Eric Johnson and Pieter Spierenburg (eds), *Social Control in Europe: Vol. 2, 1800–2000* (Columbus: Ohio State University Press, 2004), pp. 213–17

Lee, Joseph, 'Patterns of Rural Unrest in Nineteenth-Century Ireland: A preliminary survey', in L.M. Cullen and F. Furet (eds), *Ireland and France, 17th–20th Centuries: Towards a comparative study of rural history* (Ann Arbor: UMI Publishing, 1980), pp. 223–37

Leeson, D.M., *The Black and Tans: British police and auxiliaries in the Irish War of Independence, 1920–1921* (Oxford: Oxford University Press, 2011)

Lohan, Máire, *An 'Antiquarian Craze': The life, times and work in archaeology of Patrick Lyons RIC (1861–1954)* (Dublin: Edmund Burke Publisher, 2008)

Lowe, W.J., 'The War against the R.I.C., 1919–21', *Éire-Ireland*, vol. 37, nos 3 & 4, Autumn–Winter 2002, pp. 79–117

Lucey, Donncha Seán, *Land, Popular Politics and Agrarian Violence in Ireland: The case of County Kerry, 1872–86* (Dublin: UCD Press, 2011)

Luddy, Maria, *Women and Philanthropy in Nineteenth-Century Ireland* (Cambridge: Cambridge University Press, 1995)

———, *Prostitution and Irish Society, 1800–1940* (Cambridge: Cambridge University Press, 2007)

———, 'The Early Years of the NSPCC in Ireland', *Éire-Ireland*, vol. 44, nos 1 & 2, Spring–Summer 2009, pp. 62–90

——— and Mary O'Dowd, *Marriage in Ireland, 1660–1925* (Cambridge: Cambridge University Press, 2020)

Mac an Ghalloglaigh, Domhnall, 'The Land League in Leitrim 1879–1883', *Breifne*, vol. 6, no. 22, 1983–4, pp. 155–87

Macilwee, Mick, *The Liverpool Underworld: Crime in the city, 1750–1900* (Liverpool: Liverpool University Press, 2011)

MacRaild, Donald M. and Frank Neal, 'Child-Stripping in the Victorian City', *Urban History*, vol. 39, no. 3, 2012, pp. 431–52

Mac Suibhne, Breandán and Amy Martin, 'Fenians in the Frame: Photographing Irish political prisoners, 1865–68', *Field Day Review*, 2005, pp. 101–19

Malcolm, Elizabeth, *'Ireland Sober, Ireland Free': Drink and temperance in nineteenth-century Ireland* (Dublin: Gill & Macmillan, 1986)

———, '"Troops of Largely Diseased Women": The Contagious Diseases Acts and moral policing in late nineteenth-century Ireland', *Irish Economic and Social History*, vol. 26, 1999, pp. 1–14

———, *The Irish Policeman, 1822–1922: A life* (Dublin: Four Courts Press, 2006)

———, 'Between Habitual Drunkards and Alcoholics: Inebriate women and reformatories in Ireland, 1899–1919', in Margaret H. Preston and Margaret Ó hÓgartaigh (eds), *Gender and Medicine in Ireland 1700–1950* (Syracuse: Syracuse University Press, 2012), pp. 108–22

——— and W.J. Lowe, 'The Domestication of the Royal Irish Constabulary, 1836–1922', *Irish Economic and Social History*, vol. 19, 1992, pp. 27–48

Malcomson, A.P.W., *Virtues of a Wicked Earl: The life and legend of William Sydney Clements, 3rd earl of Leitrim (1806–78)* (Dublin: Four Courts Press, 2009)

Mark-FitzGerald, Emily, 'An Alien in Wexford: Harry Furniss, *Punch*, and *Zozimus* (The "Irish *Punch*")', *Visual Culture in Britain*, vol. 20, no. 2, 2019, pp. 135–51

Matson, Leslie, *Méiní: The Blasket nurse* (Dublin and Cork: Mercier Press, 1996)

McAvoy, Sandra, 'Sexual Crime and Irish Women's Campaign for a Criminal Law Amendment Act, 1912–35', in Maryann Gialanella Valiulis (ed.), *Gender and Power in Irish History* (Dublin: Irish Academic Press, 2009), pp. 84–99

McCabe, Ciaran, '"Are You Mad Also?": The Murder of Sergeant Michael Rogan and His Family in Ballinadrimna, Co. Kildare in 1892', *Journal of the Kildare Archaeological Society*, vol. 20, no. 2, 2010–11, pp. 159–72

McCabe, Desmond, 'Open Court: Law and the expansion of magisterial jurisdiction at petty sessions in nineteenth-century Ireland', in Norma M. Dawson (ed.), *Reflections on Law and History* (Dublin: Four Courts Press, 2006), pp. 126–62

McCluskey, Fergal, *The Irish Revolution, 1912–23: Tyrone* (Dublin: Four Courts Press, 2014)

McCracken, Donal P., *Inspector Mallon: Buying Irish nationalism for a five-pound note* (Dublin: Irish Academic Press, 2009)

———, *'You Will Dye at Midnight': Threatening letters in Victorian Ireland* (Dublin: Eastwood, 2021)

McDonnel, Randal, *Cushendun in the Glens of Antrim* (Cushendun: Randal McDonnel, n.d.)

McDowell, R.B., *The Irish Administration 1801–1914* (London: Routledge & Kegan Paul, 1964)

McGarry, Fearghal, *Eoin O'Duffy: A self-made hero* (Oxford: Oxford University Press, 2005)

McGee, Owen, *The IRB: The Irish Republican Brotherhood from the Land League to Sinn Féin* (Dublin: Four Courts Press, 2005)

McGuire, E.B., *Irish Whiskey: A history of distilling, the spirit trade and excise controls in Ireland* (Dublin: Gill & Macmillan, 1973)

McGuire, James and James Quinn (eds), *Dictionary of Irish Biography* (Cambridge: Cambridge University Press, 2009)

McLoughlin, Dympna, 'Infanticide in Nineteenth-Century Ireland', in Angela Bourke, Siobhán Kilfeather, Maria Luddy, Margaret MacCurtain, Gerardine Meaney, Máirín Ní Dhonnchadha, Mary O'Dowd and Clair Wills (eds), *Field Day Anthology of Irish Writing*, (Cork: Cork University Press, 2002), vol. 4, pp. 915–22

McMahon, Kevin, 'The "Crossmaglen Conspiracy" Case. Part I', *Seanchas Ardmhacha*, vol. 6, no. 2, 1972, pp. 251–86

———, 'The "Crossmaglen Conspiracy" Case. Part II', *Seanchas Ardmhacha*, vol. 7, no. 1, 1973, pp. 65–107

———, 'The "Crossmaglen Conspiracy" Case. Part III', *Seanchas Ardmhacha*, vol. 7, no. 2, 1974, pp. 326–63

Mc Mahon, Richard, 'Urbanisation and Interpersonal Violence in Europe and North America', *Informationen zur modernen Stadtgeschichte*, vol. 2, 2013, pp. 21–30

McNally, Gerry, 'Probation in Ireland: A brief history of the early years', *Irish Probation Journal*, vol. 4, no. 1, 2007, pp. 5–24

McNamara, Conor, *War and Revolution in the West of Ireland: Galway 1913–1922* (Dublin: Irish Academic Press, 2018)

Mitchell, Arthur, *Revolutionary Government in Ireland: Dáil Éireann, 1919–22* (Dublin: Gill & Macmillan, 1995)

Moffitt, Miriam, 'Protestant Tenant Farmers and the Land League in North Connacht', in Carla King and Conor McNamara (eds), *The West of Ireland: New perspectives* (Dublin: History Press Ireland, 2011), pp. 93–116

Moloney, Senan, *The Phoenix Park Murders: Conspiracy, betrayal and retribution* (Cork: Mercier Press, 2006)

Molony, Thomas, 'The Prevention and Punishment of Crime', in Ian O'Donnell and Finbarr McAuley (eds), *Criminal Justice History: Themes and controversies from pre-independence Ireland* (Dublin: Four Courts Press, 2003), pp. 82–97

Moran, Gerard, 'The Origins and Development of Boycotting', *Journal of the Galway Archaeological and Historical Society*, vol. 40, 1985-6, pp. 49–64

———, 'Matthew Harris, Fenianism and Land Agitation in the West of Ireland', in Fergus Campbell and Tony Varley (eds), *Land Questions in Modern Ireland* (Manchester: Manchester University Press, 2013), pp. 218–37

Morris, Robert M., '"Lies, Damned Lies, and Criminal Statistics": Reinterpreting the criminal statistics of England and Wales, 1850–1960', *Crime, Histoire et Sociétés*, vol. 5, no. 1, 2001, pp. 111–27

Muenger, Elizabeth A., *The British Military Dilemma in Ireland: Occupation politics, 1886–1914* (Lawrence: University of Kansas Press, 1991)

Mulhall, Daniel, *A New Day Dawning: A portrait of Ireland in 1900* (Cork: Collins Press, 1999)

Mulholland, Marc, 'Land War Homicides', in Senia Pašeta (ed.), *Uncertain Futures: Essays about the Irish past for Roy Foster* (Oxford: Oxford University Press, 2016), pp. 81–96

Murphy, Clare C., 'Conflict in the West: The Ranch War continues, 1911–1912, Part I', *Cathair na Mart*, vol. 15, 1995, pp. 84–105

———, 'Conflict in the West: The Ranch War Continues, 1911–1912, Part II', *Cathair na Mart*, vol. 16, 1997, pp. 112–39

Murphy, Desmond, 'The Land War in Donegal 1879–1891', *Donegal Annual*, vol. 32, 1980, pp. 476–86

Murphy, Maura, 'The Ballad Singer and the Role of the Seditious Ballad in Nineteenth-Century Ireland', *Ulster Folklife*, vol. 25, 1979, pp. 79–102

Murphy, William, 'Sport in a Time of Revolution: Sinn Féin and the hunt in Ireland, 1919', *Éire-Ireland*, vol. 48, nos 1 & 2, Spring–Summer 2013, pp. 112–47

Murray, A.C., 'Agrarian Violence and Nationalism in Nineteenth-Century Ireland: The myth of Ribbonism', *Irish Economic and Social History*, vol. 13, 1986, pp. 56–73

Murtagh, Ann, *Portrait of a Westmeath Tenant Community, 1879–85: The Barbavilla murder* (Dublin: Irish Academic Press, 1999)

Nelson, Thomas, *The Land War in County Kildare* (Maynooth: St Patrick's College Maynooth, 1985)

Nye, Robert A., *Crime, Madness and Politics in Modern France: The medical concept of national decline* (Princeton: Princeton University Press, 1984)

O'Brien, Joseph V., *'Dear, Dirty Dublin': A city in distress, 1899–1916* (Berkeley and London: University of California Press, 1982)

Ó Broin, Leon, 'The Invincibles', in T. Desmond Williams (ed.), *Secret Societies in Ireland* (Dublin: Gill & Macmillan, 1973), pp. 113–25

O'Callaghan, Margaret, 'Parnellism and Crime: Constructing a conservative strategy of containment 1887–91', in Donal McCartney (ed.), *Parnell: The politics of power* (Dublin: Wolfhound Press, 1991), pp. 102–24

Ó Cathaoir, Brendan, 'Another Clare: Ranchers and moonlighters, 1700–1945', in Matthew Lynch and Patrick Nugent (eds), *Clare: History and society. Interdisciplinary essays on the history of an Irish county* (Dublin: Geography Publications, 2008), pp. 359–423

Ó Cuirreáin, Seán, *The Queen v. Patrick O'Donnell: The man who shot the informer James Carey* (Dublin: Four Courts Press, 2021)

O'Donnell, Ian, 'Lethal Violence in Ireland, 1841 to 2003: Famine, celibacy and parental pacification', *British Journal of Criminology*, vol. 45, 2005, pp. 671–95

——, 'The Fall and Rise of Homicide in Ireland', in Sophie Body-Gendrot and Pieter Spierenburg (eds), *Violence in Europe: Historical and contemporary perspectives* (New York: Springer, 2008), pp. 79–92

O'Hegarty, P.S., *A History of Ireland under the Union 1801 to 1922* (London: Methuen, 1952)

O'Mahony, Colman, *In the Shadows: Life in Cork 1750–1930* (Ballincollig: Tower Books, 1997)

O'Riordan, Tomás, 'The Theft of the Irish Crown Jewels, 1907', *History Ireland*, vol. 9, no. 4, Winter 2001, pp. 23–8

Osborough, Nial, *Borstal in Ireland: Custodial provision for the young adult offender 1906–1974* (Dublin: Institute of Public Administration, 1975)

O'Sullivan, Donal J., *The Irish Constabularies 1822–1922: A century of policing in Ireland* (Dingle: Brandon, 1999)

O'Sullivan, Eoin, '"This Otherwise Delicate Subject": Child sexual abuse in early twentieth-century Ireland', in Paul O'Mahony (ed.), *Criminal Justice in Ireland* (Dublin: Institute of Public Administration, 2002), pp. 176–201

O'Sullivan, Niamh, *Every Dark Hour: A history of Kilmainham jail* (Dublin: Liberties Press, 2007)

Palmer, Stanley H., *Police and Protest in England and Ireland 1780–1850* (Cambridge: Cambridge University Press, 1988)

Partridge, Pádraig, 'Crime in the Dublin Metropolitan Police District, 1894–1914', *Retrospect*, vol. 2, 1982, pp. 36–43

Pavlich, George, 'The Emergence of Habitual Criminals in 19th-Century Britain: Implications for criminology', *Journal of Theoretical and Philosophical Criminology*, vol. 2, no. 1, 2010, pp. 1–62

Preston, Margaret H., *Charitable Words: Women, philanthropy, and the language of charity in nineteenth-century Dublin* (Westport, CT: Praeger, 2004)

Prior, Pauline M., *Madness and Murder: Gender, crime and mental disorder in nineteenth-century Ireland* (Dublin: Irish Academic Press, 2008)

Prunty, Jacinta, *Dublin Slums 1800–1925: A study in urban geography* (Dublin: Four Courts Press, 1998)

Radford, Mark, '"Closely Akin to Actual Warfare": The Belfast riots of 1886 and the RIC', *History Ireland*, vol. 7, no. 4, Winter 1999, pp. 27–31

————, 'The "Social Volcano": Policing Victorian Belfast', in Christine Kinealy and Roger Swift (eds), *Politics and Power in Victorian Ireland* (Dublin: Four Courts Press, 2006), pp. 166–77

————, *The Policing of Belfast 1870–1914* (London: Bloomsbury, 2015)

Raftery, Mary and Eoin O'Sullivan, *Suffer the Little Children: The inside story of Ireland's industrial schools* (Dublin: New Island, 1999)

Rains, Stephanie, 'Reading the Hand: Palmistry, graphology and alternative literacies', in Rebecca Anne Barr, Sarah-Anne Buckley and Muireann O'Cinneide (eds), *Literacy, Language and Reading in Nineteenth-Century Ireland* (Liverpool: Liverpool University Press, 2019), pp. 176–90

Rattigan, Clíona, '"I Thought From Her Appearance that She was in the Family Way": Detecting infanticide cases in Ireland, 1900–1921', *Family and Community History*, vol. 11, no. 2, November 2008, pp. 134–51

Raymond, Raymond James, 'Pawnbrokers and Pawnbroking in Dublin: 1830–1870', *Dublin Historical Record*, vol. 32, no. 1, December 1978, pp. 15–26

Reidy, Conor, *Ireland's 'Moral Hospital': The Irish borstal system 1906–1956* (Dublin: Irish Academic Press, 2010)

————, 'Inebriate Women in Early Twentieth-Century Ireland', *History Ireland*, vol. 22, no. 6, November–December 2014, pp. 26–9

Reynolds, John, *46 Men Dead: The Royal Irish Constabulary in County Tipperary, 1919–22* (Cork: Collins Press, 2016)

Rose, Lionel, *'Rogues and Vagabonds': Vagrant underworlds in Britain 1815–1986* (Abingdon: Routledge, 1988)

Rouse, Paul, *Sport and Ireland: A history* (Oxford: Oxford University Press, 2015)

Ruxton, Dean, *When the Hangman Came to Galway: A gruesome true story of murder in Victorian Ireland* (Dublin: Gill & Macmillan, 2018)

Ryan, Louise, 'Publicising the Private: Suffragists' Critique of Sexual Abuse and Domestic Violence', in Louise Ryan and Margaret Ward (eds), *Irish Women and the Vote: Becoming citizens* (Dublin: Irish Academic Press, 2007), pp. 75–89

Rynne, Frank, 'Permanent Revolutionaries: The IRB and the Land War in west Cork', in Fearghal McGarry and James McConnel (eds), *The Black Hand of Republicanism: Fenianism in modern Ireland* (Dublin: Four Courts Press, 2009), pp. 55–71

——, 'Redressing Historical Imbalance: The role of grassroots leaders Richard Hodnett and Henry O'Mahony in the Land League revolution in west Cork, 1879–82', in Brian Casey (ed.), *Defying the Law of the Land: Agrarian radicals in Irish history* (Dublin: History Press Ireland, 2013), pp. 133–53

Settle, Louise, *Sex for Sale in Scotland: Prostitution in Edinburgh and Glasgow, 1900–1939* (Edinburgh: Edinburgh University Press, 2016)

Shepherd, W.E., 'Murder at Mullingar', *Journal of the Irish Railway Record Society*, vol. 18, 1992, pp. 80–8

Shore, Heather, *Artful Dodgers: Youth and crime in early nineteenth-century London* (Woodbridge: Boydell Press, 1999)

Sindall, R.S., 'The Criminal Statistics of Nineteenth-Century Cities: A new approach', *Urban History Yearbook*, 1986, pp. 28–36

Smith, Beverly A., 'Ireland's Ennis Inebriates' Reformatory: A 19th century example of failed institutional reform', *Federal Probation*, vol. LIII, no. 1, March 1989, pp. 53–64

Smyth, William J., 'Conflict, Reaction and Control in Nineteenth-Century Ireland: The archaeology of revolution', in John Crowley, Donal Ó Drisceoil and Mike Murphy (eds), *Atlas of the Irish Revolution* (New York: New York University Press, 2017), pp. 21–55

Solow, Barbara, *The Land Question and the Irish Economy, 1870–1903* (Cambridge, MA: Harvard University Press, 1971)

Spierenburg, Pieter, *A History of Murder: Personal violence in Europe from the Middle Ages to the present* (Cambridge: Polity, 2008)

Springhall, John, *Coming of Age: Adolescence in Britain 1860–1960* (Dublin: Gill & Macmillan, 1986)

Starr, Douglas, *The Killer of Little Shepherds: The case of the French Ripper and the birth of forensic science* (London: Simon Schuster, 2011)

Steiner-Scott, Elizabeth, '"To Bounce a Boot Off Her Now & Then …": Domestic violence in post-Famine Ireland', in Maryann Gialanella Valiulis and Mary O'Dowd (eds), *Women and Irish History: Essays in honour of Margaret MacCurtain* (Dublin: Wolfhound Press, 1997), pp. 125–43

Stevenson, S.J., 'The "Habitual Criminal" in Nineteenth-Century England: Some observations', *Urban History Yearbook*, vol. 13, 1986, pp. 37–60

Summerscale, Kate, *The Wicked Boy: An infamous murder in Victorian London* (London: Penguin, 2017)

Suodenjoki, Sami, 'Mobilising for Land, Nation and Class Interests: Agrarian agitation in Finland and Ireland, 1879–1918', *Irish Historical Studies*, vol. 41, no. 160, November 2017, pp. 200–20

Taylor, David, *Policing the Victorian Community: The development of the police in Middlesbrough, c. 1840–1914* (Basingstoke: Palgrave Macmillan, 2002)

————, 'Beyond the Bounds of Respectable Society: The "dangerous classes" in Victorian and Edwardian England', in Julia Rowbotham and Kim Stevenson (eds), *Criminal Conversations: Victorian crimes, social panic, and moral outrage* (Columbus: Ohio State University Press, 2005), pp. 3–22

Taylor, Howard, 'Rationing Crime: The political economy of crime statistics since the 1850s', *Economic History Review*, new series, vol. 51, no. 3, August 1998, pp. 569–90

Thompson, Frank, 'The Land War in County Fermanagh', in Eileen M. Murphy and William J. Roulston (eds), *Fermanagh History and Society: Interdisciplinary essays on the history of an Irish county* (Dublin: Geography Publications, 2004), pp. 287–305

Toal, Ciaran, '"The Brutes": Mrs Metge and the Lisburn Cathedral Bomb, 1914', *History Ireland*, vol. 22, no. 6, November–December 2014, pp. 30–3

Townshend, Charles, *The British Campaign in Ireland 1919–1921: The development of political and military policies* (Oxford: Oxford University Press, 1975)

————, *The Republic: The fight for Irish independence* (London: Allen Lane, 2013)

Urquhart, Diane, *Women in Ulster Politics 1890–1940: A history not yet told* (Dublin: Irish Academic Press, 2000)

————, 'Irish Divorce and Domestic Violence, 1857–1922', *Women's History Review*, vol. 22, no. 5, 2013, pp. 820–37

Van Hattum, M., 'The Language of "Ribbonmen": A CDA approach to identity construction in nineteenth-century Irish English threatening notices', *Journal of Historical Sociolinguistics*, vol. 3, no. 2, 2017, pp. 241–62

Vaughan, W.E., 'Landlord and Tenant Relations in Ireland between the Famine and the Land War, 1850–1878', in L.M. Cullen and T.C. Smout (eds), *Comparative Aspects of Scottish and Irish Economic and Social History 1600–1900* (Edinburgh: John Donald, 1977), pp. 216–26

————, *Landlords and Tenants in Ireland 1848–1904* (Dundalk: Dundalgan Press, 1984)

————, *Landlords and Tenants in Mid-Victorian Ireland* (Oxford: Oxford University Press, 1994)

————, *Murder Trials in Ireland, 1836–1914* (Dublin: Four Courts Press, 2009)

Waldron, Jarlath, *Maamtrasna: The murders and the mystery* (Dublin: Edmund Burke Publisher, 1992)

Ward, Brian, 'Cockfighting in Ireland, 1900 to 1925', *New Hibernia Review*, vol. 20, no. 3, Autumn 2016, pp. 97–111

Warwick-Haller, Sally, *William O'Brien and the Irish Land War* (Dublin: Irish Academic Press, 1990)

Watkins, Emma and Barry Godfrey, *Criminal Children: Researching juvenile offenders, 1820–1920* (Barnsley: Pen & Sword, 2018)

Weeks, Jeffrey, 'Inverts, Perverts and Mary Annes: Male prostitution and the regulation of homosexuality in England in the nineteenth and early twentieth centuries', *Journal of Homosexuality*, vol. 6, nos 1–2, 1981, pp. 113–34

Wheatley, Michael, *Nationalism and the Irish Party: Provincial Ireland 1910–1916* (Oxford: Oxford University Press, 2005)

Whelehan, Niall, 'Labour and Agrarian Violence in the Irish Midlands, 1850–1870', *Saothar*, vol. 37, 2012, pp. 7–18

————, 'Revolting Peasants: Southern Italy, Ireland, and cartoons in comparative perspective, 1860–1882', *International Review of Social History*, vol. 60, no. 1, 2015, pp. 1–35

Wingfield, Nancy Meriwether, *The World of Prostitution in Late Imperial Austria* (Oxford: Oxford University Press, 2017)

Winstanley, Michael, *Ireland and the Land Question 1800–1922* (London and New York: Methuen, 1984)

Yeates, Pádraig, *Lockout: Dublin, 1913* (Dublin: Gill & Macmillan, 2000)

————, 'Who Were Dublin's Looters in 1916? Crime and society in Dublin during the Great War', *Saothar*, vol. 41, 2016, pp. 111–23

DISSERTATIONS

Ball, Stephen, 'Policing the Land War: Official responses to political protest and agrarian crime in Ireland, 1879–91', unpublished PhD dissertation, Goldsmith's College, University College London, 2000

Boyle, Michael, 'Women and Crime in Belfast, 1900–13', unpublished PhD dissertation, Queen's University Belfast, 1997

Bridgeman, Ian Robert, 'Policing Rural Ireland: A study of the origins, development and role of the Irish Constabulary, and its impact on crime prevention and detection in the nineteenth century', unpublished PhD dissertation, Open University, 1993

Delaney, Gerard Martin Mary, 'The Role of the Fenians in the Early Years of the Land War in Mayo', unpublished MA in Local History dissertation, University of Limerick, 2022

Goldsmith, Alasdair Lindsay, 'The Development of the City of Glasgow Police, *c.* 1800 – *c.* 1939', unpublished PhD dissertation, University of Strathclyde, 2002

Radford, Mark, 'A Trial of Strength: The policing of Belfast 1870–1914', unpublished PhD dissertation, University of Liverpool, 2002

Stanford, Terence George, 'The Metropolitan Police, 1850–1914: Targeting, harassment and the creation of a criminal class', unpublished PhD dissertation, University of Huddersfield, 2007

Index